Digital Fingerprinting

Cliff Wang · Ryan M. Gerdes
Yong Guan · Sneha Kumar Kasera
Editors

Digital Fingerprinting

 Springer

Editors
Cliff Wang
Computing and Information Science
    Division
Army Research Office
Durham, NC
USA

Yong Guan
Department of Electrical and Computer
    Engineering
Iowa State University
Ames, IA
USA

Ryan M. Gerdes
Department of Electrical and Computer
    Engineering
Virginia Polytechnic Institute
Arlington, VA
USA

Sneha Kumar Kasera
Computer Science Department
University of Utah
Salt Lake City, UT
USA

ISBN 978-1-4939-8247-9   ISBN 978-1-4939-6601-1   (eBook)
DOI 10.1007/978-1-4939-6601-1

Contents

Introduction... 1
Yong Guan, Sneha Kumar Kasera, Cliff Wang and Ryan M. Gerdes
1 Overview... 1
2 Applications and Requirements of Fingerprints 2
3 Types of Fingerprints....................................... 2

Types and Origins of Fingerprints............................... 5
Davide Zanetti, Srdjan Capkun and Boris Danev
1 Introduction 5
2 Physical-Layer Device Identification 6
   2.1 General View 6
   2.2 Device Under Identification 8
   2.3 Identification Signals 9
   2.4 Features 9
   2.5 Device Fingerprints 12
   2.6 Physical-Layer Identification System 13
   2.7 System Performance and Design Issues 14
   2.8 Improving Physical-Layer Identification Systems 15
3 State of the Art... 17
   3.1 Transient-Based Approaches 17
   3.2 Modulation-Based Approaches 21
   3.3 Other Approaches 22
   3.4 Attacking Physical-Layer Device Identification 23
   3.5 Summary and Conclusion 24
4 Future Research Directions.................................. 25
5 Conclusion.. 26
References 27

Device Measurement and Origin of Variation 31
Ryan M. Gerdes, Mani Mina and Thomas E. Daniels
1   Introduction 31
     1.1   ABCD Parameters 33
     1.2   Proposed Model 33
2   Measuring Parameters 34
3   Determining Component Significance. 36
     3.1   Constructing Model Input 36
     3.2   Producing Model Output 36
     3.3   Evaluating Model Output 37
4   Conclusion 38
References 38

Crytpo-Based Methods and Fingerprints 39
Joe H. Novak, Sneha Kumar Kasera and Yong Guan
1   Introduction 39
     1.1   Authentication 39
     1.2   Key Generation 40
2   Techniques 41
     2.1   Physical Unclonable Functions 41
     2.2   Controlled Physical Unclonable Functions 49
     2.3   Clock Skew 52
     2.4   Wireless Devices 58
     2.5   Optical Media 61
     2.6   Trojan Detection 63
     2.7   Software Control 63
3   Tradeoffs 64
     3.1   Benefits 64
     3.2   Drawbacks 65
4   Summary 65
References 66

Fingerprinting by Design: Embedding and Authentication 69
Paul L. Yu, Brian M. Sadler, Gunjan Verma and John S. Baras
1   Background 69
     1.1   Intrinsic Fingerprints 69
     1.2   Fingerprint Embedding 70
     1.3   Fingerprinting and Communications 71
2   Introduction to Embedded Authentication. 72
3   Framework for Embedded Authentication 72
     3.1   Authentication System—Transmitter 73
     3.2   Authentication System—Receiver 74
     3.3   Authentication Performance 77
4   Metrics for Embedded Fingerprint Authentication 77
     4.1   Impact on Data BER 77
     4.2   Authentication Performance 78

4.3   Security Analysis 79
4.4   Complexity 81
5   Experimental Results 82
5.1   Authentication Performance 82
5.2   Key Equivocation 82
5.3   Impact on Data BER 84
6   Conclusions 85
Appendix: Precoding and Power-Allocation with CSI 85
No CSI 85
Perfect CSI 86
Statistical CSI 86
References 87

Digital Fingerprint: A Practical Hardware Security Primitive 89
Gang Qu, Carson Dunbar, Xi Chen and Aijiao Cui
1   Introduction 89
2   Digital Fingerprinting for IP Protection 93
2.1   Background on Fingerprinting 93
2.2   The Need and Challenge of Digital
        Fingerprinting IPs 94
2.3   Requirements of Digital Fingerprinting 94
2.4   Iterative Fingerprinting Techniques 95
2.5   Fingerprinting with Constraint-Addition 98
3   Observability Don't Care Fingerprinting 100
3.1   Illustrative Example 100
3.2   Observability Don't Care Conditions 101
3.3   Finding Locations for Circuit Modification Based
        on ODCs 101
3.4   Determining Potential Fingerprinting Modifications 102
3.5   Maintaining Overhead Constraints 103
3.6   Security Analysis 103
4   Satisfiability Don't Care Fingerprinting 104
4.1   Satisfiability Don't Care and Illustrative Example 104
4.2   Assumptions for SDC Based Fingerprinting 105
4.3   SDC Based Fingerprinting Technique 106
4.4   Fingerprint Embedding Scheme 107
4.5   Security Analysis 108
5   Scan Chain Fingerprinting 109
5.1   Illustrative Example 109
5.2   Basics on Scan Chain Design 110
5.3   Scan Chain Fingerprinting 111
5.4   Security Analysis 111
6   Conclusion 113
References 113

Operating System Fingerprinting................................ 115
Jonathan Gurary, Ye Zhu, Riccardo Bettati and Yong Guan
1   Overview of Operating System Fingerprinting.................... 115
2   Major Operating System Fingerprinting Techniques............... 116
     2.1   OS Fingerprinting 116
     2.2   Reconnaissance Through Packet-Content Agnostic Traffic
            Analysis.. 122
     2.3   Analysis of Smartphone Traffic....................... 123
     2.4   Analysis of Encrypted Traffic 124
3   Case Study: Smartphone OS Reconnaissance.................... 124
     3.1   System and Threat Model 127
     3.2   Identifying Smartphone Operating Systems 128
     3.3   Empirical Evaluation 132
4   Summary and Future Directions............................ 135
Appendix A: Detailed Descriptions of Algorithms 136
References 137

**Secure and Trustworthy Provenance Collection for Digital
Forensics**... 141
Adam Bates, Devin J. Pohly and Kevin R.B. Butler
1   Introduction 141
2   Provenance-Aware Systems 142
     2.1   Disclosed Provenance-Aware Systems 143
     2.2   Automatic Provenance-Aware Systems 144
3   Ensuring the Trustworthiness of Provenance 147
     3.1   Security Challenges to Provenance Collection 147
     3.2   The Provenance Monitor Concept 149
4   High-Fidelity Whole Systems Provenance 150
     4.1   Design of Hi-Fi 150
     4.2   Handling of System-Level Objects 151
     4.3   Hi-Fi Implementation 154
     4.4   Limitations of Hi-Fi 158
5   Linux Provenance Modules 159
     5.1   Augmenting Whole-System Provenance 159
     5.2   Threat Model 160
     5.3   Design of LPM 161
     5.4   Deploying LPM 164
6   Analyzing the Security of Provenance Monitors................. 165
     6.1   Completeness Analysis of Hi-Fi 165
     6.2   Security Analysis of LPM 169
7   Current and Future Challenges to Provenance for Forensics......... 171
References 173

Conclusion 177
Yong Guan, Sneha Kumar Kasera, Cliff Wang and Ryan M. Gerdes
1   Overview 177
2   Measurements of Fingerprints 178
3   Fingerprints and Crypto-Based Methods. 179
4   Science of Fingerprints. 179
5   Security of Fingerprints 180

Index 183

Introduction

Yong Guan, Sneha Kumar Kasera, Cliff Wang and Ryan M. Gerdes

Abstract Authentication of a user or a device is absolutely essential before it can be allowed access to critical and protected resources or services. Most of the existing fingerprint-based authentication systems have focused on authenticating human beings only. There is a strong need to extend the fingerprinting ideas to devices for the purpose of building robust and more convenient authentication systems for the next generation connected devices. Furthermore, device fingerprints have many other related applications including forensics, intrusion detection, and assurance monitoring that need to be explored as well. In this chapter, we introduce important aspects of device fingerprints.

1 Overview

Authentication, the process of reliably verifying the identity of a person or a device, continues to pose serious challenges in an increasingly networked and mobile world. Authentication of a user or a device is absolutely essential before it can be allowed access to critical and protected resources or services. Authentication is mainly achieved through one of the following techniques

- What you know: passwords, secret keys, private keys, etc.
- What you have: physical keys, smart cards, etc.
- What you are: fingerprints, face recognition, keystrokes, etc.

Y. Guan (✉)
Iowa State University, Ames, IA 50011, USA
e-mail: guan@iastate.edu

S.K. Kasera
University of Utah, Salt Lake City, UT 84112, USA
e-mail: kasera@cs.utah.edu

C. Wang
Army Research Office, Research Triangle Park, Durham, NC 27709, USA
e-mail: cliff.x.wang.civ@mail.mil

R.M. Gerdes
Utah State University, Logan, UT 84341, USA
e-mail: ryan.gerdes@usu.edu

© Springer Science+Business Media New York 2016
C. Wang et al. (eds.), *Digital Fingerprinting*,
DOI 10.1007/978-1-4939-6601-1_1

The first two techniques are subject to theft of the passwords or physical objects. The third technique is robust against such thefts. However, most of the existing fingerprint-based authentication systems have focused on authenticating human beings only. There is a strong need to extend the fingerprinting ideas to devices for the purpose of building robust and more convenient authentication systems for devices. Furthermore, device fingerprints may also have many other related applications including forensics, intrusion detection, and assurance monitoring that need to be explored as well. Device fingerprint research requires cross-disciplinary expertise in hardware and software spanning different branches of engineering and computer science.

2 Applications and Requirements of Fingerprints

Fingerprints have broad applications and are useful in many contexts, security and otherwise, including in

1. determining whether an entity is a friend or a foe,
2. detecting intrusions,
3. collecting and analyzing data for forensic purposes,
4. authenticating before allowing access to resources, services, or networks, and
5. assurance monitoring.

Fingerprints must be robust to environmental changes and aging, resistant to attacks, accurate (low false negative and false positives), easy to measure in a predictable manner, and convenient to use. Some applications, e.g., deciding whether someone is a friend or foe, would require a very quick decision-making and thus the fingerprints must lend themselves to quick measurement and verification, while other applications, e.g., forensics, could allow for more time to measure and verify fingerprints. For some applications, gross classification may be enough. In the preceding, The choice of the fingerprinting method depends largely on the consequences of incorrect authentication.

Fingerprints should be immutable and inimitable (at least with a high probability). Fingerprints, not necessarily of the same kind, should be able to deal with different types of adversaries, potentially those that can spoof and reproduce fingerprints, and/or can jam the communication channel. Fingerprints and fingerprinting techniques must be adaptive depending on the nature of the applications and the adversary.

3 Types of Fingerprints

The possibility of fingerprinting a specific device comes from the fact that each individual device has variations in some features (in some components) when it is manufactured or in its context. Environment, channel and many other factors have their imprints branded in the output from a device.

Properly employed, device fingerprints allow one to perform various types of authentication and verification such as

1. infer from a multimedia object/information, if a specific device (e.g., video recorder) generates the multimedia and where and when it was generated,
2. determine which networking device produces a given RF signal, and
3. differentiate between microphones and cell phones that either record or produce sound.

Furthermore, fingerprinting may not be limited to device fingerprinting. Other important fingerprinting contexts include: network traffic fingerprinting and watermarking (e.g., from packet timing and size, we can identify an encrypted VoIP flow or the content of VoIP); CPU heat pattern and other things related to CPU; fingerprint computers via clock skew and other features; and distinguishing users and host applications via measuring the HCI device output such as Bluetooth frame size and frequency or other features.

In what follows, these issues are discussed with regard to the methodology of fingerprinting, the origins and design of fingerprints, how cryptographic operations may be strengthened using fingerprints, operating systems fingerprints, provence collection for fingerprints, and protection of intellectual property using fingerprints.

Types and Origins of Fingerprints

Davide Zanetti, Srdjan Capkun and Boris Danev

Abstract We present a systematic review of physical-layer identification systems and provide a summary of current state-of-the-art techniques. We further review the types of fingerprints that were discussed in prior work and highlight issues that are still open and need to be addressed in future work.

1 Introduction

Devices are traditionally identified by some unique information that they hold such as a public identifier or a secret key. Besides by what they hold, devices can be identified by what they *are*, i.e., by some unique characteristics that they exhibit and that can be observed. Examples include characteristics related to device components such operating system, drivers, clocks, radio circuitry, etc. Analyzing these components for identifiable information is commonly referred to as *fingerprinting*, since the goal is to create fingerprints similar to their biometric counterparts [2].

Here, we focus on techniques that allow wireless devices to be identified by unique characteristics of their analog (radio) circuitry; this type of identification is also referred to as *physical-layer device identification*. More precisely, physical-layer device identification is the process of fingerprinting the analog circuitry of a device by analyzing the device's communication at the physical layer for the purpose of identifying a device or a class of devices. Physical-layer device identification is possible due to hardware imperfections in the analog circuitry introduced at the manufacturing process. These hardware imperfections appear in the transmitted signals which makes them measurable. While more precise manufacturing and quality con-

D. Zanetti (✉)
Institute of Information Security, ETH Zurich, Zürich, Switzerland
e-mail: zanettid@inf.ethz.ch

S. Capkun
e-mail: capkuns@inf.ethz.ch

B. Danev
e-mail: boris.danev@inf.ethz.ch

© Springer Science+Business Media New York (outside the USA) 2016
C. Wang et al. (eds.), *Digital Fingerprinting*,
DOI 10.1007/978-1-4939-6601-1_2

trol could minimize such artifacts, it is often impractical due to significantly higher production costs.[1]

The use of physical-layer device identification has been suggested for defensive and offensive purposes. It has been proposed for intrusion detection [4, 15, 45], access control [3, 48], wormhole detection [33], cloning detection [6, 23], malfunction detection [49], secure localization [44], rogue access point detection [21], etc. It has also been discussed as one of the main hurdles in achieving anonymity and location privacy [29, 30]. Wireless platforms for which physical-layer identification has been shown to be feasible include HF Radio Frequency IDentification (RFID) transponders, UHF (CC1000) sensor nodes, analog VHF transmitters, IEEE 802.11 and 802.15.4 (CC2420) transceivers.

Being able to assess, for a given wireless platform, if physical-layer identification is feasible and under which assumptions, accuracy, and cost is important for the construction of accurate attacker models and consequently for the analysis and design of security solutions in wireless networks. So far, to the best of our knowledge, physical-layer device identification has not been systematically addressed in terms of feasibility, design, implementation and evaluation. This lack of systematization often results in misunderstanding the implications of device identification on the security of wireless protocols and applications.

The goal of this work is to enable a better understanding of device identification and its implications by systematizing the existing research on the topic. We review device identification systems, their design, requirements, and properties, and provide a summary of the current state-of-the-art techniques. We finally summarize issues that are still open and need to be addressed for this topic to be fully understood.

2   Physical-Layer Device Identification

In this section we present the main components of a physical-layer device identification system and discuss the system properties and requirements.

2.1   General View

Physical-layer device identification involves three entities as shown in Fig. 1: a wireless device, a device identification system, and an application system requesting the identification.

Physical-layer device identification systems aim at identifying (or verifying the identity of) devices or their affiliation classes based on characteristics of devices that are observable from their communication at the physical layer. That is, physical-layer device identification systems acquire, process, store, and compare signals generated

---

[1]This work is largely based on [8].

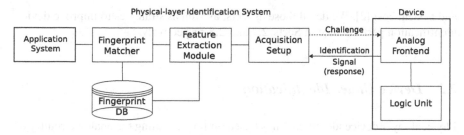

Fig. 1 Entities involved in the physical-layer identification of wireless devices and their main components

from devices during communications with the ultimate aim of identifying (or verifying) devices or their affiliation classes.

Such an identification system can be viewed as a pattern recognition system typically composed of (Fig. 1): an acquisition setup to acquire signals from devices under identification, also referred to as *identification signals,* a feature extraction module to obtain identification-relevant information from the acquired signals, also referred to as *fingerprints,* and a fingerprint matcher for comparing fingerprints and notifying the application system requesting the identification of the comparison results.

Typically, there are two modules in an identification system: one for enrollment and one for identification. During enrollment, signals are captured from either each device or each (set of) class-representative device(s) considered by the application system. Fingerprints obtained from the feature extraction module are then stored in a database (each fingerprint may be linked with some form of unique ID representing the associated device or class). During identification, fingerprints obtained from the devices under identification are compared with reference fingerprints stored during enrollment. The task of the identification module can be twofold: either recognize (identify) a device or its affiliation class from among many enrolled devices or classes (1:N comparisons), or verify that a device identity or class matches a claimed identity or class (1:1 comparison).

The typical operation of an identification module flows as follows: the acquisition setup (Sect. 2.6) acquires the signals transmitted (Sect. 2.3) from the device under identification (Sect. 2.2), which may be a response to a specific challenge sent by the acquisition setup. Then, the feature extraction module (Sect. 2.6) extracts features (Sect. 2.4) from the acquired signals and obtains device fingerprints (Sect. 2.5). Subsequently, the fingerprint matcher (Sect. 2.6) retrieves the reference fingerprints associated to the device under identification from the fingerprint database and compares them against the obtained fingerprints to determine or verify the identity (or the class) of the device under identification. The results of the fingerprint matcher can then be incorporated in the decision making process of the application system requesting the identification (e.g., to grant or not to grant access to a certain location).

The design specification of an identification system usually includes requirements for system accuracy (allowable error rates), computational speed, exception handling, and system cost [2]. We detail those aspects, as well as strategies to improve device identification performance in Sects. 2.7 and 2.8 respectively.

2.2 Device Under Identification

Physical-layer device identification is based on fingerprinting the analog circuitry of devices by observing their radio communication. Consequently, any device that uses radio communication may be subject to physical-layer identification. So far, it has been shown that a number of devices (or classes of devices) can be identified using physical-layer identification. These include analog VHF transmitters [18, 42, 43, 45–47], IEEE 802.11 transceivers [3, 14–16, 25, 40, 48], IEEE 802.15.4 transceivers [5], Bluetooth transceivers [17], UHF sensor nodes [33], HF RFID [6, 37] and UHF RFID [31, 51] transponders. All these devices are composed of antennas, analog frontends, and logic units, but have different levels of complexity, e.g., IEEE 802.11 transceivers (Fig. 2b) are complex whereas RFID transponders are relatively simple (Fig. 2a).

Although what makes a device or a class of devices to be uniquely identified among other devices or classes of devices is known to be due to imperfections introduced at the manufacturing phase of the analog circuitry, the actual device's components causing those have not been always clearly identified in all systems. For example, Toonstra and Kinsner [45, 46] based their identification system on the uniqueness of VHF transmitter's frequency synthesizers (local oscillators), while Danev et al. [6] only suggested that the proposed identification system may rely on imperfections caused by RFID device's antennas and charge pumps. Identifying the exact components may become more difficult when considering relatively-complex devices. In these cases, it is common to identify in the whole analog circuitry, or in a specific sub-circuit, the cause of imperfections. For example, Brik et al. [3] identified IEEE 802.11 transceivers considering modulation-related features; the cause of hard-

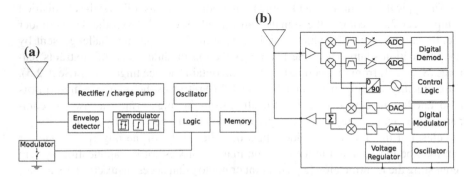

Fig. 2 Block diagrams of two classes of wireless devices. **a** RFID transponder. **b** IEEE 802.11 transceiver

ware artifacts can be then located in the modulator sub-circuit of the transceivers. Table 1 shows a non-exhaustive list of reported identification experiments together with the considered devices and (possible) causes of imperfections. Knowing the components that make devices uniquely identifiable may have relevant implications on both attacks and applications, which makes the investigation on such components an important open problem and research direction.

2.3 Identification Signals

Considering devices communicating through radio signals, i.e., sending data according to some defined specification and protocol, identification at the physical layer aims at extracting unique characteristics from the transmitted radio signals and to use those characteristics to distinguish among different devices or classes of devices. We defined *identification signals* as the signals that are collected for the purpose of identification. Signal characteristics are mainly based on observing and extracting information from the properties of the transmitted signals, like amplitude, frequency, or phase over a certain period of time. These time-windows can cover different parts of the transmitted signals. Mainly, we distinguish between data and non-data related parts. The data parts of signals directly relate to data (e.g., preamble, midamble, payload) transmission, which leads to considered data-related properties such as modulation errors [3], preamble (midamble) amplitude, frequency and phase [25, 34], spectral transformations [17, 25]. Non-data-related parts of signals are not associated with data transmission. Examples include the turn-on transients [45, 46], near-transient regions [35, 50], RF burst signals [6]. Figure 3 shows an non-exhaustive list of signal regions that have been used to identify active wireless transceivers (IEEE 802.11, 802.15.4) and passive transponders (ISO 14443 HF RFID).

2.4 Features

Features are characteristics extracted from identification signals. Those can be *predefined* or *inferred*. Table 1 shows a non-exhaustive list of reported identification experiments together with the deployed features.

Predefined features relate to well-understood signal characteristics. Those can be classified as *in-specification* and *out-specification*. Specifications are used for quality control and specify error tolerances. Examples of in-specification characteristics include modulation errors such as frequency offset, I/Q origin offset, magnitude and phase errors [3], as well as time-related parameters such as the duration of the response [32]. Examples of out-specification characteristics include clock skew [21] and the duration of the turn-on transient [33]. Figure 4a, b show a predefined, in-specification feature used to identify EPC C1G2 RFID tags [52]. The explored feature relates to the tags' transmitted data rate ($BLF = 1/T_{cycle}$). The EPC C1G2

Table 1 Non-exhaustive list of reported identification experiments together with feature-related information

Device[a]	Signal Part[b]	Feature[c]	Type[d]	Cause of Imperfections[e]	Reference
Analog VHF txmtr	Transient	Wavelets	Inferred	Frequency synthesizer	Toonstra and Kinsner [45]
Bluetooth trx	Transient	Wavelets	Inferred	–	Hall et al. [17]
IEEE 802.15.4 trx	Transient	FFT spectra	Inferred	–	Danev and Capkun [5]
IEEE 802.11 trx	Data	Modulation errors	Predefined (in-spec)	Modulator circuitry	Brik et al. [3]
ISO 14443 RFID txpndr	RF burst	FFT spectra	Inferred	Antenna, charge pump	Danev et al. [6]
IEEE 802.11 trx	Data	Clock skew	Predefined (out-spec)	Trx analog circuitry	Jana and Kasera [21]
UHF trx	Transient	Transient length	Predefined (out-spec)	–	Rasmussen and Capkun [33]
IEEE 802.11 trx	Data (preamble)	Wavelets	Inferred	–	Klein et al. [25]
EPC C1G2 RFID txpndr	Data	Timing errors	Predefined (out-spec)	Oscillator	Zanetti et al. [51]
GSM trx	Near-transient, Data	Amp., freq., phase	Predefined	–	Williams et al. [50]

[a]Device: class of considered devices.

[b]Signal Part: the signal part used to extract fingerprints.

[c]Feature: basic signal characteristic.

[d]Type: type of the considered features. *Predefined*—well-understood signal characteristics. *Inferred*—various signal transformations.

[e]Cause of Imperfections: device component likely to be the cause of exploited hardware variations.

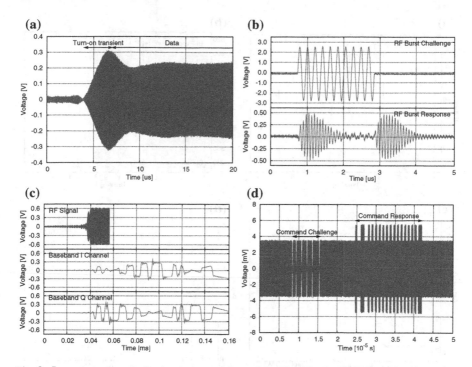

Fig. 3 Several signal parts (regions) commonly used for identification. **a** Turn-on transient of an IEEE 802.15.4 (CC2420) transceiver. **b** ISO 14443 HF RFID tag response to an out-of-specification RF burst signal. **c** Preamble and data modulated regions in IEEE 802.11 transceivers. Signal parts can be either analyzed at RF or at baseband (I/Q). **d** HF/UHF RFID tag response to in-specification commands

standard [11] allows a maximum tolerance of ±22 % around the nominal data rate: different tags transmit at different data rates.

Differently from predefined features, where the considered characteristics are known in advance prior to recording of the signals, we say that features are inferred when they are extracted from signals, e.g., by means of some spectral transformations such as Fast Fourier Transform (FFT) or Discrete Wavelet Transform (DWT), without a-priori knowledge of a specific signal characteristic. For example, wavelet transformations have been applied on signal turn-on transients [17, 18] and different data-related signal regions [25, 26]. The Fourier transformation has also been used to extract features from the turn-on transient [5] and other technology-specific device responses [6]. Figure 4c, d show an inferred feature used to identify EPC C1G2 RFID tags [51]. The explored feature relies on the spectral transformation (FFT) of the tag's data-related signal region: different tags present different signal spectra.

Both predefined and inferred features can be subject to further statistical analysis in order to improve their quality. We discuss more in detail such improvements in Sect. 2.8.

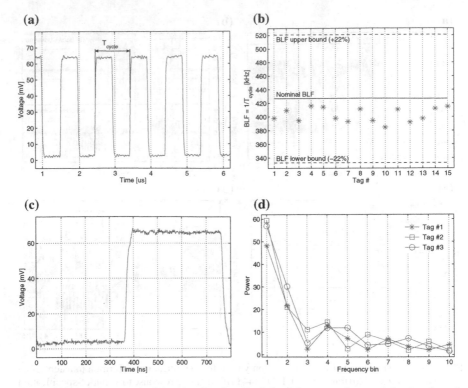

Fig. 4 Different features used for identification. Predefined feature: **a** data-modulated region of EPC C1G2 RFID tags [52] and **b** the considered predefined feature, i.e., the tags' data rate ($BLF = 1/T_{cycle}$) for different tags, as well as the given nominal data rate and tolerances according to the EPC C1G2 specifications [11]. Inferred feature: **c** data-modulated region of EPC C1G2 RFID tags [51] and **d** the considered inferred feature, i.e., the signal spectral transformation (FFT), for different tags

2.5 Device Fingerprints

Fingerprints are sets of features (or combinations of features, Sect. 2.8) that are used to identify devices. The properties that fingerprints need to present in order to achieve practical implementations (adapted from [2]) are:

- Universality: every device (in the considered device-space) should have the considered features.
- Uniqueness: no two devices should have the same fingerprints.
- Permanence: the obtained fingerprints should be invariant over time.
- Collectability: it should be possible to capture the identification signals with existing (available) equipments.

When considering physical-layer identification of wireless devices, we further consider:

- Robustness: fingerprints should not be subject, or at least, they should be evaluated with respect to (i) external environmental aspects that directly influence the signal propagation like radio interferences due to other radio signals, surrounding materials, signal reflections, absorption, etc., as well as positioning aspects like the distance and orientation between the devices under identification and the identification system, and (ii) device-related aspects like temperature, voltage level, and power level. Many types of robustness can be acceptable for a practical identification system. Generally, obtaining robust features helps in building more reliable identification systems.
- Data-dependency: fingerprints can be obtained from features extracted from a specific bit pattern (data-related part of the identification signal) transmitted by a device under identification (e.g., the claimed ID sent in a packet frame). This dependency has particularly interesting implications given that fingerprints are associated to both devices and data transmitted by those devices.

2.6 Physical-Layer Identification System

A physical-layer identification system (Fig. 1) has the tasks to acquire the identification signals (acquisition setup), extract features and obtain fingerprints from the identification signals (feature extraction module), and compare fingerprints (fingerprint matcher). The system may either passively collect identification signals or it may actively challenge devices under identification to produce the identification signals.

The acquisition setup is responsible for the acquisition and digitalization of the identification signals. We refer to a single acquired and digitalized signal as sample. Depending on the considered features to extract, before digitalizing the identification signals, those may be modified, e.g., downconverted. The acquisition process should neither influence nor degrade (e.g., by adding noise) the signals needed for the identification, but should preserve and bring into the digital domain the unique signal characteristics on which the identification relies on. Therefore, high-quality (and expensive) equipment may be necessary. Typically, high-quality measurement equipment has been used to capture and digitize signal turn-on transients [17] and baseband signals [3].

The acquisition setup may also challenge devices under identification to transmit specific identification signals. Under *passive* identification, the acquisition setup acquires the identification signals without interacting with the devices under identification, e.g., identification signals can simply relate to data packets sent by devices under identification during standard communication with other devices. Differently, under *active* identification, the acquisition setup acquires the identification signals after challenging the devices under identification to transmit them. Besides the advantages of obtaining identification signals "on demand", active identification may exploit challenges, and consequently replies that contain identification signals, that are rare, or not present at all, in standard communications. For example, RFID transponders can be challenged with out-specification signal requests as shown in [6, 51].

The feature extraction module is responsible for extracting characteristics from signals that can then be used to distinguish devices or classes of devices. To improve the accuracy of an identification system, the feature extraction module may combine several features together (Sect. 2.8). In the case of predefined features, the feature extraction module implements functions that directly relate an input sample to the features. For example, when considering features like modulation errors, the feature extraction module implements a demodulator and several other functions to quantify these errors. Differently, in the case of inferred features, feature extraction can be a form of dimensionality reduction, where an input sample of dimension (random variables) d containing both relevant and redundant (for the identification) information is reduced to a new sample of dimension $m \leq d$ containing only relevant information. For example, dimensionality reduction techniques have not only been used to reduce the dimensionality [48], but also to find more discriminant subspaces [41]. Reducing the dimensionality of a sample makes it processable and highlights relevant features that may be hidden by noisy dimensions.

The fingerprint matcher compares newly extracted device fingerprints with reference fingerprints enrolled in the fingerprint database. Depending on the application system, it can provide a yes/no answer if a device fingerprint matches a chosen reference fingerprint (identity verification) or a list of devices that the device fingerprint most likely originated from (identification). The matcher is commonly implemented by some distance measure (e.g., Euclidean and Mahalanobis distances) or a more complex pattern recognition classifier such as Probabilistic Neural Networks (PNN) and Support Vector Machines (SVM) [1]. The choice of the matching technique highly depends on the extracted device fingerprints and the requirements of the application system (Sect. 3).

2.7 System Performance and Design Issues

The performance evaluation of a physical-layer device identification system is an important requirement for the system specification. Performance should be investigated in terms of identification accuracy, computational speed, exception handling, cost, and security [2].

The system accuracy is usually expressed in error rates that cannot be theoretically established, but only statistically estimated using test databases of device fingerprints. As physical-layer device identification systems are inherently similar to biometric identification systems, they can be evaluated using already established accuracy metrics [2]. More precisely, the error rates should include the probability of accepting an imposter device (False Accept Rate or FAR) and the probability of rejecting a genuine device (False Reject Rate or FRR). These error rates are usually expressed in the Receiver Operating Characteristic (ROC) that shows the FRRs at different FAR levels. The operating point in ROC, where FAR and FRR are equal, is referred to as the Equal Error Rate (EER). The EER is a commonly used accuracy metric because it is a single value metric and also tells that one recognition system is better than another for the range of FAR/FRR operating points encompassing the EER. For the accuracy at other operating points, one has to consider the ROC. We note that it is also common to provide the FRR for certain benchmark operating points such as FAR of 0.01, 0.1, 1 %.

The ROC and EER are the mostly commonly used metrics for the comparison of identification (verification) systems [13].

We note that physical-layer device identification systems in current state-of-art works (Sect. 3) were often evaluated as classification systems [1]. In a classification system, unknown device fingerprints are classified (correctly or incorrectly) to their respective reference device fingerprints. The error rate is referred to as the classification error rate and shows the ratio of the number of incorrectly classified device fingerprints over all classified fingerprints. The classification error rate does not capture the acceptance of imposters nor the rejection of genuine devices, and therefore is typically not an appropriate metric for the evaluation of the accuracy of identification (verification) systems.

The requirement on computational resources, cost, and exception handling need to be considered as well. In physical-layer identification techniques the complexity of the extracted fingerprints directly relates to the quality and speed of signal acquisition and processing; the higher the quality and speed, the higher the cost. Acquisition setups depend on environmental factors which make exception handling a critical component (e.g., signals may be difficult to acquire from certain locations; alternatively, acquired signals may not have the acceptable quality for feature extraction). Therefore, appropriate procedures need to be devised in order to fulfill given requirements.

Last but not least, the evaluation of a physical-layer device identification system must address related security and privacy issues. Can the device fingerprints be forged and therefore compromise the system? How can one defend against attacks on the integrity of the system? Related works on these systems have largely neglected these issues.

2.8 Improving Physical-Layer Identification Systems

Before enrollment and identification modules can be deployed, the identification system must go through a building phase where design decisions (e.g., features, feature extraction methods, etc.) are tested and, in case, modified to fulfill the requirements on the above-mentioned system properties: accuracy, computational speed, exception handling, and costs.

Although these last three may significantly affect the design decisions, accuracy is usually the most considered property to test and evaluate an identification system. Typically, to improve the accuracy of a (physical-layer) identification system (for wireless devices), i.e., to improve its overall error rates, different strategies can be deployed: (i) acquire signals with multiple acquisition setups, (ii) acquire signals from multiple transmitters on the same device (e.g., when devices are MIMO[2] systems), (iii) consider several acquisitions of the same signals, (iv) consider different signal parts (e.g., both transients and data) and different features, and (v) deploy different approaches for both feature extraction and matching.

So far, neither MIMO systems as devices under identification nor multiple acquisition setups have been considered yet. MIMO systems as devices under identification may offer a wider range of characteristics which the identification process can be based on. This can lead to more robust fingerprints (by analogy with human fingerprints, it is like verifying a human identity by scanning two different fingers). Using multiple acquisition setups may increase the accuracy of the identification, e.g., by acquiring a signal from different location at the same time may lead to more robust fingerprints. The impact of MIMO systems and of multiple acquisition setups is still unexplored.

Considering several acquisitions (samples) of the same signal is the common approach to obtain more reliable fingerprints [5, 17, 33]. Generally, the acquired samples are averaged out into one significant sample, which is then used by the feature extractor module to create fingerprints.

Considering different signal parts, features, and feature extraction methods is often referred to as multi-modal biometrics, where different modalities are combined to increase the identification accuracy and bring more robustness to the identification process [38]. Several works have already considered combining different modalities. For example, different signal properties (e.g., frequency, phase) were used in [3, 17], different signal regions, signal properties and statistics (e.g., skewness, kurtosis) were explored in [25, 35]. Different modalities extracted from device responses to various challenge requests were studied in [6]. The use of more modalities have resulted in significant improvement of the overall device identification accuracy. It should be noted that the above modalities were mostly combined before the feature matching (classification) procedure. Therefore, the combination of different classification techniques remains to be explored [20, 24].

In addition to the above-mentioned strategies to improve the accuracy of an identification system, it is worth to mention *feature selection* and *statistical feature extraction*. Feature selection aims at selecting from a set of features, the sub-set that leads to the best accuracy [19] (that sub-set will then be used in enrollment and identification modules). Statistical feature extraction exploits statistical methods to choose and/or transform features of objects (in our case, devices) such that the similarities

---

[2]MIMO refers to multiple-input and multiple-output. Such wireless systems use multiple antennas for transmitting and receiving for the purpose of improving communication performance.

between same objects are preserved, while the differences between different objects are enhanced [1]. Statistical feature extraction is a powerful technique to improve the features' discriminant quality.

3 State of the Art

Identification of radio signals gained interest in the early development of radar systems during the World War II [22, 28]. In a number of battlefield scenarios it became critical to distinguish own from enemy radars. This was achieved by visually comparing oscilloscope photos of received signals to previously measured profiles [28]. Such approaches gradually became impractical due to increasing number of transmitters and more consistency in the manufacturing process.

In mid and late 90's a number of research works appeared in the open literature to detect illegally operated radio VHF FM transmitters [4, 18, 45, 46]. Subsequently, physical-layer identification techniques were investigated for device cloning detection [6, 23], defective device detection [49], and access control in wireless personal and local area networks [3, 15, 16, 21, 33]. A variety of physical properties of the transmitted signals were researched and related identification systems proposed.

Here we review the most prominent techniques to physical-layer identification available in the open literature. We structure them in three categories, namely transient-based, modulation-based, and other approaches based on signal part used for feature extraction. For each category, we discuss the works in chronological order. A concise summary is provided in Table 2.

3.1 Transient-Based Approaches

Physical-layer identification techniques that use the turn-on/off transient of a radio signal are usually referred to as transient-based approaches to physical-layer device identification. These approaches require accurate transient detection and separation before feature extraction and matching. The detection and separation of the turn-on transient depend on the channel noise and device hardware and have been shown to be critical to these systems [39, 47].

The open literature on transient-based device identification can be traced back to the early 90s. Toonstra and Kinsner [45, 46] introduced wavelet analysis to characterize the turn-on transients of 7 VHF FM transmitters from 4 different manufacturers. Device fingerprints were composed of wavelet spectra extracted from signal transients captured at the FM discriminator circuit. All extracted fingerprints were correctly classified by means of a genetic algorithm (neural network). Gaussian noise was added to the original transients in order to simulate typical field conditions. Hippenstiel and Payal [18] also explored wavelet analysis by filter banks in order to characterize the turn-on transients of 4 different VHF FM transmitters. They showed

Table 2 Summary of physical-layer device identification techniques

Approach	Signal	Features	Evaluation data			Evaluated factors	Methodology	Error rate
			Device Type	#	Origin[a]			
Toonstra and Kinsner [45]	Transient	Wavelets	Analog VHF txmtr	7	D1	–	Classification	0%
Ellis and Serinken [10]	Transient	Amplitude, phase	Analog VHF txmtr	28	D1	Fixed distance	Visual inspection	n/a
Tekbas et al. [42]	Transient	Amplitude, phase	Analog VHF txmtr	10	D1	Wide temp. range, voltage and SNR	Classification	5%
Hall et al. [15]	Transient	Amplitude, phase, power, DWT coeffs.	IEEE 802.11 trx	14	D2	Close proximity and temperature	Classification	8%
Hall et al. [17]	Transient	Amplitude, phase, power, DWT coeffs.	Bluetooth trx	10	D2	Close proximity	Classification	7%
Ureten and Serinken [48]	Transient	Amplitude envelope	IEEE 802.11 trx	8	D2	Close proximity	Classification	2%
Rasmussen and Capkun [33]	Transient	Length, amplitude, DWT coeffs.	UHF trx	10	D3	Close proximity	Classification	30%
Brik et al. [3]	Data	Frequency, sync, I/Q, magnitude, phase	IEEE 802.11 trx	138	D3	Varied distance and location	Classification	0.34%

(continued)

Table 2 (continued)

Approach	Signal	Features	Evaluation data			Evaluated factors	Methodology	Error rate
			Device Type	#	Origin[a]			
Jana and Kasera [21]	Data	Clock skew	IEEE 802.11 Access Point	5	D1	Virtual AP, temp. and NTP sync.	Classification, attacks	0%
Danev and Capkun [5]	Transient	FFT spectra	IEEE 802.15.4 trx	50	D3	Distance, location, voltage, temp.	Verification, attacks	0.24%
Suski et al. [40]	Preamble	Power spectrum density	IEEE 802.11 trx	3	D3	Proximity, SNR	Classification	13%
Danev et al. [6]	RF burst	FFT spectra, modulation	ISO 14443 HF RFID txpndr	50	D3	Varied position, distance	Verification	4%
Periaswamy et al. [31]	Preamble	Minimum power response	EPC C1G2 UHF RFID txpndr	50	D3	fixed position	Verification	5%
Williams et al. [50]	Data, near transient	Amplitude, frequency, phase, statistics	GSM trx.	16	D1	Fixed position, SNR	Verification	5–20%

[a]D1: Devices from different manufacturers and some of the same model; D2: Devices from different manufacturers and models; D3: Devices from the same manufacturer and model (identical)

that Euclidean distance was an accurate similarity measure to classify extracted device fingerprints from different manufacturers. Choe et al. [4] presented an automated device identification system based on wavelet and multi-resolution analysis of turn-on transient signals and provided an example of transmitter classification of 3 different transmitters.

Ellis and Serinken [10] studied the properties of turn-on transients exhibited by VHF FM transmitters. They discussed properties of universality, uniqueness, and consistency in 28 VHF FM device profiles characterized by the amplitude and phase of the transients. By visual inspection, the authors showed that there were consistent similarities between device profiles within the same manufacturer and model and device profiles from different models that could not be visually distinguished. Moreover, some devices did not exhibit stable transient profiles during normal operation. The authors suggested that further research is needed to quantify environmental factors (e.g., doppler shift, fading, temperature). Following these recommendations, Tekbas, Serinken and Ureten [42, 43] tested 10 VHF FM transmitters under ambient temperature, voltage, and noise level changes. The device fingerprints were composed of transient amplitude and phase features obtained from the signal complex envelope. A probabilistic neural network (PNN) was used for classifying the fingerprints. The experimental results showed that the system needed to be trained over a wide temperature range and the operational supply-voltage levels in order to achieve low classification error rates of 5 %. Classification accuracy of low-SNR transients could be improved by estimating the SNR and modifying its level in the training phase [43].

Transient-based approaches were also investigated in modern wireless local and personal area networks (WLAN/WPAN), primarily for intrusion detection and access control. Hall et al. [15–17] focused on Bluetooth and IEEE 802.11 transceivers. The authors captured the transient signals of packet transmissions from close proximity (10 cm) with a spectrum analyzer. They extracted the amplitude, phase, in-phase, quadrature, power, and DWT coefficients and combined them in device fingerprints. Classification results on 30 IEEE 802.11 transceivers composed of different models from 6 different manufacturers [14, 16] showed error rates of 0–14 % depending on the model and manufacturer. The average classification error rate was 8 %. The same technique was also applied to a set of 10 Bluetooth transceivers and showed similar classification error rates [17]. The authors also introduced dynamic profiles, i.e., each device fingerprint was updated after some amount of time, in order to compensate internal temperature effects in the considered devices.

Ureten and Serinken [48] proposed extracting the envelope of the instantaneous amplitude of IEEE 802.11 transient signals for device classification. The authors classified signals captured at close proximity from 8 different manufacturers using a probabilistic neural network. The classification error rates fluctuated between 2–4 % depending on the size of the device fingerprints.

In the above works, signal transients were captured at close proximity to the fingerprinting antenna, approximately 10–20 cm. The classification error rates were primarily estimated from a set of different model/manufacturer devices; only a few devices possibly had identical hardware. Physical-layer identification of same model and same manufacturer devices was considered by Rasmussen and Capkun [33]. Each device fingerprint contained the transient length, amplitude variance, number of peaks of the carrier signal, difference between normalized mean and the normalized maximum value of the transient power, and the first DWT coefficient. Experimental results on 10 UHF (Mica2/CC1000) sensor devices with identical hardware showed a classification error rate of 30 % from close proximity. A follow-up work [5] showed that a carefully designed hardware setup with high-end components and statistically selected features can also accurately identify same model and manufacturer sensor devices. The authors built device fingerprints with statistically filtered FFT spectra of transient signals and used Mahalanobis distance as a similarity measure. The system accuracy was evaluated using identity verification on 50 IEEE 802.15.4 (CC2420) Tmote Sky sensor devices from the same model and manufacturer. Low equal error rates (EER) of 0.24 % were achieved with signals captured from distances up to 40 m. The authors also concluded that large fixed distances and variable voltage preserve fingerprint properties, whereas varying distance and antenna polarization distort them enough to significantly decrease the accuracy (EER = 30 %).

3.2 Modulation-Based Approaches

Modulation-based approaches to device identification focus on extracting unique features from the part of the signal that has been modulated, i.e., the data. Such features have only recently being proposed for device identification. More precisely, Brik et al. [3] used five distinctive signal properties of modulated signals, namely the frequency error, SYNC correlation, I/Q origin offset, and magnitude and phase errors as features for physical-layer identification. The latter were extracted from IEEE 802.11b packet frames, previously captured using a high-end vector signal analyzer. Device fingerprints were built using all five features and classified with k-NN and SVM classifiers specifically tuned for the purpose. The system was tested on 138 identical 802.11b NICs and achieved a classification error rate of 3 and 0.34 % for k-NN and SVM classifiers respectively. The signals were captured at distances from 3 to 15 m from the fingerprinting antenna. Preliminary results on varying devices' locations showed that the extracted fingerprints are stable to location changes.

Modulation-based approaches were also applied to classifying RFID devices. Danev et al. [6] showed that the modulation of tag responses of different model ISO 14443 RFID transponders shows distinctive and consistent characteristics when challenged with various out-specification commands. They tested their proposal on RFID transponders from 4 different classes.

3.3 Other Approaches

A number of physical-layer identification techniques have been proposed [6, 21, 40] that could not be directly related to the aforementioned categories. These approaches usually targeted a specific wireless technology and/or exploited additional properties from the signal and logical layer.

Suski et al. [40] proposed using the baseband power spectrum density of the packet preamble to uniquely identify wireless devices. A device fingerprint was created by measuring the power spectrum density (PSD) of the preamble of an IEEE 802.11a (OFDM) packet transmission. Subsequently, device fingerprints were matched by spectral correlation. The authors evaluated the accuracy of their approach on 3 devices and achieved an average classification error rate of 20 % for packet frames with SNR greater than 6 dB. Klein et al. [25, 26] further explored IEEE 802.11a (OFDM) device identification by applying complex wavelet transformations and multiple discriminant analysis (MDA). The classification performance of their technique was evaluated on 4 same model Cisco wireless transceivers. The experimental results showed SNR improvement of approx. 8 dB for a classification error rate of 20 %. Varying SNR and burst detection error were also considered.

Various signal characteristics, signal regions and statistics were recently investigated on GSM devices [34, 35, 50]. The authors used the near-transient and midamble regions of GSM-GMSK burst signals to classify devices from 4 different manufacturers. They observed that the classification error using the midamble is significantly higher than using transient regions. Various factors were identified as potential areas of future work on the identification of GMSK signals. In a follow-up work [35], it has been shown that near-transient RF fingerprinting is suitable for GSM. Additional performance analysis was provided for GSM devices from the same manufacturer in [50]. The analysis revealed that a significant SNR increase (20–25 dB) was required in order to achieve high classification accuracy within same manufacturer devices.

Recently, a number of works investigated physical-layer identification of different classes of RFID [6, 31, 32, 36, 37, 51]. Periaswamy et al. [31, 32] considered fingerprinting of UHF RFID tags. In [31], the authors showed that the minimum power response characteristic can be used to accurately identify large sets of UHF RFID tags. An identification accuracy of 94.4 % (with FAR of 0.1 %) and 90.7 % (with FAR of 0.2 %) was achieved on two independent sets of 50 tags from two manufacturers. Timing properties of UHF RFID tags have been explored in two independent works [32, 51]. The authors showed that the duration of the response can be used to distinguish same manufacturer and type RFID tags independent of the environment. This poses a number of privacy concerns for users holding a number of these tags, e.g., user unauthorized tracking can be achieved by a network of readers with a high accuracy [51].

In the context of HF RFID, Danev et al. [6] explored timing, modulation, and spectral features extracted from device responses to purpose-built in- and out-specification signals. The authors showed that timing and modulation-shape features could only be used to identify between different manufacturers. On the other hand, spectral features would be the preferred choice for identifying same manufacturer and model transponders. Experimental results on 50 identical smart cards and a set of electronic passports showed an EER of 2.43 % from close proximity. Similarly, Romero et al. [36] demonstrated that the magnitude and phase at selected frequencies allow fingerprinting different models of HF RFID tags. The authors validated their technique on 4 models, 10 devices per model. Recently, the same authors extended their technique to enable identification of same model and manufacturer transponders [37]. The above works considered inductive coupled HF RFID tags and the proposed features work from close proximity.

Jana and Kasera [21] proposed an identification technique based on clock skews in order to protect against unauthorized access points (APs) in a wireless local area network. A device fingerprint is built for each AP by computing its clock skew at the client station; this technique has been previously shown to be effective in wired networks [27]. The authors showed that they could distinguish between different APs and therefore detect an intruder AP with high accuracy. The possibility to compute the clock skew relies on the fact that the AP association request contains time-stamps sent in clear.

3.4 Attacking Physical-Layer Device Identification

The large majority of works have focused on exploring feature extraction and matching techniques for physical-layer device identification. Only recently the security of these techniques started being addressed [5, 7, 9]. In these works, attacks on physical-layer identification systems can be divided into *signal replay* and *feature replay* attacks. In the former, the attacker's goal is to observe analog identification signals of a targeted device, capture them in a digital form, and then transmit (replay) these signals towards the identification system by some appropriate means (e.g., through purpose-built devices or more generic ones like software-defined radios [12], high-end signal analyzers, or arbitrary waveform generators). Differently, feature replay attacks aim at creating, modifying, or composing identification signals that reproduce only the features considered by the identification system. Such attacks can be launched by special devices such as arbitrary waveform generators that produce the modified or composed signals, by finding a device that exhibits similar features to the targeted device, or to replicate the entire circuitry of the targeted device or at least the components responsible for the identification features.

Edman and Yener [9] developed impersonation attacks on modulation-based identification techniques [3]. They showed that low-cost software-defined radios [12] could be used to reproduce modulation features (feature replay attacks) and impersonate a target device with a success rate of 50–75 %. Independently, Danev et al. [7] have designed impersonation attacks (both feature and signal replay attacks) on transient and modulation-based approaches using both software-defined radios and high-end arbitrary waveform generators. They showed that modulation-based techniques are vulnerable to impersonation with high accuracy, while transient-based techniques are likely to be compromised only from the location of the target device. The authors pointed out that this is mostly due to presence of wireless channel effects in the considered device fingerprints; therefore the channel needed to be taken into consideration for successful impersonation. In addition, Danev and Capkun [5] showed that their identification system may be vulnerable to hill-climbing attacks if the number of signals used for building the device fingerprint is not carefully chosen. This attack consists of repeatedly sending signals to the device identification system with modifications that gradually improve the similarity score between these signals and a target genuine signal. They also demonstrated that transient-based approaches could easily be disabled by jamming the transient part of the signal while still enabling reliable communication.

3.5 Summary and Conclusion

A detailed look of the state of the art shows a number of observations with respect to the design, properties, and evaluation of physical-layer identification systems.

A broad spectrum of wireless devices (technologies) have been investigated. The devices under identification cover VHF FM transmitters, IEEE 802.11 network access cards (NIC) and access points (AP), IEEE 802.15.4 sensor node devices, Bluetooth mobile phones, and RFID transponders. Identification at the physical layer has been shown to be feasible for all the considered types of devices.

In terms of feature extraction, most works explored inferred features for device identification [5, 10, 15, 40, 42, 45, 48]. Few works used predefined features [3, 21, 33] with only one work [3] exploiting predefined in-specification features. Typically, predefined features would be more controlled by device manufacturers (e.g., standard compliance) and are therefore likely to exhibit less discriminative properties compared to inferred features. The inferred features are however more difficult to discover and study given that purpose-built equipment and tailored analysis techniques are required. Both transient and data parts of the physical-layer communication were used for extracting device fingerprints.

The majority of works used standard classifiers such as Neural Network, Nearest Neighbor, and Support Vector Machines classifiers [1] to classify (match) fingerprints from different devices. Classification error rate was used as a metric of accuracy in [3, 10, 15, 33, 40, 42, 45, 48], while identification (verification) accuracy in terms of FAR, FRR and EER metrics is used in [5, 6]. In Sect. 2.7, we discuss the differences between those metrics and suggest an appropriate usage.

In terms of system evaluation, earlier works mostly considered heterogeneous devices from different manufacturers and models, while recent works focused on the more difficult task of identifying same model and manufacturer devices (see Table 2). In addition to hardware artifacts in the analog circuitry introduced at the manufacturing process, physical-layer identification of devices that present different hardware design, implementation, and were subject to a different manufacturing process may benefit from those differences. Differently, physical-layer identification of devices that present the same hardware design, implementation, and manufacturing process is exclusively based on hardware variability in the analog circuitry introduced at the manufacturing process, which makes the physical-layer identification of those devices a harder task.

Proper investigations on the actual components that make devices uniquely identifiable have been so far neglected. Although in some (few) works these components can be easily identified (e.g., Toonstra and Kinsner [45] based their device identification on signals generated by the local frequency synthesizer), in most of the other works only suggestions were provided (e.g., the device antenna and charge pump [6] or the modulator sub-circuit of the transceiver [3]).

Only few works considered evaluating the robustness of the extracted fingerprints to environment and in-device effects (see Table 2). Although parameters like temperature and voltage (at which the device under identification is powered) were considered, robustness evaluations mainly focused on determine the impact of distance and orientation of the device under identification with respect to the identification system. Obviously, features not (or only minimally) affected by distance and orientation will be easily integrated in real-world applications. Results show that inferred features based on spectral transformations such as Fast Fourier Transform or Discrete Wavelet Transform are particularly sensitive to distance and orientation [5, 6] (i.e., the identification accuracy significantly decreases when considering different distances and orientations), while features less affected by the transmission medium (i.e., the wireless channel) like clock skews or (some) modulation errors [3] are less sensitive.

In general, the proposed system evaluations rarely considered acquisition cost and time, feature extraction overhead and device fingerprint size. For example, some brief notes on feature extraction overhead and fingerprint size can be found in [5, 6] and on signal acquisition time in [3], but they are rather an exception in the reviewed state-of-the-art works.

Security and privacy considerations were largely neglected. Only recently, researchers considered attacks on selected physical-layer techniques [7, 9], but no comprehensive security and privacy analysis has been attempted.

4 Future Research Directions

Although physical-layer identification has been increasingly investigated within the last decade, several questions related to the performance of identification systems, fingerprint robustness, and applicability of physical-layer identification in real-world scenarios are still unanswered. In particular, during the presented work, we highlighted the following aspects:

- The causes of unique identification.
  Identify the components that make devices uniquely identifiable is a difficult task, but have relevant implications on both applications and attacks. Application

systems can benefit from more tailored features and detailed attack analysis, while attackers can use this information for advanced feature replay attacks.

- Robust fingerprints.

  Analyze the robustness of fingerprints with respect to application-related environmental and in-device aspects would help in both understanding the limitations and finding improvements on the considered features. Potential, and currently not-explored areas of improvement include MIMO systems, multiple acquisition setups, and multi-modal fingerprints. Deploying multiple acquisition setups may increase the accuracy of the identification while MIMO systems as devices under identification may offer a wider range of identification features. Considering different signal parts, features, and feature extraction methods and combining them to obtain multi-modal fingerprints may increase the identification accuracy and bring more robustness to the identification process.

- Security and privacy of device identification.

  Attacks on both security and privacy of physical-layer identification entities need to be thoroughly investigated and appropriate countermeasures designed and evaluated. Investigation of data-dependent properties in device fingerprints might be a promising direction to improve the resilience against replay attacks.

5 Conclusion

Physical-layer identification has been investigated on a broad spectrum of wireless technologies, but primarily as a defensive technique in order to enhance wireless security against identity-targeted attacks. The feasibility of physical-layer device identification has been largely neglected in the security analysis of protocols aiming at ensuring device (user) identity and location privacy. Moreover, the proposed techniques often lack proper performance evaluation and their resilience to attacks is rarely analyzed.

By systematizing the main concepts of these systems and analyzing the state-of-the-art approaches in the open literature, we provide a comprehensive overview of physical-layer identification and highlight the different types and origins of fingerprints.

Despite the existence of a number of works on the subject, understanding physical-layer identification in terms of feasibility, accuracy, cost, assumptions, and implications still remains a challenge. Further research is required to address a number of questions such as: what are the exact causes of identification? What is the impact of diversity on the identification accuracy? What are the properties of different physical-layer device fingerprints in terms of robustness and security guarantees? How much information entropy do fingerprints contain? Understanding the exact causes of fingerprinting would enable more tailored pattern analysis techniques and provide insights on how offensive uses could be mitigated. Diversity (e.g., MIMO, multi-modal features) can be exploited for improving the accuracy and increasing the robustness of these systems. Similarly, data-dependent properties could largely enhance the resilience to replay attacks.

References

1. Bishop, C.: Pattern Recognition and Machine Learning. Springer (2006)
2. Bolle, R., Connell, J., Pankanti, S., Ratha, N., Senior, A.: Guide to Biometrics. Springer (2003)
3. Brik, V., Banerjee, S., Gruteser, M., Oh, S.: Wireless device identification with radiometric signatures. In: Proceedings of ACM International Conference on Mobile Computing and Networking (MobiCom), pp. 116–127 (2008)
4. Choe, H., Poole, C., Yu, A., Szu, H.: Novel identification of intercepted signals for unknown radio transmitters. Proc. SPIE **2491**, 504–517 (1995)
5. Danev, B., Capkun, S.: Transient-based identification of wireless sensor nodes. In: Proceeding of ACM/IEEE Conference on Information Processing in Sensor Networks (IPSN), pp. 25–36 (2009)
6. Danev, B., Heydt-Benjamin, T.S., Capkun, S.: Physical-layer identification of RFID devices. In: Proceedings of USENIX Security Symposium, pp. 199–214 (2009)
7. Danev, B., Luecken, H., Capkun, S., Defrawy, K.E.: Attacks on physical-layer identification. In: Proceedings of ACM Conference on Wireless Network Security (WiSec), pp. 89–98 (2010)
8. Danev, B., Zanetti, D., Capkun, S.: On physical-layer identification of wireless devices. ACM Comput. Surv. **45**(1), 6:1–6:29 (2012)
9. Edman, M., Yener, B.: Active attacks against modulation-based radiometric identification. Technical report 09-02, Rensselaer Institute of Technology (August 2009)
10. Ellis, K., Serinken, N.: Characteristics of radio transmitter fingerprints. Radio Sci. **36**, 585–597 (2001)
11. EPCglobal: UHF Class 1 Gen 2 standard v. 1.2.0 (2008)
12. Ettus, M.: Universal software defined radio (USRP) (2007). http://www.ettus.com/
13. FVC: Fingerprint Verification Competition FVC (2006). http://bias.csr.uni-bo.it/fvc2006/
14. Hall, J.: Detection of rogue devices in wireless networks. Ph.D. thesis (2006)
15. Hall, J., Barbeau, M., Kranakis, E.: Enhancing intrusion detection in wireless networks using radio frequency fingerprinting. In: Proceedings of Communications, Internet, and Information Technology (CIIT), pp. 201–206 (2004)
16. Hall, J., Barbeau, M., Kranakis, E.: Radio frequency fingerprinting for intrusion detection in wireless networks. Manuscript (2005). http://wiki.uni.lu/secan-lab/Hall2005.html
17. Hall, J., Barbeau, M., Kranakis, E.: Detecting rogue devices in Bluetooth networks using radio frequency fingerprinting. In: Proceedings of IASTED International Conference on Communications and Computer Networks (CCN), pp. 108–113 (2006)
18. Hippenstiel, R., Payal, Y.: Wavelet based transmitter identification. In: Proceedings of International Symposium on Signal Processing and Its Applications (ISSPA), pp. 740–742 (1996)
19. Jain, A., Zongker, D.: Feature selection: evaluation, application, and small sample performance. IEEE Trans. Pattern Anal. Mach. Intell. **19**(2), 153–158 (1997)
20. Jain, A.K., Duin, R.P.W., Mao, J.: Statistical pattern recognition: a review. IEEE Trans. Pattern Anal. Mach. Intell. **22**(1), 4–37 (2000)
21. Jana, S., Kasera, S.K.: On fast and accurate detection of unauthorized wireless access points using clock skews. In: Proceedings of ACM International Conference on Mobile Computing and Networking (MobiCom), pp. 104–115 (2008)
22. Jones, R.: Most Secret War: British Scientific Intelligence 1939–1945. Hamish Hamilton (1978)
23. Kaplan, D., Stanhope, D.: Waveform collection for use in wireless telephone identification. US Patent 5999806 (1999)

24. Kittler, J., Hatef, M., Duin, R., Matas, J.: On combining classifiers. IEEE Trans. Pattern Anal. Mach. Intell. **20**(3), 226–239 (1998)
25. Klein, R.W., Temple, A., Mendenhall, M.J.: Application of wavelet-based RF fingerprinting to enhance wireless network security. Secur. Commun. Netw. **11**(6), 544–555 (2009)
26. Klein, R.W., Temple, M.A., Mendenhall, M.J.: Application of wavelet denoising to improve OFDM-based signal detection and classification. Secur. Commun. Netw. **3**(1), 71–82 (2010)
27. Kohno, T., Broido, A., Claffy, K.: Remote physical device fingerprinting. IEEE Trans. Dependable Secure Comput. **2**(2), 93–108 (2005)
28. Margerum, D.: Pinpointing Location Of Hostile Radars. Microwaves (1969)
29. Mitra, M.: Privacy for RFID systems to prevent tracking and cloning. Int. J. Comput. Sci. Netw. Secur. **8**(1), 1–5 (2008)
30. Pang, J., Greenstein, B., Gummadi, R., Seshan, S., Wetherall, D.: 802.11 user fingerprinting. In: Proceedings of ACM International Conference on Mobile Computing and Networking (MobiCom), pp. 99–110 (2007)
31. Periaswamy, S.C.G., Thompson, D., Di, J.: Fingerprinting RFID tags. IEEE Trans. Dependable Secure Comput. **8**(6), 938–943 (2011)
32. Periaswamy, S.C.G., Thompson, D.R., Romero, H.P.: Fingerprinting radio frequency identification tags using timing characteristics. In: Proceedings of Workshop on RFID Security (RFIDSec Asia) (2010)
33. Rasmussen, K., Capkun, S.: Implications of radio fingerprinting on the security of sensor networks. In: Proceedings of International ICST Conference on Security and Privacy in Communication Networks (SecureComm) (2007)
34. Reising, D.R., Temple, M.A., Mendenhall, M.J.: Improved wireless security for GMSK-based devices using RF fingerprinting. Int. J. Electron. Secur. Digit. Forensics **3**(1), 41–59 (2010)
35. Reising, D.R., Temple, M.A., Mendenhall, M.J.: Improving intra-cellular security using air monitoring with RF fingerprints. In: Proceedings of IEEE Wireless Communications and Networking Conference (WCNC) (2010)
36. Romero, H.P., Remley, K.A., Williams, D.F., Wang, C.M.: Electromagnetic measurements for counterfeit detection of radio frequency identification cards. IEEE Trans. Microwave Theory Tech. **57**(5), 1383–1387 (2009)
37. Romero, H.P., Remley, K.A., Williams, D.F., Wang, C.M., Brown, T.X.: Identifying RF identification cards from measurements of resonance and carrier harmonics. IEEE Trans. Microw. Theory Tech. **58**(7), 1758–1765 (2010)
38. Ross, A., Jain, A.: Multimodal biometrics: an overview. In: Proceedings of European Signal Processing Conference (EUSIPCO), pp. 1221–1224 (2004)
39. Shaw, D., Kinsner, W.: Multifractal modeling of radio transmitter transients for classification. In: Proceedings of IEEE Conference on Communications, Power and Computing (WESCANEX), pp. 306–312 (1997)
40. Suski, W., Temple, M., Mendenhall, M., Mills, R.: Using spectral fingerprints to improve wireless network security. In: Proceedings of IEEE Global Communications Conference (GLOBECOM), pp. 1–5 (2008)
41. Suski, W.C., Temple, M.A., Mendenhall, M.J., Mills, R.F.: Radio frequency fingerprinting commercial communication devices to enhance electronic security. Int. J. Electron. Secur. Digital Forensics **1**(3), 301–322 (2008)
42. Tekbas, O., Ureten, O., Serinken, N.: An experimental performance evaluation of a novel radio-transmitter identification system under diverse environmental conditions. Can. J. Electr. Comput. Eng. **29**(3), 203–209 (2004)
43. Tekbas, O., Ureten, O., Serinken, N.: Improvement of transmitter identification system for low SNR transients. Electron. Lett. **40**(3), 182–183 (2004)
44. Tippenhauer, N.O., Rasmussen, K.B., Pöpper, C., Capkun, S.: Attacks on public WLAN-based positioning. In: Proceedings of ACM/USENIX International Conference on Mobile Systems, Applications and Services (MobiSys), pp. 29–40 (2009)
45. Toonstra, J., Kinsner, W.: Transient analysis and genetic algorithms for classification. In: Proceedings of IEEE Conference on Communications, Power, and Computing (WESCANEX), pp. 432–437, vol. 2 (1995)

46. Toonstra, J., Kinsner, W.: A radio transmitter fingerprinting system ODO-1. In: Proceedings of Canadian Conference on Electrical and Computer Engineering, pp. 60–63, vol. 1 (1996)
47. Ureten, O., Serinken, N.: Detection of radio transmitter turn-on transients. Electron. Lett. **35**, 1996–1997 (2007)
48. Ureten, O., Serinken, N.: Wireless security through RF fingerprinting. Can. J. Electr. Comput. Eng. **32**(1), 27–33 (2007)
49. Wang, B., Omatu, S., Abe, T.: Identification of the defective transmission devices using the wavelet transform. IEEE Trans. Pattern Anal. Mach. Intell. **27**(6), 696–710 (2005)
50. Williams, M., Temple, M., Reising, D.: Augmenting bit-level network security using physical layer RF-DNA fingerprinting. In: Proceedings of IEEE Global Telecommunications Conference (GLOBECOM), pp. 1–6 (2010)
51. Zanetti, D., Danev, B., Capkun, S.: Physical-layer identification of UHF RFID tags. In: Proceedings of ACM Conference on Mobile Computing and Networking (MOBICOM), pp. 353–364 (2010)
52. Zanetti, D., Sachs, P., Capkun, S.: On the practicality of UHF RFID fingerprinting: how real is the RFID tracking problem? In: Proceedings of Privacy Enhancing Technologies Symposium (PETS), pp. 97–116 (2011)

Device Measurement and Origin of Variation

Ryan M. Gerdes, Mani Mina and Thomas E. Daniels

Abstract In this chapter a methodology is set forth that allows one to determine whether or not a particular device component causes, or contributes significantly to, the differences in signalling behaviour between devices that allow for their identification.

1 Introduction

When we speak of modelling a component or components of a device, we mean that we wish to determine what the output— either the voltage, current, or both—of said component(s) will be given a certain input voltage or current. Component behaviour may be captured in one of two ways: using a lumped, or discrete, circuit model or by viewing the component of as a kind of black box, wherein an input simply produces an output without explanation.

A discrete model consists of resistors, inductors, and capacitors arranged in such a way so as to mimic the response of the component to an input. Each of these discrete elements accounts for how energy is accounted for in the component; electrical energy is represented by capacitance, magnetic energy by inductors, and dissipated power by resistors [2]. Having constructed such a model, measurements of the component being modelled must be carried out in such a way as to reveal the values of elements used in the model. These types of models are advantageous in that not only can they provide closed form solutions for the output, but they also allow us to think about the inner-workings of the component using well understood processes (i.e. how the different circuit elements used to model the component interact, etc.).

R.M. Gerdes (✉)
Utah State University, Logan, UT 84322, USA
e-mail: ryan.gerdes@usu.edu

M. Mina · T.E. Daniels
Iowa State University, Ames, IA 50011, USA
e-mail: mmina@iastate.edu

T.E. Daniels
e-mail: daniels@iastate.edu

© Springer Science+Business Media New York (outside the USA) 2016
C. Wang et al. (eds.), *Digital Fingerprinting*,
DOI 10.1007/978-1-4939-6601-1_3

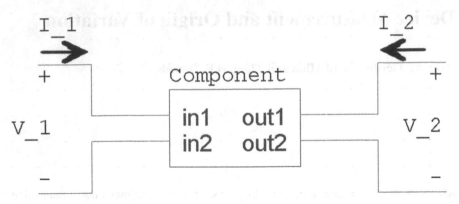

Fig. 1 Depiction of a two-port model for a component (input voltage/current denoted by V_1/I_1 and output voltage/current by V_2/I_2). *Note* it is assumed that voltage/current measurements are carried out at device terminals

The black box, or port, model of a component specifies only the port characteristics of the device—i.e. it only indicates what the voltage/current will be at one port given a voltage/current applied at another—but not why this is so. While this model may not explain the behaviour of a component, it does capture the behaviour of a component precisely, within the limits of the measured inputs/outputs and under the assumption of linearity.

In a two-port model (Fig. 1) an input voltage, V_1, and current, I_1 are related to the output voltage, V_2, and current, I_2 via linear combination. Given four variables, there are six ways to choose two dependent and two independent variables; these six choices represent the possible two-port models (also called parameters) we must choose from. (It is actually slightly more complicated than this as we must choose which dependent variable is be written first. Furthermore, linear combinations of independent variables with linear combinations of dependent variables further increases the number of possible equations to infinity. Refer to [2] for a detailed discussion.) The parameter type chosen usually depends on how multiple two-port models are to be connected [1].

Before proceeding with our discussion of how a two-port model of a component can be constructed in order to determine the influence the component has on the unique behaviour of the device, it should be noted that if the operating frequency of the component being modelled is is high, as it is in wired networking technologies beyond 10 Mb Ethernet and for wireless devices, then it may be necessary to use two-port models where the independent/dependent variables are themselves linear combinations of independent/dependent variables (see Sect. 2). In addition, a two-port model of a device is only valid if a true ground plane exists; i.e. the ground is of zero potential, zero resistance, and is continuous [2].

1.1 ABCD Parameters

For our analysis we chose ABCD parameters because of the ease of combining ABCD models for multiple components in a cascaded or chained fashion (when using ABCD parameters with multiple components connected in a cascaded configuration, it is only necessary to perform simple matrix multiplication to determine their combined response). This allows us to build more complicated models, in which additional component models are added to the chain, to see how different components affect a device's signal in combination with ease.

ABCD parameters treat V_1 and I_1 as dependent variables and V_2 and I_2 as independent ones; the input voltage/current and output voltage/current are related via

$$\begin{bmatrix} V_1 \\ I_1 \end{bmatrix} = \begin{bmatrix} A & B \\ C & D \end{bmatrix} \begin{bmatrix} V_2 \\ -I_2 \end{bmatrix} \tag{1}$$

where each of A, B, C, and D are defined as [1]

$$A = \frac{V_1}{V_2}\bigg|_{I_2=0} \tag{2a}$$

$$B = \frac{V_1}{-I_2}\bigg|_{V_2=0} \tag{2b}$$

$$C = \frac{I_1}{V_2}\bigg|_{I_2=0} \tag{2c}$$

$$D = \frac{I_1}{-I_2}\bigg|_{V_2=0} \tag{2d}$$

In characterising a device that operates over a bandwidth, it is necessary to determine ABCD parameters at multiple frequencies. The question of how ABCD parameters for a component may be obtained is discussed in Sect. 2.

1.2 Proposed Model

To determine the effect of an arbitrary device component on the voltage signal V_s, we propose the following model where Z_S represents the impedance of the source generating V_S, Z_L is an arbitrary load with ABCD parameters of $\begin{bmatrix} 1 & 0 \\ 1/Z_L & 1 \end{bmatrix}$, and the box M represents the ABCD parameters, denoted by $\begin{bmatrix} a & b \\ c & d \end{bmatrix}$, at the frequency of V_S for the component under consideration. The voltage across Z_L is then the modified signal V_S, which is found by solving the following set of equations

$$\begin{bmatrix} V_1 \\ I_1 \end{bmatrix} = \begin{bmatrix} a & b \\ c & d \end{bmatrix} \begin{bmatrix} 1 & 0 \\ Y_L & 1 \end{bmatrix} \begin{bmatrix} V_2 \\ -I_2 \end{bmatrix} \tag{3a}$$

$$= \begin{bmatrix} a + bY_L & b \\ c + dY_L & d \end{bmatrix} \begin{bmatrix} V_2 \\ -I_2 \end{bmatrix} \tag{3b}$$

where $Y_L = 1/Z_L$. As the output port is an open circuit, $I_2 = 0$; furthermore, we need only consider the output voltage, V_2, so (3b) reduces to a single equation, which after rearranging

$$V_2 = \frac{V_1}{a + bY_L} \tag{4}$$

The input voltage, V_1, may be found by means of a voltage divider

$$V_1 = \frac{Z_{IN}}{Z_{IN} + Z_S} V_S \tag{5}$$

where Z_{IN} is the input impedance of the cascade (the component plus the shunt load). As per the definition of ABCD parameters, dividing (2a) by (2c) gives $Z_{IN} = A/C$. The input impedance needed for (5) is then

$$Z_{IN} = \frac{a + bY_L}{c + dY_L} \tag{6}$$

Allowing the source impedance to equal the load impedance, $Z_S = Z_L$, substituting (6) into (5), and then using the result with (4) leads to the following expression for the output voltage

$$V_2 = \frac{V_S}{a + d + bY_L + c/Y_L} \tag{7}$$

Equation 7 thus describes how the signal V_s would be affected by passing through an arbitrary component with measured ABCD parameters of $\begin{bmatrix} a & b \\ c & d \end{bmatrix}$.

2 Measuring Parameters

As the operating frequency of a component increases, the wave-nature of input/output signals is manifested; i.e. wires are better thought of as transmission lines and signals take on the form of travelling waves. For this reason high-speed devices are often characterised using scattering parameters (S-parameters), which can be defined in terms of travelling waves, instead of ABCD parameters. As scattering parameters consist of linear combinations of voltages and currents at the input and output terminals of a component—again, depending on whether or not a measurements can be taken directly at the terminals, these may or may not be defined in terms of travelling waves—and are thus convertible to ABCD parameters.

For illustrative purposes, we shall assume that voltage and current are measured at the terminals of the component; i.e. wave phenomena may be ignored. While this simplification is acceptable for low-speed/low-frequency components of devices, high-speed networking devices, whose components operate in the radio frequency range of spectrum, would require S-parameters defined in terms of travelling waves (see chapter three of [2]).

In reference to Fig. 1, voltage-referenced S-parameters for a two-port component are defined as [2]

$$S_{11} = \left.\frac{V_1 - I_1 Z_1^*}{V_1 + I_1 Z_1}\right|_{V_2 = -I_2 Z_2} \tag{8a}$$

$$S_{21} = \left.\frac{V_2 - I_2 Z_2^*}{V_1 + I_1 Z_1} \sqrt{\frac{|Re\,(Z_1)|}{|Re\,(Z_2)|}}\right|_{V_2 = -I_2 Z_2} \tag{8b}$$

$$S_{12} = \left.\frac{V_1 - I_1 Z_1^*}{V_2 + I_2 Z_2} \sqrt{\frac{|Re\,(Z_2)|}{|Re\,(Z_1)|}}\right|_{V_1 = -I_1 Z_1} \tag{8c}$$

$$S_{22} = \left.\frac{V_2 - I_2 Z_2^*}{V_2 + I_2 Z_2}\right|_{V_1 = -I_1 Z_1} \tag{8d}$$

where Z_1 and Z_2 are the impedances of the source and load, respectively, causing the excitation of the component. Under the assumption that $Z_0 = Z_1 = Z_2$ and that the source and load impedances used in Fig. 2 are equivalent to Z_1 and Z_2, respectively, the equivalent ABCD parameters are [2]

$$A = \frac{(1 + S_{11})\,(1 - S_{22}) + S_{12}S_{21}}{2S_{21}} \tag{9a}$$

$$B = \frac{(1 + S_{11})\,(1 + S_{22}) - S_{12}S_{21}}{2S_{21}} Z_0 \tag{9b}$$

$$C = \frac{(1 - S_{11})\,(1 - S_{22}) - S_{12}S_{21}}{2S_{21}} \frac{1}{Z_0} \tag{9c}$$

$$D = \frac{(1 - S_{11})\,(1 + S_{22}) + S_{12}S_{21}}{2S_{21}} \tag{9d}$$

S-parameters can be measured using an oscilloscope and a phase meter; however, this approach becomes tedious when it is necessary to measure the parameters across a range of frequencies. Thus, network analysers are more commonly employed to determine how a component will respond to an arbitrary input, within a given bandwidth. Both vector and scalar network analysers exist; the former provides complex S-parameters, which tell how the magnitude and phase of a signal would be affected by the component, while the latter gives information only about how the magnitude of a signal would be altered. For many fingerprinting approaches, both the magnitude and phase of the signal are important for device identification so vector measurements are to be preferred.

3 Determining Component Significance

In order to discover whether a particular component plays a significant role in device variation, models of the component drawn from several of the particular device under consideration, based on their measured S-parameters, would need to be constructed. An idealised signal, derived by averaging the waveforms from each of the devices would serve as the input to the model. The fingerprinting regime for each device would be applied to the output of the model and applied to each device's output in turn. If signal variation originates at the component, we would expect to see differences in outputs, though even stronger evidence of this affect would come in the form of collisions between the simulated signals from devices known to have shown significant overlap from previous experiments. The extent to which a particular component contributes to the uniqueness of a device could be estimated using a quantity of information calculation.

3.1 Constructing Model Input

An idealised signal (i.e. a signal composed of attributes unique only to the particular brand/model i of a networking technology), A_i, could be constructed by taking n sampled signals from each device, aligning, and then averaging. This signal, A_i serves as the input, V_S, to the model depicted in Fig. 2.

3.2 Producing Model Output

The output of the model constructed for the jth device, V_2^j, is found by using (7) with $V_S = A_i$

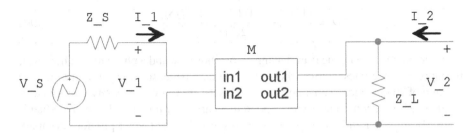

Fig. 2 Model to examine how an input signal (V_S) is affected by a component with ABCD parameters of M (Z_S is the impedance of the source generating V_S and Z_L is the impedance of a test load)

$$V_2^j = \frac{A_i}{a_j + d_j + b_j Y_L + c_j/Y_L} \tag{10}$$

where device j is a member of model i and a_j, b_j, c_j, d_j are the ABCD parameters derived from the S-parameter measurements, for the jth device, of the component being tested. The value of Z_S, and hence Z_L, according to the assumptions laid out above, should be equal to the source impedance used in the S-parameter measurements.

It must be remembered that ABCD parameters are defined as a function of frequency. Thus, it is necessary that ABCD parameters be found for each frequency bin of A_i and then be applied only to the corresponding bin. More explicitly, allowing $\mathscr{A} = \mathscr{F}\{A\}$, where $\mathscr{F}\{\cdot\}$ denotes the Fourier transform, the output for the kth bin is

$$\mathscr{V}_2^j(k) = \frac{\mathscr{A}_i(k)}{a_j(k) + d_j(k) + b_j(k)Y_L + c_j(k)/Y_L} \tag{11}$$

where $a_j(k), b_j(k), c_j(k), d_j(k)$ are the ABCD parameters measured at the frequency of the kth bin. The time-domain output of the model for the jth device's component is then $V_2^j = \mathscr{F}^{-1}\left\{\mathscr{V}_2^j\right\}$, where $\mathscr{F}^{-1}\{\cdot\}$ denotes the inverse-Fourier transform. As each bin is of finite width, it is not possible to have exact ABCD parameters; interpolation between measured parameters, to fill in for unmeasured frequencies, and/or the addition of multiple frequencies, to account for the frequencies contained within a bin, must therefore be used.

3.3 Evaluating Model Output

In seeking to determine the effects a particular component has on a signal, we are actually asking two questions: how much of an effect does the component have (i.e. how significant is the component: is it enough to explain the differences we see between cards?) and does it actually produce the unique characteristics our fingerprinting regime uses to differentiate devices?

Significance

To calculate the significance a component has in determining device identity, we can calculate how much information is added to the ideal signal by the device model and check whether it is enough to make up the difference between the information of the ideal signal and the actual measured waveforms of the device. Specifically, allowing $u_A = H(A_i)$ to be some measure of the information of A_i, we then measure the average information, u_j, contained in n of device j's records (these records must be aligned to A_i). The ratio

$$\frac{H\left(V_2^j\right) - u_A}{u_j - u_A} \times 100 \tag{12}$$

then tells us what percentage of unique information the component is responsible for.

Identity

Even if a component can be shown to add a great deal of information to a signal, we must still find out whether it is information that develops a device's identity. To do this, we generate m test signals, based upon the appropriate A_i, for each device, pass them through the device's model, select one of the modified signals to act as the device's fingerprint, and, following the procedure of the fingerprinting regime, compare each device against itself and all the other devices.

To simulate the natural variability observed in the captured waveforms, a small amount of additive white gaussian noise should be added to each test signal. So long as the variances of the devices' actual fingerprint are approximately equal, this will produce an equivalent overlap between the fingerprints, should any exist. If the fingerprints diverge, we can infer that the component does in fact contribute to a devices identify; significantly, if any collisions between two devices' fingerprints occur and happen to correspond with known collisions of devices, we can infer an even stronger relationship between the device's identity and the component.

4 Conclusion

We have proposed a methodology, based upon an empirical two-port model, capable of determining the extent to which an arbitrary component of a device contributes to its unique behaviour, as manifested by the fingerprinting regime. The methodology describes how a component should be measured to create a model that captures component behaviour over the entire bandwidth of its operation, as well as how an input signal that represents a generic device can be used with the model to evaluate the component's affect on creating device identity.

References

1. Kumar, S., Suresh, K.K.S.: Electric Circuits and Networks. Pearson Education (2009)
2. Weber, R.J.: Introduction to Microwave Circuits: Radio Frequency and Design Applications. IEEE Press (2001)

Crytpo-Based Methods and Fingerprints

Joe H. Novak, Sneha Kumar Kasera and Yong Guan

Abstract Device fingerprints primarily provide underlying seeds and keys for the cryptographic operations of authentication and secret key generation. In this chapter, we present techniques and technologies to use this information with cryptography. We also present cryptographic functions derived from authentication and key generation that use device fingerprints.

1 Introduction

Device fingerprints serve two primary functions in cryptography. Those functions are authentication and key generation. All other cryptographic operations (e.g., secure hash functions, certified code generation) involving fingerprints are derived from these.

1.1 Authentication

Because device fingerprints are unique to a device, they provide positive identification of the device. This proof of identity authenticates the device to a system. For most applications, it is not sufficient to repeatedly present the fingerprint to a system for authentication because that value may be intercepted and copied by an attacker. This issue is resolved with challenge-response models. In one model, the system mathematically derives the response a device will return given a specific challenge.

J.H. Novak (✉) · S.K. Kasera
University of Utah, Salt Lake City, UT 84112, USA
e-mail: jnovak@eng.utah.edu; joe@cs.utah.edu

S.K. Kasera
e-mail: kasera@cs.utah.edu

Y. Guan
Iowa State University, Ames, IA 50011, USA
e-mail: guan@iastate.edu

© Springer Science+Business Media New York (outside the USA) 2016
C. Wang et al. (eds.), *Digital Fingerprinting*,
DOI 10.1007/978-1-4939-6601-1_4

In another model, the manufacturer or a trusted third party applies a very large number of random challenges to the device before it is placed into service. The device combines its fingerprint with challenges to generate responses. The manufacturer stores these challenge-response pairs in a database for later retrieval. A system authenticates a device by sending a challenge to it and verifying the response it returns either against a derived response or against the challenge-response pair stored in the database.

1.2 Key Generation

In contrast to authentication, a device keeps its fingerprint secret for key generation applications. Because the key is kept secret, a device may repeatedly use its fingerprint for cryptographic key operations. Since a fingerprint is an intrinsic characteristic of a device, it is not explicitly stored on the device. This makes it difficult to forcibly extract the key. It also makes the fingerprint difficult to clone. Many cryptographic algorithms require keys of specific lengths or which have certain mathematical properties. If a device fingerprint does not natively have these properties, a hash is performed on the fingerprint to map it to a key appropriate for the algorithm [42].

1.2.1 Symmetric Keys

A symmetric or pre-shared key application uses a common secret key to encrypt and decrypt data at both sides of the exchange. Since robust fingerprints are unique to devices, each party will not know the fingerprint of the other. Only one side of the exchange has secure access to the shared secret key. The other side of the exchange must store the fingerprint in memory which may not be secure. Consequently, device fingerprints are often used in scenarios where one side of the exchange is in a secure location but the other side is not. The unsecured side does not need to store the secret key because it is intrinsic to the device. It is possible to implement cryptographic protocols so that both sides of an exchange can determine a shared secret key based on challenge-response pairs over an unsecured channel. In this case, both sides of the exchange may be located in unsecured environments.

1.2.2 Asymmetric Keys

Asymmetric key cryptography consists of a public and private key pair. In this type of cryptographic operation, the fingerprint of a device is the private key. Device fingerprints are then used in any asymmetric cryptographic algorithms and operations such as RSA, Diffie-Hellman key exchange, and digital signatures.

2 Techniques

Device fingerprints are an active area of research and few commercial devices make use of them at the time of this writing. As the area evolves, more systems will benefit from their use. This section describes how fingerprints may be used in practice.

2.1 Physical Unclonable Functions

Physical unclonable functions or PUFs are at the forefront of device fingerprint research. A PUF is a function embedded in a device that cannot be altered by an attacker without damaging the device [36]. A PUF is also known as physical random function or physical one way function. Researchers have implemented and analyzed numerous models. Models typically use intentional fingerprints to create the physical unclonable function. The function outputs a different response for each unique challenge. The function is influenced by manufacturing imperfections and each device generates a different response given the same challenge. The manufacturer or a trusted third party records the challenge-response pairs in a database. A system later authenticates the device by choosing a challenge from the database that has not been used before and submitting it to the device. If the response from the device matches the response saved in the database, then the device is authenticated. The challenge-response pair is marked in or removed from the database so that it is not reused. Because challenge-response pairs are not reused, they may be transmitted in clear-text.

The designer of a model must be careful to ensure there are an exponential number of possible challenge-response pairs. If there are not, an attacker can create a model of the device by characterizing its behavior.

2.1.1 Multiplexer-Based Arbiter Implementation

The multiplexer-based arbiter PUF [12, 42] implementation applies an input challenge sequence to the select inputs of a series of multiplexers. The device outputs the response to the challenge. The implementation generates a single bit of output in the following manner. The inputs to two 2×1 multiplexers are tied high. The device applies a single bit from the challenge to the multiplexer select input. This creates a race condition where the timing of the outputs of the multiplexers is dependent on the lengths of the wires and the switching time of the transistors. The delays will vary between microchips because of manufacturing imperfections. This is one stage of the arbiter circuit. Signals pass through a series of stages to create the delay path of the output bit. Successive bits of the challenge are applied to the select inputs of the series of multiplexers. In the final stage of the circuit, one multiplexer output is tied to the data input of a D flip-flop. The other multiplexer output is tied to the clock input of the flip-flop. If the data path bit arrives first, the output bit of the arbiter circuit is a 1. If the clock path bit arrives first, it is a 0. Multiple instances of the circuit are combined to generate an output response of any desired length.

For example, consider the eight-bit challenge 10110100 applied to an arbiter where the least significant bit is bit number zero. The device breaks the challenge into two four-bit challenges to generate two bits of output. It applies challenge bits seven through four to one sequence of multiplexers (circuit A) and it simultaneously applies bits three through zero to a separate sequence of multiplexers (circuit B). Dividing the challenge in this manner serves two purposes. First, it creates a more robust fingerprint because each sequence of multiplexers will have different wire delays. Second, it allows the response bits to be generated in parallel decreasing the amount of time required to generate the response.

The high bit of the challenge has a value of 1 which causes the signals to travel through the high inputs of the multiplexers in the first stage of circuit A. The next bit of the challenge has a value of 0 and the signals travel through the low inputs of the multiplexers. The next two bits of the challenge both have values of 1 and the signals travel through the high inputs of the third and fourth stages. Because the path lengths differ and because the switching time of the transistors in the multiplexers differ, the signals will arrive at the D-flip flop at different times. If the D-input signal arrives before the clock input, the most significant response bit will have a value of 1. If the clock input arrives before the D-input signal, the most significant response bit will have a value of 0.

The low order bits of the challenge cause the signals to flow in a similar manner through circuit B. Challenge bit three has a value of 0 which causes the signals to flow through the low inputs of the multiplexers. Challenge bit two has a value of 1 and the signals flow through the high inputs of the next stage. Bits one and zero of the challenge both have values of 0 and the signals flow through the low inputs of the third and fourth stages. The race between the D-input and the clock input paths to the D-flip flop determine the value of the least significant response bit in the same manner as circuit A determines the value of the most significant response bit.

The PUF concatenates the output bits of circuits A and B to create the response to the challenge. In an actual implementation, a challenge is typically thousands of bits in length. Each series of multiplexers consists of hundreds or thousands of stages.

2.1.2 Delay-Based Implementation

A delay-based implementation determines the response by measuring the amount of time it takes to create a response to a specific challenge. This duration is the fingerprint. One implementation creates two separate circuits through a series of switches [12]. Both inputs are initially zero. The challenge is hashed by a pseudorandom function to make the responses to the challenges more difficult for an attacker to determine. Successive output bits of the pseudorandom function are applied to the switches. The outputs of the series of switches are tied to an AND gate. The device initiates the race by applying a transition to the input of the circuit. The output of the AND gate transitions from low to high when both paths have completed. The response is the amount of time taken between applying the challenge to the input and the transition of the output of the AND gate from low to high.

As an example, assume a PUF consists of a series of 2-input by 2-output switches. Each switch either routes its two input signals straight through if the select input is 0 or routes them to the opposite outputs if the value is 1. The device applies the challenge 0101 to the delay-based circuit. The pseudorandom function permutes the input and applies the sequence 1001 to the switches. After some setup time, the control logic applies the input transition to both inputs of the first switch at the same time. The pseudorandom function applies a switch select value of 1 to the first stage of the circuit. The switch routes the input signals to the opposite outputs. The pseudorandom function applies select values of 0 to the next two stages of the circuit and the switches route the signals straight through to their respective outputs. The pseudorandom function applies a select value of 1 to the final stage and the signals are routed to the opposite outputs of the switch. The final stage feeds its output to the inputs of an AND gate. The gate transitions from low to high when both signal paths arrive at the gate. The device fingerprint is the amount of time taken from the input transition to the output transition.

Each unique challenge produces a different delay through the circuit since the path lengths and delays of individual wires vary. The lengths and delays vary between identical microchips because of manufacturing imperfections.

It is possible to implement delay-based PUFs with any suitable self-timed circuit. For example, consider a system using a self-timed floating point processor [31] as shown in Fig. 1. There is no system clock in the circuit. Control signals flow through the self-timed circuit based on delay elements rather than a system clock. A device operates this type of self-timed circuit by first applying the data, and then by sending a pulse on the request input. When the self-timed circuit has completed its operation, it sends a pulse on the acknowledge output. The challenge to this system consists of

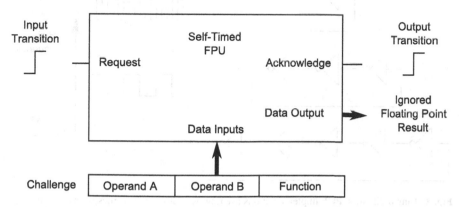

Fig. 1 Self-timed delay. A delay-based PUF implemented with a self-timed circuit. The response is the time taken to compute the output of the floating point operation

the operands and function of the floating point operation such as addition or division. The response is not the result of the computation because it is a predictable value. Instead, the response is the time taken to compute the result. The floating point result is discarded.

2.1.3 Oscillator Implementation

Another type of PUF creates fingerprints from the difference in frequencies of logically identical ring oscillators [12, 42] or other types of astable multivibrators. Physical realizations commonly use ring oscillators such as those shown in Fig. 2 because they do not require mixed analog and digital fabrication. A circuit may replace the first inverter in the chain with a NAND gate to enable or disable the oscillator based on an external logic signal. Any odd number of inverting logic gates produces a square wave output. The circuit designer adjusts the frequency of the waveform by adding or removing inverters [28]. Adding logic gates to the ring increases the time it takes for the signal to propagate through the circuit resulting in a longer period and lower frequency.

The oscillator circuit is initially not powered and the output of each inverter has a logic value of 0. When power is applied, noise causes the output of the transistors of the inverters to be some small voltage value. The inverting amplifier in the inverters will invert the voltage and increase its magnitude. This process continues through the inverter chain until the value is fed back into the loop and oscillations begin. It takes time for the signal to propagate through the chain because each inverter introduces

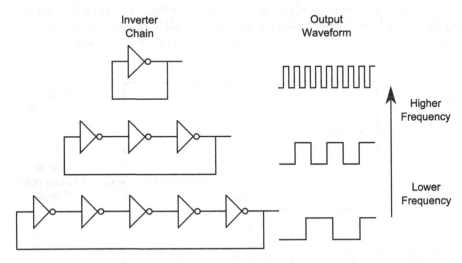

Fig. 2 Ring oscillators. PUF implementations use ring oscillators such as these. Any odd number of inverting logic gates produces a square wave output. More gates result in more delay through the circuit and lower frequency

some delay. Eventually, the voltage will be amplified to logic value of 0 or 1. This amplification combined with the propagation delay result in a square wave at the output of the circuit. The period of the square wave is proportional to the number of inverters in the chain.

Physical realizations commonly use macro blocks to create logically identical oscillator circuits on a microchip. Despite this, logically identical blocks produce slightly different frequencies. The primary contributor to this phenomenon is manufacturing variation. It is this variation which allows the circuit to compare pairs of logically identical oscillators to produce unique fingerprints per device.

The circuit generates output response bits by comparing the frequencies of logically identical pairs of self oscillating loops. The challenge consists of a bit pattern that selects the pairs of self oscillating loops to be compared. A bit in the response indicates which self oscillating loop in the respective pair has a higher frequency.

Consider a simplified implementation consisting of four oscillators (0 through 3), two multiplexers (*A* and *B*), and two counters (*A* and *B*). Oscillator 0 is tied to the 0 input of both multiplexers. Similarly, oscillator 1 is tied to the 1 input, oscillator 2 to input 2, and oscillator 3 to input 3. The outputs of multiplexers *A* and *B* are sent to counters *A* and *B*, respectively. The challenge is 4 bits in length. The two least significant bits are tied to the select input of multiplexer *A* and the two most significant bits to the select input of multiplexer *B*. The challenge selects which oscillators are compared. For example, a challenge of 1000 selects oscillator 0 from multiplexer *A* and oscillator 2 from multiplexer *B*. The circuit resets the counters and then allows them to run until the frequency of each selected oscillator is determined. The comparator compares the counter values to determine which oscillator has the highest frequency. If the frequency of multiplexer *B* is higher than that of multiplexer *A*, the output is a 1. Otherwise, the output is a 0. The output is a single bit in the response.

In an actual implementation, there are hundreds or thousands of oscillators and the challenge is much longer. The multiplexers accept more inputs and there are multiple instances of the circuit. The challenge is divided into groups and applied to the instances of the circuit to generate the response bits.

2.1.4 Noise

For cryptographic operations such as secret key generation, the response to a challenge must be repeatable. Noise caused by voltage fluctuations or temperature changes can cause bits in the response to change. Error correcting codes are used to compensate for these effects [11]. The manufacturer or a trusted third party places the device in ideal environmental conditions when challenge-response pairs are initially generated and recorded in the database. Error correcting syndrome values are computed during this initialization process. They are stored along with the challenge-response pairs. The syndrome values do not need to be kept secret but they do leak information to a potential attacker. The responses must be increased by the length of the syndrome values to compensate. The syndrome allows the user to correct bit errors in the responses to corresponding challenges.

As a simplified example, assume responses are 3 bits in length and a (6, 3) error correcting block code [35] is used with generator G and syndrome S matrices shown below.

$$
G = \begin{bmatrix} 1\,0\,0\,1\,0\,1 \\ 0\,1\,0\,0\,1\,1 \\ 0\,0\,1\,1\,1\,0 \end{bmatrix}, \; S = \begin{bmatrix} 1\,0\,1 \\ 0\,1\,1 \\ 1\,1\,0 \\ 1\,0\,0 \\ 0\,1\,0 \\ 0\,0\,1 \end{bmatrix}
$$

During the initialization phase, the manufacturer applies a challenge c to the device which generates a response of 101. The length of the challenge is determined by the implementation of the device and is not necessarily related to the length of the response. The syndrome values are computed as shown below. In the computation, w is the code word and d is the response. Error correcting matrix operations are performed *mod* 2.

$$
\begin{aligned}
w &= dG \\
&= \begin{bmatrix} 1\,0\,1 \end{bmatrix} \begin{bmatrix} 1\,0\,0\,1\,0\,1 \\ 0\,1\,0\,0\,1\,1 \\ 0\,0\,1\,1\,1\,0 \end{bmatrix} \\
&= \begin{bmatrix} 1\,0\,1\,2\,1\,1 \end{bmatrix} \; mod\, 2 \\
&= \begin{bmatrix} 1\,0\,1\,0\,1\,1 \end{bmatrix}
\end{aligned}
$$

The first three bits of the code word, 101, are the response and the last three bits, 011, are the syndrome values. The manufacturer records the response and syndrome values in the database along with the challenge c. At a later time a user presents the syndrome values 011 in addition to the challenge c to the device. The device uses the syndrome values to correct bit errors in the response before using the response for cryptographic operations. Assume the device incorrectly produces a response of 111 to challenge c because of noise. Before using the response in cryptographic operations, the device performs error correction to determine the correct value 101.

To perform the error correction, the device first generates the vector r by concatenating the uncorrected response 111 with the syndrome 011 supplied by the user. It then multiplies the vector r by the syndrome matrix S to produce an estimate $\hat{d}$ of the response.

$$\hat{d} = rS$$

$$= \begin{bmatrix} 1 & 1 & 1 & 0 & 1 & 1 \end{bmatrix} \begin{bmatrix} 1 & 0 & 1 \\ 0 & 1 & 1 \\ 1 & 1 & 0 \\ 1 & 0 & 0 \\ 0 & 1 & 0 \\ 0 & 0 & 1 \end{bmatrix}$$

$$= \begin{bmatrix} 2 & 3 & 3 \end{bmatrix} \bmod 2$$

$$= \begin{bmatrix} 0 & 1 & 1 \end{bmatrix}$$

An estimate $\hat{d}$ of all zeros indicates no bit errors within the tolerance of the block code. Since the estimate is not all zeros, the device performs an error correction step on the response before producing the final output. It matches the estimate against the rows in the syndrome matrix S. The matching row indicates the bit position of the error. In this example, the estimate 011 matches the second row in the syndrome matrix. The device knows that the second bit of the response 111 is in error. It then inverts the second bit to produce the correct response of 101.

Ring oscillator implementations are susceptible to environmental variation because the frequency changes with temperature. This is particularly a difficulty when temperature changes in one area of a microchip faster than in another area. In this situation, the frequency of one oscillator changes faster than the frequency of another and the relationship between the frequencies may be reversed resulting in bit errors [42].

Consider the system physically arranged as shown in Fig. 3. During normal operating conditions, the left side of the cryptographic device has slightly elevated temperature compared to the right side of the device. The waveforms of oscillators A, B, and C at normal temperatures are shown on the left side of Fig. 4. During periods of heavy CPU load, the temperature at oscillator A increases more than at oscillators B or C because oscillator A is physically located near the CPU which is generating heat. The waveforms during these times are shown at the center of Fig. 4. As the temperature at oscillator A increases, its frequency decreases. The frequencies of oscillators B and C decrease also but to a lesser degree. The consequence is that oscillator A is now lower in frequency than oscillator B. Comparing these two oscillators during periods of high CPU activity generates a different output than when measured at periods of low CPU activity. During periods of heavy graphics operations the temperature at

Fig. 3 Temperature variation. Physical arrangement of this system demonstrates the effects of temperature variation on oscillators in a cryptographic device

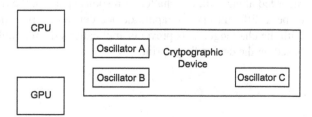

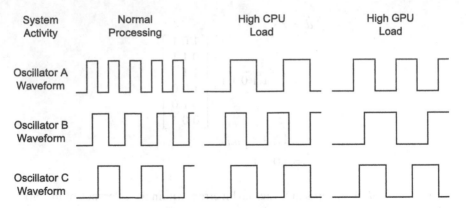

Fig. 4 Relative oscillator frequencies. Frequencies vary with temperature

oscillator *B* increases more than at oscillators *A* or *C* because of its close proximity to the GPU. The waveforms at these times are shown on the right side of Fig. 4. The frequency of oscillator *B* is significantly lowered. The frequencies of oscillators *A* and *C* decrease but to a lesser degree than oscillator *B*. Comparing oscillators *B* and *C* at these times produces a different response than when compared during periods of normal processing.

Exhaustive measurements are required to compensate for temperature effects after the device has been manufactured. Pairs of oscillators must not be compared if their frequencies are very close together during normal operating conditions. Because of manufacturing variation, it is not possible to determine which pairs of oscillators will have similar frequencies before the microchip has been produced.

2.1.5 Privacy

As with any type of hardware identifier, device fingerprints raise privacy concerns [10, 34, 38]. For example, in the case of tracking applications users may not want to be identified by their devices. One solution to this is to allow a user to provide an additional parameter that is combined with the challenge to produce the response returned by the device. The additional parameter is called a personality [10, 11].

The device combines the personality with the challenge before they are applied to the PUF. Consequently, personalities must be part of the initialization process and recorded along with the challenge-response pairs in the database. The PUF appears to be a different cryptographic device depending on which personality is applied with the challenge. This prevents applications from collaborating to identify a user based on the device fingerprint.

2.1.6 Improvements

An adversary typically attacks a PUF by attempting to create a model of the device by applying challenges and recording the responses. The number of pairs required for such attacks is polynomial in the number of delay elements in the circuit. Researchers have suggested numerous improvements to improve the security of PUFs by making this process more difficult.

One implementation adds a feed forward path to the multiplexer-based PUF [24]. In this scenario, one of the stages of the circuit feeds its output to the input of an arbiter circuit running in parallel. The result of the race from the parallel circuit is the challenge bit to a later stage of the original circuit. This adds nonlinearity to the circuit to help prevent the attack.

Another structure uses parity operations to map multiple responses to the same output value [26]. The attacker must guess which challenge correctly models the circuit. A similar improvement is to XOR multiple outputs of the circuit [42].

A more complex circuit creates an interleaved multiplexer-based array structure [27] where the challenge bits of one row are connected in reverse order to the inputs of the next row. The design incorporates feed forward and output XOR concepts.

2.2 Controlled Physical Unclonable Functions

A controlled PUF or CPUF [10] is a device capable of executing a program which also contains a physical unclonable function. In a typical operation, a user submits a program to the device for execution. Protocols and cryptographic primitives bind execution of the program to the device. Execution of the program is linked to the device such that the user can verify that the program was executed on the intended hardware. Establishing a shared secret key over an unsecured channel is possible with CPUFs.

2.2.1 Primitives

There are two cryptographic primitives on a CPUF. The first primitive generates a response to a challenge. The device computes the response by first hashing the challenge and the submitted program. The user codes a literal consisting of the challenge into the program so that a hash of the same program with a different challenge produces different results. The device submits the result of the hash to the PUF portion of the hardware to obtain the response. This process is shown at the top of Fig. 5. The second primitive generates a secret key. The device generates a secret key by first submitting a challenge to the PUF to obtain a response. It then hashes the response with the program to create the secret key. As with response generation, the user codes a literal of the challenge into the program to create a unique hash. The secret key function is shown at the bottom of Fig. 5.

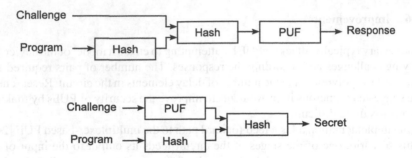

Fig. 5 CPUF primitives. Response generation generate_response (*top*) and secret key generation generate_secret (*bottom*) cryptographic primitives of a CPUF

2.2.2   Initialization

Initial challenge-response pairs must be obtained over a secure channel. The manufacturer or trusted third party obtains the initial pairs by submitting a program to the device that contains a function call to the primitive that generates a response. For example, to obtain the response to challenge 123, the manufacturer submits the following program to the device.

```
{
        response = generate_response(123);
        return response;
}
```

Assume the output of generate_response is 456. The manufacturer records the challenge-response pair (123, 456) in a database for later use.

2.2.3   Secret Key Establishment

A user establishes a shared secret key with a device by submitting a program similar to that shown in the example below. Suppose the manufacturer has given the challenge-response pair (123, 456) to the user. Further suppose the hash of the result 456 and a hash of the program below is 789. The device computes the secret by first applying 123 to the PUF to obtain the response 456. It then hashes 456 with a hash of the program to obtain the secret 789. Because the user already knows the response to the challenge which is the output of the PUF, she can compute the hash of the program and the response to create the secret. The response 456 is already known to the user. The user hashes 456 with a hash of the program to obtain the same secret 789.

```
{
        key = generate_secret(123);
}
```

2.2.4 Obtaining Challenge-Response Pairs

A user should select previously unused challenge-response pairs for each program execution to avoid leaking information to an attacker. The user obtains an initial challenge-response pair from the manufacturer over a secure channel. The manufacturer need provide only a single pair the user. The user may obtain additional challenge-response pairs directly from the device over an unsecured channel.

Suppose the user knows the challenge-response pair (123, 456) and wants to obtain a new challenge-response pair. The user selects an arbitrary number, 987 in this example. The arbitrary number is not the challenge, but it is used later to determine the challenge. To obtain the new response, the user submits the program below.

```
{
        new_response = generate_response(987);
        key = generate_secret(123);
        enc_response = encrypt(new_response, key);
        mac = create_mac(new_response, key);
        return enc_response, mac;
}
```

The program generates the new response by calling a cryptographic primitive on the argument 987. The program then computes the shared secret key for the old challenge 123. Next, the program encrypts the new response using the secret key. It also computes a message authentication code (MAC) of the new response with the secret key. The output of the program is the encrypted version of the new response and the MAC of the response. The device returns this information to the user. The user receives the information, decrypts the new response, and computes and verifies the MAC. The final step is for the user to compute the new challenge. The user creates the new challenge by computing a hash of the program and the number 987 selected at the beginning of the process. The algorithm is illustrated in Fig. 6.

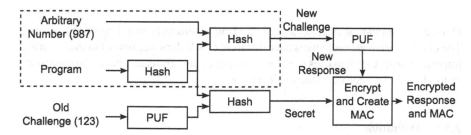

Fig. 6 Challenge-response pair generation. The device executes the program to create a new challenge-response pair. Numbers from the example are in parenthesis. The functions inside the dashed line are computed by the user to obtain the new challenge

The MAC allows the user to verify that the result came from the device and not from an attacker as a result of a person-in-the-middle attack. An attacker may attempt to modify the old challenge to obtain the new response, but this attempt fails because the new response and the secret key are partially derived from a hash of the program. Modifying the old challenge creates a different hash.

2.2.5 Certified Code Execution

In a distributed computing environment, a user may wish to know if a computation was executed on the intended device. The device generates a certificate of execution for the result of a computation by creating a MAC of the result as demonstrated by the example below.

Assume the user knows the challenge-response pair (123, 456). The user submits the following program to the device.

```
{
    key = generate_secret(123);
    result = perform_some_computation();
    mac = create_mac(result, key);
    return result, mac;
}
```

The program generates a shared secret key derived from the challenge 123. Then the program executes the user's computation. The device returns the result of the computation along with a MAC of the result. The user computes the shared secret as described in Sect. 2.2.3 and computes the MAC of the result. If the MAC returned by the device matches the MAC computed by the user, then the computation was performed on the intended device.

2.3 Clock Skew

Device authentication systems use clock skew extensively as a fingerprint feature. The clocks of two identical parts have different clock skew because of manufacturing imperfections. A system uses clock skew to either authenticate a device to a network or to identify an imposter node in a network.

2.3.1 Definition

Clock skew is defined as the difference between the frequencies of two clocks [29]. The frequency of a clock is the rate at which the clock progresses. Formally, if

$C_t(t) = t$ is true clock time, then the offset of clock $C_a(t)$ is the difference between the time reported by that clock and the time reported by $C_t(t)$. Similarly, the offset of clock $C_a(t)$ with respect to clock $C_b(t)$ is the difference between the time reported by clock $C_a(t)$ and the time reported by clock $C_b(t)$. The offset $O_a(t)$ of clock $C_a(t)$ is given by

$$O_a(t) = C_a(t) - C_t(t).$$

The offset $O_{ab}(t)$ of clock $C_a(t)$ with respect to clock $C_b(t)$ is given by

$$O_{ab}(t) = C_a(t) - C_b(t).$$

The frequency f_a of clock $C_a(t)$ is the first derivative of the clock with respect to time. It is given by

$$f_a = \frac{d}{dt}(C_a(t)).$$

The skew s_{ab} of clock $C_a(t)$ with respect to clock $C_b(t)$ is the difference between their respective frequencies. It is given by

$$s_{ab} = \frac{d}{dt}(C_a(t)) - \frac{d}{dt}(C_b(t)) = f_a - f_b.$$

Clock skew cannot be directly measured. To estimate the clock skew, an algorithm compares the clock of the device being fingerprinted to the clock of the measuring device, or fingerprinter. The clock of the device being fingerprinted is $C_a(t)$ and the clock of the fingerprinter is $C_b(t)$. Clock offset data points are plotted and an algorithm fits a line to the plot. The slope of the line is the estimate of the clock skew.

2.3.2 Estimation

Two common methods of estimating the line are a method based on linear programming and least squares fit [22, 29, 46]. These techniques are illustrated in Fig. 7. The solid line is the clock skew estimate computed with the linear programming method. The line is above all data points. The dashed line is the clocks skew estimate when computed with least squares fit. The line is through the center of the data points.

Clock offset measurements have some degree of variability from sample to sample. A line cannot therefore be drawn from the origin to an arbitrary data point to approximate the data set. The linear programming approach is to fit a line above all data points [29]. The linear programming method fits a line by minimizing the objective function

$$z = \frac{1}{N} \sum_{i=1}^{N} (mx_i + b - y_i)$$

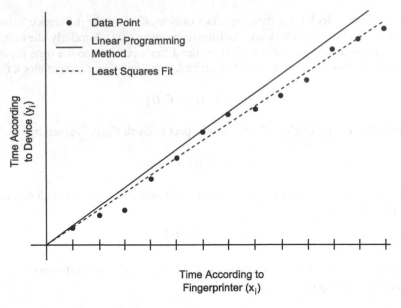

Fig. 7 Clock skew estimation. The slope of the line is the clock skew. The solid line is the clock skew computed with the linear programming method. The dashed line is the clock skew computed with least squares fit

with constraints

$$mx_i + b \geq y_i, \ \forall i = 1, ..., N.$$

In these equations, N is the number of data points, x_i is the clock offset of the device, y_i is the clock offset of the fingerprinter, m is the slope of the line, and b is the y-intercept of the line. Outputs of the linear programming method are the slope, m, and y-intercept, b. The slope is the fingerprint.

Least squares fit minimizes the sum of the squares of the errors between the actual data points and the estimate of the data points calculated with the line that is fit to the data [44]. Formally, the function

$$z = \sum_{i=i}^{N} (y_i - (mx_i + b))^2$$

is minimized.

As in the linear programming method, N is the number of data points, x_i is the clock offset of the device, y_i is the clock offset of the fingerprinter, m is the slope of the line, and b is the y-intercept of the line. The least squares fit method determines the slope, m, and the y-intercept, b, of the line. The slope is the fingerprint.

2.3.3 Network Authentication

Systems use clock skew in a number of ways to identify a node on either wired or wireless networks. Systems exploit TCP timestamps or ICMP timestamps over IEEE 802.11 and wired networks to obtain the clock skew of nodes over multiple hops [23]. They can exploit the Time Synchronization Function in the beacon probe response frames of the IEEE 802.11 protocol to obtain time stamp information in order to detect fake access points [22]. Timestamps are not readily available in some types of networks such as the IEEE 802.15.4 wireless sensor node network [18]. In these situations, systems employ additional protocols such as the Flooding Time Synchronization Protocol to capture clock skew information [17]. In a beacon-enabled IEEE 802.15.4 network, a coordinating node periodically broadcasts beacon frames. The duration between transmissions is precisely timed because other devices in the network rely on this timing information to determine when to transmit data. Systems can use the time between beacon frames to compute the clock skew of the coordinating node [32].

Regardless of the technique employed to obtain clock skew information, the procedure is similar. The system either sends a probe request to the device being fingerprinted or monitors a periodic transmission from the device. In either case, the device being fingerprinted transmits timing information. The system uses this information to estimate the clock skew of the device. The clock skew authenticates the device to the network. Figure 8 depicts a fingerprinter requesting timing information from the device being fingerprinted. The device responds with a packet containing the timestamp required for the fingerprinter to calculate the clock skew. Figure 9 illustrates a coordinating device periodically broadcasting precisely timed beacon frames.

2.3.4 Exploiting Clock Skew

From an antithetical perspective, it is possible to exploit clock skew to perform network attacks [30]. For example, consider a Tor network [37]. Tor is an overlay network that uses onion routing to hide the identity of servers from clients. Servers

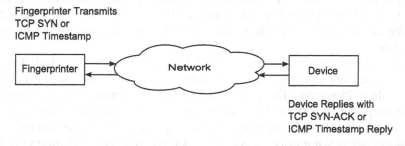

Fig. 8 Timestamp information. The fingerprinter obtains timestamp information from the device

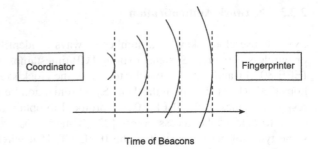

Fig. 9 Beacon-enabled IEEE 802.15.4 network. The coordinator periodically broadcasts framing information. Broadcasts are precisely timed

connect to the Tor network to advertise a service and clients request services from the Tor network. The Tor network acts as a rendezvous point so that clients and servers are hidden from each other. A server typically has a public IP address through which it accesses the Tor network. Assume an attacker determines a range of IP addresses for all servers in the Tor network but does not know which server is running a particular service. The attackers goal is to find the public IP address of the server. To perform the attack, the attacker requests the service at specific intervals which increases the load on the CPU of the server running the service. This induced load pattern affects the temperature of the CPU. The attacker additionally requests TCP timestamps of all servers through their public IP addresses to monitor each server's clock skew. Clocks are affected by temperature and the clock skew of the attacked server will have high correlation with the induced load pattern. A high correlation between load pattern and a hidden server's clock skew authenticates the hidden server to the attacker. The attacker uses this technique to determine the public IP address of the server running the targeted service.

Suppose an attacker wants to know which hidden server in a Tor network with three hidden servers contains a certain file that is 100 MB in length. The objective is to determine the public Internet IP address of the server hosting the file. The attacker repeatedly downloads the file at certain times from the hidden server through the Tor network. This induces a load pattern on the server affecting the temperature of the CPU and consequently the clock skew patterns of that server. Multiple downloads can be made simultaneously to further increase load. The measurer requests TCP timestamps from all candidate hidden servers and saves the results. The attacker performs an analysis on the TCP timestamps to determine the clock skew patterns of each server. If the attacker detects a correlation between the change in clock skews and the induced load pattern, the hidden server has been located and the attack is successful.

One possible countermeasure to the attack is to maintain a constant clock skew on the hidden servers. One way to accomplish this is to maintain a constant maximum load on the hidden server. The server runs a process that detects when the system is not running at full capacity and forces additional load on the server to return it to full capacity. The benefit of this method is that no changes to the hardware are required. The drawback is that it places unnecessary load on the system and wastes energy.

The wasted energy generates additional heat that must be expelled by the cooling system. In a server room, the additional heat generated by multiple servers may be significant and may increase energy cost. An alternative is to use different types of oscillators such as oven controlled crystal oscillators (OCXOs). The drawback to this is the expense of the oscillator and the expense of modifying the hardware to use the oscillator. Another countermeasure is to obscure or prevent access to the timing information of the hidden server. Extensive changes may be required to system software to hide timing caused by low level events such as timer interrupts.

2.3.5 Pitfalls

Crystal oscillators are affected by changes in the environment such as temperature and humidity. Because most devices are manufactured with crystal oscillators, clock skew is affected by these changes. Of these effects, temperature has the greatest impact [11, 30, 46]. However, the clock skew of a crystal oscillator varies incrementally over time in response to a change in temperature [46]. Authentication systems allow for these variations when authenticating a device by permitting some variance in the skew of the device. It is possible for the fingerprinter in a network intrusion detection system to dynamically adjust its estimate of the clock skew of a device as long as the change in skew does not exceed an appropriate threshold [22]. Tracking systems use thresholds to identify devices. As long as the estimated clock skew remains within lower and upper thresholds, the tracking system knows it is monitoring a single device.

Difficulties are created by time synchronization protocols. When the clock of a device is synchronized to a global source, the timestamp jumps by a significant amount. This causes a corresponding jump in the clock skew that may exceed the

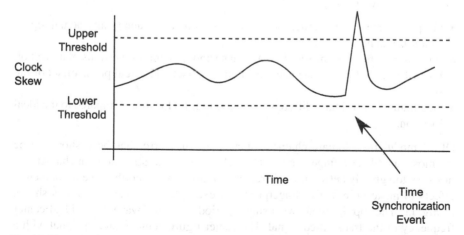

Fig. 10 Time synchronization. Authentication systems use thresholds to allow for variance. Large jumps in clock skew are ignored because they are most likely caused by time synchronization

allowed threshold [22]. Tracking and authentication systems can account for this by ignoring large jumps in clock skew. This is illustrated in Fig. 10. Similar problems occur if a device switches to an alternate power source. If a laptop computer, for instance, is switched from A/C power to battery power, the operating system may select a different clock source which affects the device characteristics including clock skew [42].

2.4 Wireless Devices

Systems use various fingerprinting techniques to authenticate and locate wireless devices. Wireless devices can exploit channel characteristics to extract shared secret keys. Some of these techniques are described in this section.

2.4.1 Radio Frequency

Extracting fingerprints from radio frequency characteristics has been in existence since at least World War II when armed forces were interested in locating the source and determining the transmitting party of radar signals [39]. Since then, radio frequency characteristics have become a popular method of uniquely identifying and authenticating wireless devices. Devices such as real-time spectrum analyzers or digital signal processing techniques are used to measure properties of the transmitted signals. Systems have used numerous radio frequency characteristics to extract fingerprint features including those described below.

Modulation domain characteristics refer to properties of the modulation scheme of the communications link such as FSK, O-QPSK, or QAM [35]. Some examples include the following [4].

- Frequency Error: Difference between ideal center frequency and actual signal center frequency.
- IQ Origin Offset: DC offset of the In-phase and Quadrature portions of a symbol.
- Phase Error: Difference between ideal phase offset and actual phase offset of the signal.
- Quadrature Error: Phase difference of the actual IQ location compared to the ideal location.

Of all modulation domain characteristics, frequency error has been shown to be the most suitable as a fingerprint feature [4]. Other modulation domain characteristics vary too greatly between measurements or are too susceptible to environmental effects to make an effective fingerprint. An example of frequency error is shown in Fig. 11. The top figure shows a single period of a sine wave at the ideal center frequency of the transmitted signal. The center figure demonstrates a signal with a small positive offset ε_1 from the ideal center frequency. The lower figure demonstrates a signal with a small negative offset ε_2 from the ideal center frequency. In

Fig. 11 Frequency error.
Frequency error is used as a
fingerprint feature

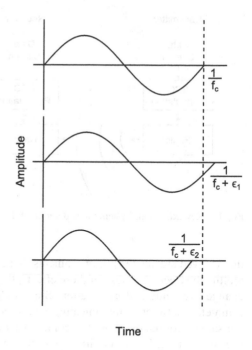

the equation for the period, ε_2 is a negative quantity. A measuring device such as a real-time spectrum analyzer must be capable of higher frequency and resolution than that of the signal from the device being fingerprinted to detect the frequency error.

Time domain methods analyze characteristics of a signal with respect to time. These methods include those listed below [13, 15, 38].

- Transients: Analysis of the initial waveform of a signal in which the amplitude rises from channel noise to full power.
- Amplitude: Differences in the overall shape of the envelope of the signal.
- Nulls: Time offset of the locations of low signal values.
- Power: Transmission power fluctuation patterns over time.

Frequency domain analysis typically analyzes similar components to time domain analysis, but does so in the frequency domain by applying Fourier or similar transforms to the waveforms [4, 38].

2.4.2 Wireless Link Key Extraction

In wireless transmission, electromagnetic waves travel in multiple paths from transmitter to receiver. This is caused by reflection and scattering as the transmitted signal comes in contact with objects in the environment. The signals traveling along each of these paths arrive at the receiver at slightly different times and from different angles. The receiver recovers the transmitted signal by probabilistically combining

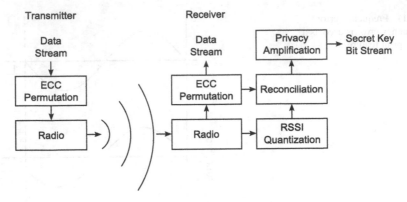

Fig. 12 Key extraction. System block diagram of the key extraction procedure

the received signals [35]. Environments that change over time lead to time varying multipath effects. Because of these effects, the characteristics of the received signal change over time and by location. Since fading channels such as this tend to be symmetric between communicating nodes, both sides of the exchange can extract the same information about the communications link [45]. Communicating nodes use bits extracted from the link between them as a secret key. Receivers at other locations cannot extract the same information mainly because of multipath effects but also because interference patterns and signal-to-noise ratios change by location.

One metric commonly available to off-the-shelf wireless components is the received signal strength indicator (RSSI). This is an indication of the strength of the signal received from the transmitter. Typical transceivers are half-duplex and cannot send and receive simultaneously. Consequently, the nodes cannot measure the strength of the signal from the other at exactly the same time. Because of this and because of hardware imperfections and limitations, the detected RSSI is not completely symmetric [21]. This results in some of the bits of the link to be interpreted differently by each side of the communication. These bit differences must be resolved before they can be used as a shared secret key. The most common method of compensating for the differences is to use a system that employs information reconciliation to correct unmatched bits and privacy amplification to prevent information about the channel characteristics from being exposed to an attacker [3]. A system block diagram of key extraction is shown in Fig. 12.

The transmitter first permutes the data stream to use in error correction at the receiver. The data are then transmitted to the receiver. The receiver quantizes the RSSI value using an upper and lower threshold. An RSSI value above the upper threshold receives a bit value of 1. An RSSI value below the lower threshold is given a bit value of 0. Any RSSI value between the two thresholds is discarded to allow for measurement inaccuracies. Higher resolution hardware may quantize the signal into more values to increase the bit extraction rate. After quantization, the system computes error correction data and feeds the data to the reconciliation stage to remove bit errors. The reconciled bit stream may contain segments that are highly correlated because sampling of the received signal may occur more frequently than changes occur in the channel characteristics. Privacy amplification eliminates correlation from the data stream by removing certain data bits [19]. This lowers the secret key bit extraction data rate, but increases the randomness of the resulting key. The device uses the resulting data stream as the secret key. Because the data is a continuous stream, devices may refresh keys periodically. Coordination between the nodes is required to determine when to discard expired key information.

To generate an uncorrelated bit stream, there must be frequent changes in the environment. Key extraction from wireless links works well in environments such as moving vehicles and crowded areas [2, 21]. It does not work well in static environments.

The benefits of wireless link key extraction are most apparent when the technique is compared to public key cryptography [2, 3, 21, 45]. Public key cryptography requires great effort in key distribution and management. With wireless links, there is no need to maintain keys in central repositories because both sides of the exchange can extract the same secret key from the link characteristics. Wireless link key extraction also requires far less computational power than public key cryptography. This is beneficial for devices such as wireless sensor nodes which have constrained resources.

2.5 Optical Media

Data are encoded on optical media such as compact discs (CDs) and digital versatile discs (DVDs) in concentric rings with a series of *lands* and *pits*. Pits are physical deformations of the disc and lands are the unmodified sections between the pits. A transition between a land and a pit indicates a logical value of 1. The length of a land or pit determines the number of consecutive 0 bits. A manufacturer mass produces a disc by pressing the pits into thermoplastic. A CD burner or DVD burner creates a disc with a laser that heats the dye on the disc to darken sections corresponding to the pits. A CD player or DVD player reads a disc by aiming a laser at the disc and monitoring the reflection. A pit diffuses the light whereas a land reflects the light without diffusing it.

Figure 13 depicts a close up view of a series of lands and pits on an optical disc. Manufacturing variation results in lands and pits with widths that are slightly different between discs that contain the same data. The differences are within tolerance of reproducing the bit stream. Variation occurs regardless of the method used to create the disc. In the case of pressing a disc, variation is caused mainly by thermal effects when the disc is created. In the case of burning a disc, variation is caused by manufacturing of the burner. These variations are used to create a certificate of authenticity for the disc. The certificate is verified by the software on the disc to ensure the disc is legitimate and has not been pirated [14].

Fig. 13 Optical disc
fingerprints. Close up view
of a section of an optical
disc. Widths of lands and pits
vary between discs that
contain the same data

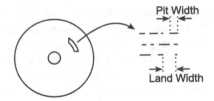

Figure 14 shows one possible method for creating and verifying a certificate of authenticity with public key cryptography techniques. The manufacturer or a trusted third party generates the certificate of authenticity. It is created by reading a specific sequence of sectors distributed across the disc to extract a fingerprint. The manufacturer signs the fingerprint with the manufacturer's private key to create a digital signature of the fingerprint. The digital signature is the certificate of authenticity. A user purchases the disc and installs the software on a computer. The manufacturer provides the certificate with the disc. The certificate is stored on the computer along with the software. When the software is executed, it reads the same sequence of sectors from the optical disc to extract the fingerprint. It also verifies the certificate with the manufacturer's public key. The additional verification step is performed to ensure the certificate originated from the manufacturer. If this step is not performed, it is possible for a counterfeiter to substitute a false manufacturing process to sell copies of the disc. If the extracted fingerprint matches the verified certificate, the software continues to execute. If they do not match, the software concludes that the disc is not an original copy and terminates. In this scheme, the disc must be physically present for the software to execute.

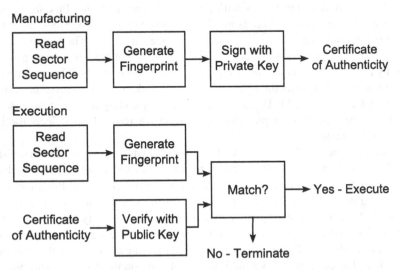

Fig. 14 Certificate of authenticity. Generation and use of a certificate of authenticity of an optical disc

Over time, the optical disc will degrade or may become scratched. Sufficient care must be taken in generating the fingerprint to account for this. The fingerprint should be generated from lands and pits distributed across the disc. Error correction and fuzzy extraction should be used to extract the fingerprint [14].

2.6 Trojan Detection

A hardware Trojan horse is malicious circuitry embedded in a microchip not intended by the manufacturer. A Trojan is typically inserted by an attacker before the microchip is manufactured. Because manufacturers outsource microchip fabrication for economic reasons, opportunity is created for attackers to insert Trojans into microchips before they are produced. Trojans can be inserted into any type of microchip, but they are especially dangerous when cryptographic processors are compromised. A Trojan in a microchip that implements the RSA algorithm, for example, can compromise the private key of cryptographic operations [1].

Trojans cannot be detected by traditional microchip testing methods such as verifying outputs for specific inputs because the malicious circuitry is typically triggered by an event that occurs infrequently or after the microchip has been powered for a long period of time. An attacker intentionally embeds this behavior into a circuit to make detection of the Trojan difficult. Manufacturers employ device fingerprints to detect Trojans before the microchip is placed into production. The manufacturer detects Trojans by creating a model of the circuit from a set of microchips that are known not to contain Trojans. The manufacturer must verify the integrity of the microchips by destructively probing the circuitry. Consequently, the model must be created before the verification process. If the manufacturer determines that a microchip on which the model is based contains a Trojan circuit, a new set of microchips must be selected and the process is repeated until a valid model is created. The manufacturer validates the remaining microchips against the model. The model includes device fingerprints consisting of side channel information such as power consumption and timing delay [43].

In the case of microchips such as PUFs, device fingerprints of Trojan detection protect device fingerprints of PUFs. PUFs must be protected to ensure keys and challenge-response pairs are not compromised [43]. Trojan detection is critical to the security of cryptographic operations that rely on these microchips.

2.7 Software Control

The authors of this chapter are investigating a new device fingerprinting technique called software controlled manifestation of hardware fingerprints. The basic idea is to execute a program on hardware such as a multicore CPU or GPU that results in different outputs depending on the processor on which the program runs. Identically manufactured devices produce different output when executing the same program. The output is the device fingerprint.

For example, one experiment creates a race condition on a multicore CPU. One core does not participate in the race because it runs the main controlling program that starts and monitors races on the remaining cores. A different response is generated depending on which core acts as the controller. Each remaining core executes exactly the same code and begins execution at the same time. In the challenge-response framework, the challenge consists of the program to be executed and the controlling core number. The response is the execution completion order. The number of unique fingerprints scales with the number of cores.

Preliminary experiments suggest that programs involving bias in memory arbitration tend to create unique fingerprints, but tests that consist of only control structures and floating point and integer arithmetic do not. We suspect this is because the state of the art in desktop multicore processors at the time of this writing uses a globally distributed clock [20]. However, as globally asynchronous locally synchronous (GALS) systems [5] in which each core has its own clock become popular, the proposed model will become viable.

3 Tradeoffs

3.1 Benefits

Systems gain numerous advantages by using device fingerprints with cryptography [4, 13, 42]. Among them are decreased memory usage, power consumption, and computing resources compared to traditional cryptographic operations. Fingerprints are resistant to attacks because attempting to forcibly extract a fingerprint from a device may damage or alter the device in a way that alters the fingerprint.

It is traditionally very difficult and expensive for a device to manage and store secrets in memory, but device fingerprints require no additional management or memory [42]. Devices traditionally store secret keys in non-volatile memories that are subject to invasive attack since they are always available even if the device is not powered. In contrast, fingerprints are not stored in memory and they are typically available only when the device is powered. They are not stored in memory because they are derived from the physical characteristics of the device. Consequently, they are difficult to duplicate.

Some platforms may not have the computing power to run traditional cryptographic primitives [42]. Resource constrained devices may use fingerprints instead of these primitives. In environments where a permanent power source is not available or where a device is difficult to access to replace the power source, it is advantageous to extend the life of the power source. Using device fingerprints instead of running resource intensive cryptographic operations aids in conserving the available power.

3.2 Drawbacks

Additional hardware real estate may be required to produce a fingerprint. For example, in the case of PUFs, a significant amount of real estate is required to implement a sufficient number of arbiters or oscillators to create a robust set of challenge-response pairs.

Adoption of device fingerprints into computer systems is an obstacle. While no modifications to standard cryptographic algorithms are required, extensive changes to system level software may be needed to supply those algorithms with the device fingerprint.

4 Summary

Device fingerprints are used with cryptography in two primary ways. Authentication algorithms use fingerprints to positively identify a device or an individual who is in possession of a device. Algorithms involving secret or private keys use a device fingerprint as the key. A fingerprint may be hashed to obtain a key with certain mathematical properties if required by an algorithm. A fingerprint may be combined with user input to allow additional features such as multiple secret keys per device. Once a secret key is derived from a fingerprint, no modifications are necessary to use the fingerprint in existing cryptographic algorithms.

There are numerous useful and important applications for device fingerprints. They have applications in criminology, cargo transport, network security, and in the military to name a few. They are used to create more secure and accurate network intrusion detection systems and to allow a system to determine when a device becomes defective. One of the more important but less cited applications is determining friend from foe in military operations.

Device characteristics may be altered by changing environmental conditions. For example, electron mobility and oscillator frequency vary with change in temperature. These changes impact fingerprinting methods to varying degrees. Characteristics of circuitry in different areas on a single microchip may be altered differently with a change in the environment [42]. Additional measures such as error correction algorithms are incorporated into the device to compensate for changing environmental conditions.

Device fingerprints are an ongoing and active area of research. Extracting robust fingerprints from devices is a difficult task. A reliable fingerprint must be hard to duplicate, resistant to attacks, and immune to environmental effects. A fingerprint feature must provide a large number of unique fingerprints to accurately and reliably identify individual devices. As advances are made in the area, combining device fingerprints with cryptography will become an increasingly important technique.

References

1. Agrawal, D., Baktir, S., Karakoyunlu, D., Rohatgi, P., Sunar, B.: Trojan detection using ic fingerprinting. In: IEEE Symposium on Security and Privacy, pp. 296–310 (2007)
2. Aono, T., Higuchi, K., Ohira, T., Komiyama, B., Sasaoka, H.: Wireless secret key generation exploiting reactance-domain scalar response of multipath fading channels. IEEE Trans. Antennas Propag. **53**(11), 3776–3784 (2005)
3. Azimi-Sadjadi, B., Kiayias, A., Mercado, A., Yener, B.: Robust key generation from signal envelopes in wireless networks. In: CCS'07: Proceedings of the 14th ACM Conference on Computer and Communications Security, pp. 401–410 (2007)
4. Brik, V., Banerjee, S., Gruteser, M., Oh, S.: Wireless device identification with radiometric signatures. In: MobiCom'08: Proceedings of the 14th ACM International Conference on Mobile Computing and Networking, New York, NY, USA, pp. 116–127 (2008)
5. Chapiro, D.M.: Globally-Asynchronous Locally-Synchronous Systems (Performance, Reliability, Digital), Ph.D. thesis, Stanford University (1985)
6. Danev, B., Capkun, S.: Transient-based identification of wireless sensor nodes. In: Proceedings of the ACM/IEEE International Conference on Information Processing in Sensor Networks (IPSN) (2009)
7. Conduct of the Persian Gulf War, Final Report to the Congress, Department of Defense, Appendix M, April 1992, pp. M-1 and M-2 (1992)
8. Douceur, J.: The Sybil attack. In: First IPTPS (2002)
9. Franklin, J., McCoy, D., Tabriz, P., Neagoe, V., Van Randwyk, J., Sicker, D.: Passive data link layer 802.11 wireless device driver fingerprinting. In: Usenix Security Symposium (2006)
10. Gassend, B., Clarke, D., van Dijk, M., Devadas, S.: Controlled physical random functions. In: Proceedings of the 18th Annual Computer Security Conference, December (2002)
11. Gassend, B., Clarke, D., van Dijk, M., Devadas, S.: Silicon physical random functions. In: Proceedings of the Computer and Communication Security Conference, November (2002)
12. Gassend, B., Clarke, D., van Dijk, M., Devadas, S.: Delay-based circuit authentication and applications. In: Proceedings of the 2003 ACM Symposium on Applied Computing, March (2003)
13. Gerdes, R., Daniels, T., Mina, M., Russell, S.: Device Identification via Analog Signal Fingerprinting: A Matched Filter Approach, NDSS (2006)
14. Hammouri, G., Dana, A., Sunar, B.: CDs have fingerprints too. In: CHES'09, Proceedings of the 11th International Workshop on Cryptographic Hardware and Embedded Systems, pp. 348–362 (2009)
15. Hall, J., Barbeau, M., Kranakis, E.: Radio frequency fingerprinting for intrusion detection in wirless networks. In: Defendable and Secure Computing (2005)
16. Hu, Y., Perrig, A., Johnson, D.: Packet leashes: a defense against wormhole attacks in wireless networks. In: IEEE Annual Conference on Computer Communications (INFOCOM), pp. 1976–1986 (2003)
17. Huang, D.-J., Teng, W.-C., Wang, C.-Y., Huang, H.-Y., Hellerstein, J.: Clock skew based node identification in wireless sensor networks. In: IEEE Globecom, LO, USA, New Orleans (2008)
18. IEEE Std 802.15.4-2006: Wireless Medium Access Control (MAC) and Physical Layer (PHY) Specifications for Low-Rate Wireless Personal Area Networks (WPANs), September (2006). http://standards.ieee.org/getieee802/download/802.15.4-2006.pdf
19. Impagliazzo, R., Levin, L., Luby, M.: Pseudo-random generation given from a one-way function. In: Proceedings of the 20th ACM Symposium on Theory of Computing (1989)
20. Intel 64 and IA-32 Architectures Software Developer's Manual, vol. 1, Basic Architecture, Intel Corporation, June (2010)
21. Jana, S., Premnath, S.N., Clark, M., Kasera, S.K., Patwari, N., Krishnamurthy, S.V.: On the effectiveness of secret key extraction from wireless signal strength in real environments. In: MobiCom (2009)
22. Jana, S., Kasera, S.K.: On fast and accurate detection of unauthorized access points using clock skews. IEEE Trans. Mobile Comput. **9**(3), 449–462 (2010)

23. Kohno, T., Broido, A., Claffy, K.: Remote physical device fingerprinting. In: Proceedings of the IEEE Symposium on Security and Privacy, May (2005)
24. Lee, J.-W., Lim, D., Gassend, B., Suh, G.E., van Dijk, M., Devadas, S.: A technique to build a secret key in integrated circuits with identification and authentication applications. In: Proceedings of the IEEE VLSI Circuits Symposium, June (2004)
25. Li, Z., Trappe, W., Zhang, Y., Nath, B.: Robust statistical methods for securing wireless localization in sensor networks. In: Proceedings of IPSN, April (2005)
26. Majzoobi, M., Koushanfar, F., Potkonjak, M.: Lightweight secure pufs. In: Proceedings of the 2008 IEEE/ACM International Conference on Computer-Aided Design, IEEE Press, pp. 670–673 (2008)
27. Majzoobi, M., Koushanfar, F., Potkonjak, M.: Testing techniques for hardware security. In: Proceedings of the International Test Conference (ITC), pp. 1–10 (2008)
28. Michal, V.: On the low-power design, stability improvement and frequency estimation of the CMOS ring oscillator. In: Radioelektronika, 2012 22nd International Conference, IEEE (2012)
29. Moon, S.B., Skelly, P., Towsley, D.: Estimation and removal of clock skew from network delay measurements. In: Proceedings of IEEE INFOCOM, vol. 1, March 1999, pp. 227–234 (1999)
30. Murdoch, S.J.: Hot or not: revealing hidden services by their clock skew. In: 13th ACM Conference on Computer and Communications Security (CCS 2006), Alexandria, VA, November (2006)
31. Novak, J.H., Brunvand, E.: Using FPGAs to prototype a self timed floating point co-processor. In: Proceedings of Custom Integrated Circuit Conference (CICC), pp. 85–88 (1994)
32. Novak, J.H., Kasera, S.K., Patwari, N.: Preventing wireless network configuration errors in patient monitoring using device fingerprints. In: 14th International Symposium and Workshops on a World of Wireless, Mobile and Multimedia Networks (WoWMoM), IEEE, pp. 1–6 (2013)
33. Patwari, N., Hero III, A.O., Perkins, M., Correal, N.S., O'Dea, R.J.: Relative location estimation in wireless sensor networks. IEEE Trans. Signal Process. **51**(8), 2137–2148 (2003)
34. Race is on to 'Fingerprint' Phones, PCs, The Wall Street Journal. http://online.wsj.com/article/SB10001424052748704679204575646704100959546.html. Accessed January 10, 2012
35. Rappaport, T.S.: Wireless Communications Principles and Practice, 2nd edn. Prentice-Hall PTR, New Jersey (2002)
36. Ravikanth, P.S.: Physical One-Way Functions, Ph.D. thesis, Massachusetts Institute of Technology (2001)
37. Reed, M.G., Syverson, P.F., Goldschlag, D.M.: Anonymous connections and onion routing. IEEE J. Sel. Areas Commun. **16**(4), 482–494 (1998)
38. Remley, K.A., Grosvenor, C.A., Johnk, R.T., Novotny, D.R., Hale, P.D., McKinley, M.D., Karygiannis, A., Antonakakis, E: Electromagnetic signatures of WLAN cards and network security. In: ISSPIT (2005)
39. Rasmussen, K.B., Capkun, S.: Implications of radio fingerprinting on the security of sensor networks. In: Proceedings of IEEE SecureComm (2007)
40. Saadah, D.M.: Friendly fire: will we get it right this time? In: 31st U.S. Army Operations Research Symposium, Fort Lee, Virginia, November (1992)
41. Sigg, S., Budde, M., Yusheng, J., Michael, B.: Entropy of audio fingerprints for unobtrusive device authentication. In: Lecture Notes in Computer Science. Modeling and Using Contexts, vol. 6967, 296–299 (2011)
42. Suh, G.E., Devadas, S.: Physical unclonable functions for device authentication and secret key generation. In: Proceedings of the 44th Design Automation Conference, IEEE, pp. 9–14 (2007)
43. Tehranipoor, M., Koushanfar, F.: A survey of hardware trojan taxonomy and detection. IEEE Des. Test Comput. **27**(1), 10–25 (2010)
44. Thomas Jr., G.B., Finney, R.L.: Calculus and analytic geometry, 6th edn. Addison-Wesley, Reading (1984)
45. Tope, M.A., McEachen, J.C.: Unconditionally secure communications over fading channels. In: Military Communications Conference (MILCOM 2001), vol. 1, October 2001, pp. 54–58 (2001)

46. Uddin, M., Castelluccia, C.: Toward clock skew based wireless sensor node services. In: Wireless Internet Conference (WICON), 2010 The 5th Annual ICST, March 2010, pp. 1–9 (2010)
47. Zanetti, C., Danev, B., Capkun, S.: Physical-layer identification of UHF RFID tags. In: Proceedings of the 16th ACM Conference on Mobile Computing and Networking—MobiCom'10, ACM SIGMOBILE, pp. 353–364 (2010)

Fingerprinting by Design: Embedding and Authentication

Paul L. Yu, Brian M. Sadler, Gunjan Verma and John S. Baras

Abstract In this chapter we consider the design of fingerprints for the purpose of authenticating a message. We begin with a background discussion of fingerprinting and related ideas, progressing to a communications point of view. Fingerprint embedding for message authentication is motivated by the desire to make an authentication tag less accessible to an eavesdropper. We consider metrics for good fingerprint design, and apply these to develop an embedding scheme for wireless communications. Wireless software defined radio experiments validate the theory and demonstrate the applicability of our approach.

1 Background

In this section we give an overview of intrinsic and intentionally embedded fingerprinting, and discuss the relationship with identification, communications, secrecy, and authentication.

1.1 Intrinsic Fingerprints

A *fingerprint* is literally the impression of a fingertip, but more broadly is a characteristic that identifies. This is often associated with an intrinsic property of uniqueness,

P.L. Yu (✉) · B.M. Sadler · G. Verma
Army Research Lab, Adelphi, MD 20783, USA
e-mail: paul.l.yu.civ@mail.mil

B.M. Sadler
e-mail: brian.m.sadler6.civ@mail.mil

G. Verma
e-mail: gunjan.verma.civ@mail.mil

J.S. Baras
Institute for Systems Research, University of Maryland, College Park, MD 20742, USA
e-mail: baras@umd.edu

© Springer Science+Business Media New York 2016
C. Wang et al. (eds.), *Digital Fingerprinting*,
DOI 10.1007/978-1-4939-6601-1_5

69

or at least uniqueness viewed as a realization of a random process with structure. Identifying humans via biometrics now includes fingerprints, iris scans, DNA, voice features, and behavioral patterns [11]. Given a sensor with sufficient resolution it is possible to differentiate unique individuals based on sensor output signatures. Note, however, that these signatures can be copied and/or altered, so there remains important additional questions regarding security.

More generally, measurable intrinsic characteristics of nominally identical devices or objects can be used to identify a specific device [14]. Examples include printers [13], cameras [2], scanners [10, 12] and photocopiers, as well as radios and their components such as filters and oscillators. Several investigators have considered applying these ideas to radio transmissions, including identification of radios based on signal transients [6, 21], and study of vulnerability of these methods to impersonation [5]. In wired communications, identification of ethernet cards has been demonstrated [7].

It follows that a good intrinsic fingerprint is unique. We would also like that the fingerprint can be measured with a sensor that is convenient and technologically feasible, and that the resulting signature is robust to measurement noise. In addition, security features may be desirable, but these are not necessarily inherent in the fingerprint.

So, given a range of human subjects or some class of devices, the inherent randomness can be exploited to develop measures of uniqueness. With sufficient understanding of the biological or physical processes, and the sensing technology, fingerprint based identification can be assigned a statistical reliability.

1.2 Fingerprint Embedding

A next step is to purposefully embed a fingerprint in a device in a designed way, so that each device can be uniquely identified. Now, in addition to the above characteristics of goodness, a good fingerprint will enable security measures, including the ability to defeat cloning and tampering. Not only is the fingerprint unique and identifiable, but it may be embedded in such a way that it is very difficult to copy. Thus, for example, a manufacturer can label and recognize each manufactured device, while at the same time making it difficult to produce a counterfeit that cannot be differentiated from the genuine original. Needless to say, this has important implications for commercial enterprise.

Fingerprint embedding into devices is of course dependent on the specifics of the device, and so can take many forms. The fingerprint may take advantage of some randomness inherent in the production of the device, that is, it may be intrinsic in the manufacturing process and this can be exploited (e.g., when a transparent material is doped with light scattering particles then laser illumination yields a unique speckle pattern). Such an intrinsic fingerprint can be measured and cataloged, like a serial number. The inherent randomness that is exploited for the intrinsic fingerprint may be uncontrollable at the micro-scale, and so it may be very difficult or impossible to manufacture a similar device with a pre-specified fingerprint.

An important application of fingerprint embedding is in circuits and chip manufacturing. A key idea here is a physically unclonable function (PUF). These are based on a challenge-response paradigm to enable authentication of a specific device, and are closely linked with cryptography and secret keys; e.g., see [22, 24].

1.3 Fingerprinting and Communications

A fingerprint conveys information, whether intrinsic or embedded by design, so we can consider fingerprinting in the context of communications. With an intrinsic fingerprint, the person or device is conveying its identity, and we strive to receive the message with sufficient fidelity to uniquely recognize the message originator. When we embed a fingerprint, we are designing a message for some specific purpose.

A closely related idea is *steganography,* conveying hidden messages (originally from Greek, meaning concealed writing). In recent years digital steganography, sometimes called data hiding, has been developed as a way of altering binary data to include a hidden message [20]. The message may have some specific purpose, such as watermarking to ensure data integrity, or inserting a copyright notice. Digital steganography has been extensively applied to data intended for human consumption, such as imagery, video, or audio. In this case the data is modified in a small and generally imperceptible way, while the message is discernible to the user with knowledge of the data hiding algorithm.

Communications channels, especially in wireless communications, are subject to eavesdroppers. Messages are typically encoded for secrecy (*encrypted*), and decoding relies on a shared secret key. It is also fundamentally important to *authenticate* a message, i.e., to verify the originator of the message. This counters the ability of the eavesdropper to use impersonation or substitution attacks. Information theoretic analysis incorporating fading wireless channel models has been used to study the level of communications secrecy relative to an eavesdropper [15, 27].

Traditional authentication and secrecy encoding rely on shared secret keys, whose use is complicated by the need for pre-distribution and storage. Information about keys is leaked and so keys become stale, and updating the keys over a network is then a potential vulnerability due to eavesdropping. If the users have access to some common random information source, while the eavesdropper does not, then this can be exploited to derive a new shared secret key [18]. For example, a common random wireless fading channel can be used to derive a key, under the assumption that an eavesdropper will have a statistically independent realization of the channel due to her physical displacement [28].

2 Introduction to Embedded Authentication

Authentication of the message source is fundamental to secure communications, providing identity validation and defense against impersonation attacks by an adversary. Authentication defeats message tampering, and enables trust to be established between users. This is especially critical in wireless communications using an open and shared medium, where an adversary can eavesdrop, spoof, and jam. In the rest of the chapter we focus on this case.

Conventional authentication schemes transmit both the data message and a separate authentication message, referred to as a tag [19]. Each authentication tag is dependent on the associated data and a secret key that is shared only between the transmitter and receiver. The tag generator employed at the transmitter is often a cryptographic hash function. It is highly nonlinear and difficult to invert, so that an adversary cannot easily recover the key given the message and the associated tag. This assumes the hash function is cryptographically secure.

In the conventional approach, the authentication tag is appended to the message, and so is available to an eavesdropper. Also, the tag utilizes additional bandwidth. This motivates the use of an embedded fingerprint to carry the authentication tag. Because the fingerprint is embedded, it can be designed so that it is difficult to recover by an adversary. And, the fingerprint can be designed so that it is does not require additional bandwidth. However, the receiver observes the message with a slight signal-to-noise ratio penalty because some message power is allocated for the tag.

We show how this can be accomplished in wireless communications by embedding a fingerprint at the physical layer [29–31]. Consequently, while an eavesdropper may recover the data message error-free, she observes the tag at a reduced signal-to-noise ratio. As we will show, this leads to uncertainty about the secret key that is not readily defeated by an increase in her computational ability. Thus, the embedding provides additional security and unlike the conventional authentication approach, does not solely rely on cryptographic security.

3 Framework for Embedded Authentication

The basic system is diagrammed in Fig. 1. The transmitter (Alice) generates the authentication tag using the data and a shared secret symmetric key. The problem of key distribution is well studied and we assume that the keys have already been distributed. (A key might also be available through some other means, such as deriving it from the common channel [32].) The tag is embedded into the MIMO transmission by employing small coded modulation shifts as a fingerprint. This symbol synchronous approach ensures low complexity of the overall authentication process. At the receiver (Bob), the message is validated by comparing the received authentication

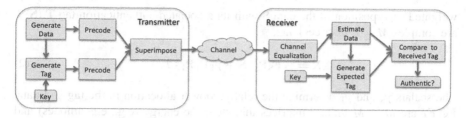

Fig. 1 System Diagram. The transmitter generates a data-dependent authentication tag and super-imposes it with the data. The receiver estimates the data and generates the corresponding expected authentication tag. This is compared with the received tag to validate the transmitters identity [31, Fig. 1]

tag with the expected authentication that is locally generated at the receiver using the demodulated data and the shared key.

3.1 Authentication System—Transmitter

We consider the general case of an $M \times N$ MIMO system, where Alice has M transmit antennas and Bob has $N > M$ receive antennas [31]. (Single antenna cases are easily treated in the following framework, and multi-carrier cases are treated in [29].) The adversary Eve has M transmit and N receive antennas that she can use to eavesdrop or spoof Alice's transmissions.

We use the following notation. $|| \cdot ||^2$ denotes the Frobenius norm, $\cdot^\dagger$ denotes complex conjugate, $\text{Tr}(\cdot)$ denotes matrix trace, and $\mathbf{I}$ denotes the identity matrix.

We assume that data is separated into frames represented by $M \times L$ complex matrices. Thus, each frame contains L symbols for each of the M antennas. We denote a particular transmitted frame by $\mathbf{X}$. The received frame is

$$\mathbf{Y} = \mathbf{HX} + \mathbf{W} \tag{1}$$

where $\mathbf{H}$ is the MIMO channel matrix ($N \times M$), $\mathbf{Y}$ is the received signal ($N \times L$), and $\mathbf{W}$ is white Gaussian noise ($N \times L$).

We introduce a stealthy fingerprint to the transmitted frame $\mathbf{X}$ so that it contains both data and a unique authentication tag. Alice and Bob have exclusive knowledge of their shared secret key K that is used to generate the authentication tag. Figure 1 shows the overall approach. We first detail the construction of the authenticated frame, and then describe the receiver processing to carry out the authentication hypothesis test.

There are many possible ways to combine data and tag, e.g., through convolution. However, to keep the scheme conceptually clear we adopt the symbol-synchronous superposition approach. Note that when the tag is not symbol synchronous, the basis expansion model is a useful tool to describe the signal [8]. The frame $\mathbf{X}$ is the weighted superposition of the data $\mathbf{S}$ with its associated authentication tag $\mathbf{T}$ ($\mathbf{S}$, $\mathbf{T}$ are complex $M \times L$ matrices), i.e.,

$$\mathbf{X} = \gamma_S \mathbf{F}_S \mathbf{P}_S^{\frac{1}{2}} \mathbf{S} + \gamma_T \mathbf{F}_T \mathbf{P}_T^{\frac{1}{2}} \mathbf{T}. \tag{2}$$

The scalars γ_S and γ_T determine the relative power allocation in the tag and data. $\mathbf{F}_S$, $\mathbf{F}_T$ are $M \times M$ unitary matrices that steer the energy (e.g., eigenmodes) and $\mathbf{P}_S$ (respectively, $\mathbf{P}_T$) are $M \times M$ diagonal matrices that allocate power between the columns of $\mathbf{F}_S$ (respectively, $\mathbf{F}_T$). Appendix contains a brief review of capacity-optimal precoding and power allocation strategies for the cases of (1) no channel state information (CSI), (2) perfect CSI, or (3) statistical CSI, available at the transmitter.

The tag is generated using a cryptographic hash [19], that is,

$$\mathbf{T} = g(\mathbf{S}, K), \tag{3}$$

for the data $\mathbf{S}$ given the shared key K. By design, it is infeasible to find the input given the output of a cryptographic hash. Therefore it is reasonable to assume that the data and tag are uncorrelated, i.e.,

$$E[\mathbf{S}^\dagger \mathbf{T}] = \mathbf{0}. \tag{4}$$

We assume each element of the $\mathbf{S}$ and $\mathbf{T}$ matrices has the same expected power. To ensure that adding authentication to the signal does not change the signal's expected power, γ_S and γ_T are chosen to ensure that

$$\gamma_S^2 \mathrm{Tr}(\mathbf{P}_S) + \gamma_T^2 \mathrm{Tr}(\mathbf{P}_T) = M \tag{5}$$

where $\mathrm{Tr}(\mathbf{P}_S) = \mathrm{Tr}(\mathbf{P}_T) = M$.

3.2 Authentication System—Receiver

The receiver processing and authentication steps are shown in Fig. 1. The receiver first equalizes the channel and obtains a data estimate. From this data estimate and the shared key the receiver generates the expected authentication tag and compares it with the received tag, declaring authentication if a match is obtained.

The receiver first obtains a noisy channel estimate $\hat{\mathbf{H}}$ in a conventional manner, for example, through the use of training symbols [3]. We model the channel estimate by

$$\hat{\mathbf{H}} = \mathbf{H} + \mathbf{Z} \tag{6}$$

where $\mathbf{Z}$ is an $N \times M$ channel estimation error matrix. We assume that if training symbols are used they do not contain the authentication fingerprint, so that channel estimation is essentially independent of the presence of the authentication process.

Next we describe the data recovery, followed by the authentication recovery and test. It will be useful to rewrite the received signal $\mathbf{Y}$ in (1) with the simple substitution of (2) to obtain

$$\begin{aligned} \mathbf{Y} &= \mathbf{HX} + \mathbf{W} \\ &= \mathbf{H}(\gamma_S \mathbf{F}_S \mathbf{P}_S^{\frac{1}{2}} \mathbf{S} + \gamma_T \mathbf{F}_T \mathbf{P}_T^{\frac{1}{2}} \mathbf{T}) + \mathbf{W}. \end{aligned} \tag{7}$$

To equalize the channel, the receiver assumes $\hat{\mathbf{H}}$ is the true channel. The frame estimate is obtained by inverting $\hat{\mathbf{H}}$ to find

$$\hat{\mathbf{X}} = \hat{\mathbf{H}}^{-1}\mathbf{Y}. \tag{8}$$

Note that the frame is corrupted through the channel estimation error as well as the additive noise.

We assume the receiver knows the CSI available to the transmitter, and so can undo any transmitter-applied precoding. Therefore the receiver estimates the data signal via

$$\tilde{\mathbf{S}} = \gamma_S^{-1} \mathbf{P}_S^{-\frac{1}{2}} \mathbf{F}_S^{-1} \hat{\mathbf{X}}. \tag{9}$$

Because the authentication tag $\mathbf{T}$ is data-dependent, the receiver is unable to remove it prior to decoding the data, and thus it acts as interference. We note that a joint detector for both data and tag can be designed, but this requires very high complexity. Instead, we keep the tag power allocation low to obtain a stealthy fingerprint that has very little negative impact on the data recovery. Having obtained $\tilde{\mathbf{S}}$, the receiver completes the data recovery using conventional demodulation and decoding steps.

Referring again to Fig. 1, having estimated the data, the receiver can now proceed to complete the authentication process. To do this, the received tag is estimated and compared against the expected tag conditioned on the assumption that the received data is uncorrupted. The comparison is given by

H_0: not authentic ($\mathbf{Y}$ does not contain correct tag)
H_1: authentic ($\mathbf{Y}$ contains correct tag).

Formally, we perform the threshold hypothesis test

- Decide H_0 if $\tau \leq \tau_0$
- Decide H_1 if $\tau > \tau_0$

where test statistic τ is calculated from the received data and the desired probability of false alarm determines the threshold τ_0.

To generate the expected tag given the current frame, the receiver needs to generate the data matrix that he believes the transmitter used in forming the tag via (3). Let us denote the receiver's estimate of this as $\hat{\mathbf{S}}$, which is readily obtained from $\tilde{\mathbf{S}}$ in (9). Note that $\tilde{\mathbf{S}}$ does not necessarily equal $\hat{\mathbf{S}}$ due to the presence of modulation and error correction coding. Given $\tilde{\mathbf{S}}$ and knowledge of the transmission format then it is straightforward for the receiver to obtain $\hat{\mathbf{S}}$. The receiver then uses the received data and shared key to construct the corresponding expected authentication tag (cf., Eq. (3))

$$\tilde{\mathbf{T}} = g(\hat{\mathbf{S}}, K). \tag{10}$$

If the data was correctly recovered then $\tilde{\mathbf{T}} = \mathbf{T}$. When the data is recovered incorrectly, then $\tilde{\mathbf{T}} \neq \mathbf{T}$ with high probability, since $g(\cdot)$ is a collision-resistant function. We are only concerned with the case where $\hat{\mathbf{S}} = \mathbf{S}$ because if this were not the case then the data would have been received in error, and authentication should not proceed.

To facilitate the comparison of the expected tag with the received tag, we compensate $\tilde{\mathbf{T}}$ for the transmission processing using

$$\hat{\mathbf{Q}} = \gamma_{\mathbf{T}} \hat{\mathbf{H}} \mathbf{F}_{\mathbf{T}} \mathbf{P}_{\mathbf{T}}^{\frac{1}{2}} \tilde{\mathbf{T}}. \tag{11}$$

This compensates for the precoding, power loading, and propagation through the channel, yielding an estimate of the tag as it appears at the receiver, denoted $\hat{\mathbf{Q}}$.

Having generated the expected tag given the received data, the receiver also must recover the received tag for comparison. We do this by calculating the residual

$$\mathbf{Q} = \mathbf{Y} - \gamma_{\mathbf{S}} \hat{\mathbf{H}} \mathbf{F}_{\mathbf{S}} \mathbf{P}_{\mathbf{S}}^{\frac{1}{2}} \hat{\mathbf{S}}. \tag{12}$$

Here, we compensate the error-corrected data $\hat{\mathbf{S}}$ for precoding, power loading, and propagation through the channel so that it can be directly subtracted from the receiver input $\mathbf{Y}$ to form residual matrix $\mathbf{Q}$.

To carry out the authentication hypothesis test, we correlate the expected authentication tag $\hat{\mathbf{Q}}$ against the received tag $\mathbf{Q}$, so our test statistic is given by

$$\tau = \Re[\mathrm{Tr}(\hat{\mathbf{Q}}^{\dagger} \mathbf{Q})]. \tag{13}$$

We set the detection threshold τ_0 to limit the probability of false alarm $p_{\mathrm{fa}} = p(\tau > \tau_0 | H_0)$. By the central limit theorem τ is approximately Gaussian distributed and simulations verify that this is a good assumption, even for small M and N. Thus, the receiver sets the detection threshold according to the allowable false alarm probability

$$\tau_0 = \sigma F^{-1}(p_{\mathrm{fa}}) \tag{14}$$

where σ is the standard deviation of τ when no authentication is transmitted, and $F(\cdot)$ is the cumulative distribution function (CDF) of the standard Gaussian distribution.

3.3 Authentication Performance

When no authentication tag is transmitted, we expand Eq. (12) with (2) and (6) to see that

$$\mathbf{Q}|H_0 = \left[(1 - \gamma_\mathrm{S})\hat{\mathbf{H}} + \mathbf{Z}\right]\mathbf{F_S P_S}^{\frac{1}{2}}\mathbf{S} + \mathbf{W} . \tag{15}$$

Now, using (15) in (13), and applying our assumption that the data and tag are uncorrelated (4), then we can show that $\tau|H_0$ is approximately zero mean and has variance approximated by

$$\sigma^2|H_0 = \gamma_\mathrm{T}^2\mathrm{Var}\left[\mathrm{Tr}((\hat{\mathbf{H}}\mathbf{F_T P_T}^{\frac{1}{2}}\mathbf{T})^\dagger\mathbf{W})\right] . \tag{16}$$

Using this in (14) we obtain the detection threshold.

We can also characterize τ under H_1, authentication present, as follows. The mean is found to be

$$E[\tau|H_1] = \gamma_\mathrm{T}^2||\hat{\mathbf{H}}\mathbf{F_T P_T}^{\frac{1}{2}}\mathbf{T}||^2 \neq 0, \tag{17}$$

and from (12) we obtain

$$\begin{aligned}\mathbf{Q}|H_1 &= \gamma_\mathrm{T}\hat{\mathbf{H}}\mathbf{F_T P_T}^{\frac{1}{2}}\mathbf{T} \\ &+ \mathbf{Z}(\gamma_\mathrm{S}\mathbf{F_S P_S}^{\frac{1}{2}}\mathbf{S} + \gamma_\mathrm{T}\mathbf{F_T P_T}^{\frac{1}{2}}\mathbf{T}) + \mathbf{W} .\end{aligned} \tag{18}$$

Using (13) and carrying out some lengthy algebra we can find $\sigma^2|H_1$, the variance of τ in (13). Thus, the authentication test corresponds to a Gaussian problem with zero mean under H_0 and non-zero mean under H_1, and generally different variance expressions under the two hypotheses. These expressions can be used to predict the test performance.

4 Metrics for Embedded Fingerprint Authentication

4.1 Impact on Data BER

The impact of superimposing the authentication tag is twofold: it takes power from the data signal and acts as interference to its demodulation. When the tag is superimposed at low power ($\gamma_\mathrm{T}^2 < 1\%$), the interference to data demodulation may be modeled as an increase in noise, i.e., as a decrease in data SNR. For example, suppose that a given channel eigenmode has 10 dB SNR. If the tag uses 1 % of the power on that eigenmode, the data SNR becomes 9.942 dB. With 0.1 % power for the tag, the data SNR becomes 9.996 dB. Hence, the data BER is essentially unchanged at such low authentication powers and the interference caused by the tag is minimal. Simulation and experimental results show this to be the case. In Sect. 5 we show that while the change in coded data BER is small for apparently minuscule tag powers, these low tag power levels are sufficient for authentication.

4.2 Authentication Performance

The performance of the authentication system depends on the amount of channel information available at the transmitter as well as the algorithm used to load the power onto the antennas. In the following we consider three cases of CSI: perfect, statistical, and none. (See Appendix for a discussion on power-loading for these cases of CSI).

In Rayleigh fading, the authentication probability for 4×256 symbol authentication tags is shown in Fig. 2. In this figure, we compare two tag allocation policies (how the tag is loaded across the antennas) and three CSI cases (how much channel state information is available to the transmitter). For either tag allocation policy, the perfect CSI case gives the best authentication performance and the statistical CSI case has a 1–2 dB advantage over the no-CSI case. Authentication performance can be improved by increasing the tag energy, whether through increasing the tag power, increasing the tag size, or some combination of the two.

One policy concentrates the tag energy in the strongest eigenmode and the other spreads it across all eigenmodes. Placing the authentication energy in the strongest channel eigenmode greatly improves the authentication detection by improving the tag SNR. The difference is especially apparent at low SNR and less apparent at high SNR when more channel modes are available with higher SNR.

Fig. 2 Authentication performance versus SNR for various CSI scenarios and tag policies in the Rayleigh fading case. The false alarm probability is set to 2^{-32}, corresponding to the probability of guessing a 32-bit word, and the tag power is 0.1 % of the total transmit power. Putting authentication tags into the strongest eigenmodes greatly improves authentication detection [31, Fig. 9]

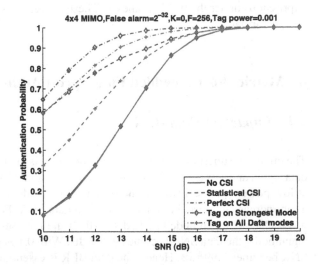

4.3 Security Analysis

Though Eve does not initially have the secret key K shared by Alice and Bob, she gains key information by observing their communications. When she learns K, she is able to impersonate Alice at will by generating legitimate tags for her messages using Eq. (3). The protection of K against Eve is therefore crucial to the security of the authentication system.

For a given data frame, the number of distinct tags that can be assigned to it is bounded by the number of keys. If sufficiently many tags are observed without noise, as is the case with conventional message authentication codes (MACs), Eve will eventually obtain the key and can mount successful impersonation or substitution attacks [17]. However, if the tags are viewed in noise as with our approach, there is a non-zero probability of error in the observed tag and the effort required to recover the secret key can be significantly increased. The following analysis quantifies this increase.

In the following we assume that Eve, just as Bob, is able to recover the data $\mathbf{S} = s$ from her observation $\mathbf{Y}$ without error. Further, we assume that Eve knows the tag generating function $g(\cdot)$ which defines the dependency of $\mathbf{T}$ on $\mathbf{S}$ and K as per (3).

4.3.1 Key Equivocation

The equivocation, or conditional entropy [4], of the key is defined as $H(K|\mathbf{Y})$. It is a measure of Eve's uncertainty about the secret key given her observation and infinite computational resources. Equivocation is non-negative and bounded by the entropy of the secret key. Zero key equivocation is the worst case for security because brute-force attacks are guaranteed to succeed.

Noiseless Observations:
First let us consider the key equivocation under the typical MAC assumption of noiseless observations. Then, observing Y is equivalent to observing $\mathbf{S}, \mathbf{T}$ without error, so

$$H(K|\mathbf{Y}) = H(K|\mathbf{S}, \mathbf{T}) = \sum_{s \in \mathscr{S}, t \in \mathscr{T}} p(s, t) H(K|s, t) \tag{19}$$

$$H(K|s, t) \triangleq - \sum_{k \in \mathscr{K}} p(k|s, t) \log p(k|s, t) \tag{20}$$

where $\mathscr{K}, \mathscr{S}, \mathscr{T}$ are the domains of $K, \mathbf{S}, \mathbf{T}$, respectively, and $p(k|s, t) \triangleq p(K = k|\mathbf{S} = s, \mathbf{T} = t)$.

From (20) it follows that equivocation is related to the invertibility of $g(\cdot)$. In particular, when $g(\cdot)$ is not invertible in k, there are multiple possible k that satisfy $t = g(s, k)$. Thus, observing a particular (s, t) tuple still leaves uncertainty about the key and the key equivocation is positive. By the pigeonhole principle [9], a sufficient condition for positive key equivocation is $|\mathscr{K}| > |\mathscr{T}|$.

Similarly, when $g(\cdot)$ is invertible in k, key equivocation is zero. A necessary (but not sufficient) condition for zero equivocation is therefore $|\mathcal{K}| \le |\mathcal{T}|$.

Noisy Observations:
For the purposes of the following discussion we will assume zero key equivocation and study the impact of noise on Eve's key equivocation.

Because Eve knows the set of possible keys, she knows the set of tags than can be associated with the transmitted data,

$$\mathcal{T}^s = \{t_i = g(s, k_i) | k_i \in \mathcal{K}\} . \tag{21}$$

With no key equivocation, $\mathcal{T}^s$ contains no duplicates and $|\mathcal{T}^s| = |\mathcal{K}|$.

Eve makes an estimate of the tag $\hat{t}$ from her observation. There is no guarantee that $\hat{t} \in \mathcal{T}^s$ because of noise. To determine the uncertainty of the tag (and therefore key), she first calculates the Hamming distance $d(\hat{t}, t_i)$ (in bits) from each valid tag $t_i \in \mathcal{T}^s$. With an iid tag bit error probability p_e, the probability that t_i was transmitted is

$$p(t_i | \hat{t}) = p_e^{h(\hat{t}, t_i)} (1 - p_e)^{\log_2 |\mathcal{T}| - h(\hat{t}, t_i)} . \tag{22}$$

Note that when $|\mathcal{K}| < |\mathcal{T}|$, it follows that $\sum_i p(t_i | \hat{t}) < 1$ and therefore $p(\cdot)$ is not a probability distribution. Therefore we construct the probability distribution given $\hat{t}$

$$f(t_i | \hat{t}) = \frac{p(t_i | \hat{t})}{\sum_{t_i \in \mathcal{T}^s} p(t_i | \hat{t})} . \tag{23}$$

The key equivocation in the noisy channel is

$$H(K|\mathbf{Y}) \approx H(K|S, \hat{T}) \approx - \sum_{k_i \in \mathcal{K}} f(k_i | \hat{t}) \log f(k_i | \hat{t})$$

$$= - \sum_{k \in \mathcal{K}} f(t_i | \hat{t}) \log f(t_i | \hat{t}) , \tag{24}$$

where $f(k_i | \hat{t}) = f(t_i | \hat{t})$ because we assume zero key equivocation in the noiseless channel, i.e., knowledge of the key is equivalent to knowledge of the tag.

Multiple Observations:
The analysis is easily extended to multiple observations of data/tag pairs, assuming the same key is used. With the data $s^1, s^2, \ldots, s^n$, Eve enumerates the possible tags

$$t_i = t_i^1 | t_i^2 | \cdots | t_i^n = g(s^1, k_i) | g(s^2, k_i) | \cdots | g(s^n, k_i) \tag{25}$$

where we use the symbol | to denote concatenation.

The estimated tag is similarly extended over multiple observations

$$\hat{t} = \hat{t}^1 | \hat{t}^2 | \cdots | \hat{t}^n . \tag{26}$$

The subsequent analysis is identical, except in Eq. (22) the term $\log_2 |\mathcal{T}|$ is replaced with $n \log_2 |\mathcal{T}|$ due to making n observations.

4.3.2 Impersonation and Substitution Attacks

When the authentication false alarm probability $p_{fa} = 0$ (see Eq. (14)), the probability of a successful impersonation attack given the previous observations $t_1, \ldots, t_{i-1}$ is lower bounded as follows [17, Theorem 3]:

$$P_{I,i} \geq 2^{-I(t_i; K | t_1, \ldots, t_{i-1})} . \tag{27}$$

The decrease in the key equivocation is approximately linear in the number of observations [31], so

$$I(t_i; K | t_1, \ldots, t_{i-1}) = H(K | t_1, \ldots, t_{i-1}) - H(K | t_1, \ldots, t_i)$$
$$\approx H(K | t_1) \tag{28}$$

as long as $H(K | t_1, \ldots, t_i) > 0$. Thus, $P_{I,i} \geq 2^{-H(K | t_1)}$.

The probability of a successful substitution attack given the previous observations $t_1, \ldots, t_{i-1}$ is lower bounded as follows [17, Theorem 6]:

$$P_{S,i} \geq 2^{-H(K | t_1, \ldots, t_{i-1})} . \tag{29}$$

This bound indicates that the probability of a successful substitution attack may grow rapidly as the key equivocation drops. For example, when the equivocation drops by 1, the lower bound on the success probability doubles. In the following section, Fig. 4 shows the key equivocation for an example authentication system.

The above theorems bound performance from below, therefore the adversary may be able to do much better. An interesting question is how well the bounds can predict adversary success probability. We note that in some cases the bound is necessarily tight: with typical MACs, there is no key equivocation and therefore the substitution attack is successful w.p. 1. As our method guarantees positive key equivocation, we assert that we protect the key better than typical MAC systems.

4.4 Complexity

The additional complexity required by our approach is linear in the size of the transmitted signal. First, the transmitter must calculate the authentication tag using the function $g(\cdot)$, as in conventional MACs. Typically this is easy to calculate. Then, depending on her power allocation strategy for the tag, she scales the data and tag and adds them together. This involves $O(ML)$ additions and multiplications (recall that the transmitted matrices are of dimension $M \times L$).

The receiver calculates the residual by re-encoding the estimated data and subtracting it from his observation. This includes any modulation, error-correction coding, and pulse shaping that may occur. Then, he calculates the expected authentication tag using $g(\cdot)$. He calculates the threshold for the given false alarm probability and SNR. This involves a single inverse normal CDF calculation. Finally, he correlates the residual with the expected authentication tag and compares the result with the threshold. This involves another $O(ML)$ complex multiplications.

5   Experimental Results

We conduct a series of SISO experiments with NI-USRP software-defined radios [1]. We use two USRP1 devices, with transmit/receive frequency of 2.44 GHz. The two radios are placed about 12 feet apart with line of sight. QPSK modulation is used for both the data and the tag. By scaling the power of the transmitter, various SNR levels are attained. Between 25,000 and 30,000 packets were transmitted at each data point. We use MATLAB to control the USRPs [26]. For each packet received, the receiver logs important information (such as the test statistic in (13)) that we analyze after the experiment.

5.1 Authentication Performance

Figure 3 shows the authentication probability for various tag powers. The packets contain 400 data symbols and the tag power ranges from 0.1 to 1 % of the transmit power. Thus, each packet contains 400 QPSK tag symbols, i.e., each packet contains an 800 bit tag. The false alarm probability is 1 %.

As previously discussed, authentication performance is improved by increasing the tag energy. This figure shows the effect of changing the tag power while holding the packet length constant. Other experiments show that modifying the packet length has similar effect and we again obtain a very good agreement between theory and experiment.

5.2 Key Equivocation

Figure 4 shows the key equivocation in Eq. (24) for various tag powers. The key equivocation is calculated based on the observed tag bit error rate for each SNR. Recalling the discussion from Sect. 4.3.1, this figure considers the case where

Fig. 3 Results from SDR experiment. Authentication probability for various tag powers (from 0.1 to 1 % of the transmit power). Packets contain 400 QPSK symbols and false alarm probability is 1 %. High-powered tags have high authentication performance

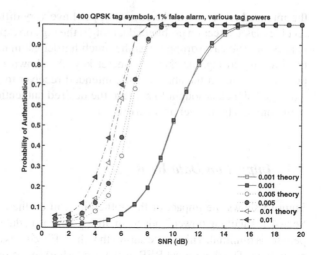

$K = 256$ bits and $T = 800$ bits. We assume that there is zero key equivocation in the noiseless case (i.e., each (message, tag) pair is associated with a unique key). This is a pessimistic assumption, so typical results will be better than those shown in Fig. 4.

Note that higher channel SNR decreases the key equivocation. Intuitively, a cleaner observation leads to less uncertainty of the tag and hence the key. (Taken to the extreme, a perfect observation leads to zero key equivocation.) For the scenarios of interest (low tag power), the key equivocation is seen to be very high as a proportion of its 256-bit maximum.

Also note that lower tag power increases the key equivocation. As with the effect of channel SNR, reducing the tag power reduces the ability of the receiver to make an accurate estimate of the tag. A large increase in key equivocation is apparent when reducing the tag power from 1 to 0.1 %. It should be noted, however, that

Fig. 4 Results derived from SDR experiment. Key equivocation for various tag powers (from 0.1 to 1 % of the transmit power). Low-powered tags have high key equivocation

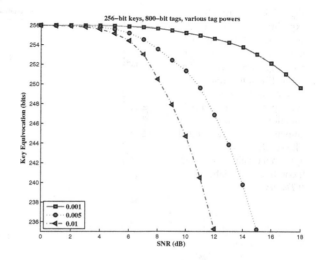

the intended receiver and the eavesdropper have very different goals. The intended receiver has a detection problem: deciding if the tag corresponding to the data and key is present. The eavesdropper has the much harder estimation problem: determining the transmitted tag and then the secret key. As shown in Fig. 3, reducing the tag power does impact the ability of the intended receiver to authenticate properly. So, a design balance is sought to achieve the desired authentication performance while maintaining a high level of security.

5.3 Impact on Data BER

Figure 5 shows the impact of the authentication on the data BER. As discussed in Sect. 4.1, small tag power leads to small reductions in data SNR, and hence the SNR penalty is minimal. This figure shows that the BER curves are, for practical purposes, coincident. The theoretical BER curve is overlaid for comparison. The experimental results show good agreement with the theoretical curve, though the experimental variability increases slightly with SNR.

Because the impact on data BER is shown to be so slight for tag powers as high as 1 %, this gives ample room for the designer to choose the appropriate operating point that balances authentication probability and key equivocation. For example, suppose we have 800-bit QPSK tags with 0.5 % of the total power. Then, from the figures above, we have > 99 % authentication probability, 252 bits of key equivocation, and < 10^{-3} message BER at 10 dB.

We emphasize the flexibility of this framework. If the tag was lengthened (e.g., by spreading over multiple messages), the power of the tag could be reduced while maintaining or increasing the authentication probability. The lower-powered tag then yields higher key equivocation as well as having lower impact on the message BER.

Fig. 5 Results from SDR experiment. Low-powered authentication has minimal impact on the data bit error rate. Tag powers range from 0.1 to 1 % of the transmit power. The 0 tag power case corresponds to the data-only situation where no authentication is transmitted. The results show good agreement with the overlaid theoretical curve labeled *0 Theory*

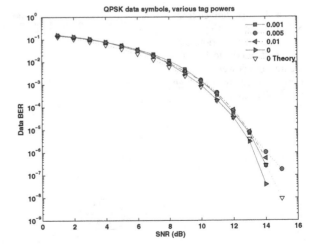

6 Conclusions

Fingerprint embedding for message authentication is motivated by the desire to make the authentication tag less accessible to an eavesdropper, and to reduce or eliminate the extra bandwidth needed for tag transmission. We established metrics for authentication fingerprint design, including security, encoding and tag length, and the impact on the ability to recover the message. We applied these ideas to wireless communications, and developed an additive embedding approach with digital modulation that is simple and readily incorporated into existing communications schemes. Wireless experiments with a software defined radio validated the theory and demonstrated the applicability of the approach. While we focused on a simple additive embedding scheme, more general approaches are easily developed.

Appendix: Precoding and Power-Allocation with CSI

Alice can improve the performance of the system by shaping her transmissions based on her available CSI. Generally, the frame can be decomposed as

$$\mathbf{X} = \mathbf{F}_S \mathbf{P}_S^{\frac{1}{2}} \mathbf{S} \tag{30}$$

where $\mathbf{F}_S$ is an $M \times M$ unitary matrix, $\mathbf{P}_S$ is an $M \times M$ diagonal matrix that allocates power between the columns of $\mathbf{F}_S$, and $\mathbf{S}$ is the modulated and possibly coded $M \times L$ data matrix. In general, to achieve optimality as described below, Alice allocates energy among the eigenvectors of either the channel covariance or its expectation. That is, the columns of $\mathbf{F}_S$ are the channel eigenvectors, and the entries of $\mathbf{P}_S$ allocate the transmission energy between them. The total power budget is constrained by

$$\mathrm{Tr}(\mathbf{P}_S) = M . \tag{31}$$

In the following we consider three cases where Alice has (1) no CSI, (2) perfect CSI, or (3) knowledge of the statistics of the channel. We briefly review the capacity-optimal precoding and power allocation strategies for each case.

No CSI

When the transmitter has no CSI, e.g., in the absence of feedback from the receiver, then there are no preferred transmission modes and transmission is isotropic, so that

$$\mathbf{F}_S = \mathbf{I} \tag{32}$$

$$\mathbf{P}_S = \mathbf{I} \tag{33}$$

resulting in $\Phi = \mathbf{I}$.

Perfect CSI

In this case the transmitter has knowledge of the realization of $\mathbf{H}$, and the capacity-achieving channel input covariance Φ has eigenvectors equal to those of $\mathbf{H}^\dagger \mathbf{H}$. Because the eigenvectors are orthogonal, the optimal power allocation is given by the water-filling solution [23]. That is, the transmissions are shaped using

$$\mathbf{F_S} = \mathbf{V} \tag{34}$$
$$P_S(i) = (v - n(i))^+ , \tag{35}$$
$$\text{where } \mathbf{H}^\dagger \mathbf{H} = \mathbf{VDV}^\dagger . \tag{36}$$

Here $P_S(i)$ (resp., $D(i)$) is the ith element on the diagonal of $\mathbf{P_S}$ (resp., $\mathbf{D}$), $n(i) = \sigma_w^2 / D(i)$ is the ith channel noise component, and v is chosen to satisfy the power constraint

$$\sum_{i=1}^{M} P_S(i) = M . \tag{37}$$

In Rayleigh fading ($K = 0 \Rightarrow \bar{\mathbf{H}} = 0$), we have $\mathbf{F_S} = \mathbf{U}_T$.

Statistical CSI

Although not as good as precise knowledge of the realization of $\mathbf{H}$, when the transmitter has knowledge of the Gaussian channel statistics (mean and covariance), she is still able to improve beyond isotropic transmissions. Conditioned on the knowledge of the channel statistics, the capacity-achieving channel input has eigenvectors equal to those of $E[\mathbf{H}^\dagger \mathbf{H}]$ [25]. That is, the transmissions are shaped using

$$\mathbf{F_S} = \mathbf{V} \tag{38}$$
$$\text{where } E[\mathbf{H}^\dagger \mathbf{H}] = \mathbf{VDV}^\dagger . \tag{39}$$

In Rayleigh fading ($K = 0$), we have $\mathbf{F_S} = \mathbf{U}_T$.

We note that this power allocation does not correspond to a water-filling solution. When the transmitter does not know $\mathbf{H}$, precoding the input with $\mathbf{F_S}$ does not yield orthogonal channels because energy spills across eigenmodes. Thus in the case of statistical CSI application of water-filling does not yield an optimal solution. An efficient iterative algorithm to determine the optimal $\mathbf{P_S}$ is given in [16].

References

1. Ettus Research—Product Detail (2013). https://www.ettus.com/product/details/USRP-PKG
2. Chen, M., Fridrich, J., Goljan, M., Lukas, J.: Determining image origin and integrity using sensor noise. IEEE Trans. Inf. Forensics Secur. **3**(1), 74–90 (2008)
3. Coldrey, M., Bohlin, P.: Training-based MIMO systems-part I: performance comparison. IEEE Trans. Signal Process. **55**(11), 5464–5476 (2007). doi:10.1109/TSP.2007.896107
4. Cover, T., Thomas, J.: Elements of Information Theory. Wiley-Interscience (1991)
5. Danev, B., Luecken, H., Čapkun, S., Defrawy, K.: Attacks on physical-layer identification. In: WiSec'10: Proceedings of the 3th ACM Conference on Wireless Network Security, pp. 89–98. ACM (2010)
6. Danev, B., Čapkun, S.: Transient-based identification of wireless sensor nodes. In: Proceedings of ACM/IEEE IPSN (2009)
7. Gerdes, R., Mina, M., Russell, S., Daniels, T.: Physical-layer identification of wired ethernet devices. IEEE Trans. Inf. Forensics Secur. **7**(4), 1339–1353 (2012)
8. Giannakis, G., Tepedelenlioglu, C.: Basis expansion models and diversity techniques for blind identification and equalization of time-varying channels. Proc. IEEE **86**(10), 1969–1986 (1998). doi:10.1109/5.720248
9. Grimaldi, R.: Discrete and Combinatorial Mathematics: An Applied Introduction. Addison-Wesley (2004). http://books.google.com/books?id=aQkgAQAAIAAJ
10. Ivanov, V., Baras, J.: Authentication of fingerprint scanners. In: IEEE International Conference on Acoustics, Speech and Signal Processing (ICASSP), pp. 1912–1915 (2011)
11. Jain, A.K., Ross, A.A., Nandakumar, K.: Introduction to Biometrics. Springer (2011)
12. Khanna, N., Mikkilineni, A.K., Delp, E.J.: Scanner identification using feature-based processing and analysis. IEEE Trans. Inf. Forensics Secur. **4**(1), 123–139 (2009)
13. Khanna, N., Mikkilineni, A.K., Delp, E.J.: Texture based attacks on intrinsic signature based printer identification. In: Proceedings of the SPIE/IS&T Conference on Media Forensics and Security XIIConference on Media Forensics and Security XII (2010)
14. Khanna, N., Mikkilineni, A.K., Martone, A.F., Ali, G.N., Chiu, G.T.C., Allebach, J.P., Delp, E.J.: A survey of forensic characterization methods for physical devices. Digit. Invest. Int. J. Digit. Forensics Incident Response **3**, 17–28 (2006). doi:10.1016/j.diin.2006.06.014
15. Lai, L., El Gamal, H., Poor, H.: Authentication over noisy channels. IEEE Trans. Inf. Theory **55**(2), 906–916 (2009). doi:10.1109/TIT.2008.2009842
16. Li, X., Jin, S., Gao, X., Wong, K.K.: Near-optimal power allocation for MIMO channels with mean or covariance feedback. IEEE Trans. Commun. **58**(1), 289–300 (2010). doi:10.1109/TCOMM.2010.01.070377
17. Maurer, U.: Authentication theory and hypothesis testing. IEEE Trans. Inf. Theory **46**(4), 1350–1356 (2000). doi:10.1109/18.850674
18. Maurer, U., Renner, R., Wolf, S.: Unbreakable keys from random noise. In: P. Tuyls, B. Skoric, T. Kevenaar (eds.) Security with Noisy Data. Springer (2007)
19. Menezes, A.J., van Oorschot, P.C., Vanstone, S.A.: Handbook of Applied Cryptography. CRC Press (2001). http://www.cacr.math.uwaterloo.ca/hac/
20. Petitcolas, F.A.P., Anderson, R.J., Kuhn, M.G.: Information hiding—a survey. Proc. IEEE **87**(7), 1062–1078 (1999)
21. Rasmussen, K., Čapkun, S.: Implications of radio fingerprinting on the security of sensor networks. In: Proceedings of IEEE SecureComm (2007)
22. Ruhrmair, U., Devadas, S., Koushanfar, F.: Security based on physical unclonability and disorder. In: M. Tehranipoor, C. Wang (eds.) Introduction to Hardware Security and Trust. Springer (2011)
23. Telatar, E.: Capacity of multi-antenna Gaussian channels. Eur. Trans. Telecommun. **10**(6), 585–596 (1999)
24. Tuyls, P., Skoric, B., Kevenaar, T.: Security with Noisy Data; On Private Biometrics, Secure Key Storage and Anti-Counterfeiting. Springer (2007)

25. Venkatesan, S., Simon, S., Valenzuela, R.: Capacity of a Gaussian MIMO channel with nonzero mean. In: Vehicular Technology Conference (VTC), vol. 3, pp. 1767–1771 (2003). doi:10.1109/VETECF.2003.1285329
26. Verma, G., Yu, P.L.: A MATLAB Library for Rapid Prototyping of Wireless Communications Algorithms with the USRP radio family. Tech. rep., U.S. Army Research Laboratory (2013)
27. Wyner, A.D.: The wire-tap channel. Bell Syst. Tech. J. **54**, 1355–1387 (1975)
28. Xiao, L., Greenstein, L., Mandayam, N., Trappe, W.: Using the physical layer for wireless authentication in time-variant channels. IEEE Trans. Wirel. Commun. **7**(7), 2571–2579 (2008). doi:10.1109/TWC.2008.070194
29. Yu, P., Baras, J., Sadler, B.: Multicarrier authentication at the physical layer. In: International Symposium on a World of Wireless, Mobile and Multimedia Networks WoWMoM, pp. 1–6 (2008). doi:10.1109/WOWMOM.2008.4594926
30. Yu, P., Baras, J., Sadler, B.: Physical-layer authentication. IEEE Trans. Inf. Forensics Secur. **3**(1), 38–51 (2008). doi:10.1109/TIFS.2007.916273
31. Yu, P., Sadler, B.: MIMO Authentication via deliberate fingerprinting at the physical layer. IEEE Trans. Inf. Forensics Secur. **6**(3), 606–615 (2011). doi:10.1109/TIFS.2011.2134850
32. Zhou, Y., Fang, Y.: Scalable and deterministic key agreement for large scale networks. IEEE Trans. Wirel. Commun. **6**(12), 4366–4373 (2007). doi:10.1109/TWC.2007.06088

Digital Fingerprint: A Practical Hardware Security Primitive

Gang Qu, Carson Dunbar, Xi Chen and Aijiao Cui

Abstract Digital fingerprinting was introduced for the protection of VLSI design intellectual property (IP). Since each copy of the IP will receive a distinct fingerprint, it can also be used as an identification for the IP or the integrated circuits (IC). This enables the IP/IC designer to trace each piece of the IP/IC and thus identify the dishonest user should piracy or misuse occurs. In this chapter, after defining the basic requirements of fingerprinting, we focus on how to solve the core challenge in digital fingerprinting, namely, how to effectively create large amount of distinct but functionally identical IPs. We first use the graph coloring problem as an example to demonstrate a general approach based on constraint manipulation; then we show how the popular iterative improvement paradigm can be leveraged for fingerprinting; the highlight will be three recently developed post silicon fingerprinting techniques that can be automatically integrated into the design and test phases: the first two approaches take advantages of the Observability Don't Cares and Satisfiability Don't Cares, which are almost always present in IC designs, to generate fingerprints. The third method utilizes the different interconnect styles between flip flops in a scan chain to create unique fingerprints that can be detected with ease. These techniques have high practical values.

1 Introduction

In recent years, the system on a chip (SoC) paradigm has increased in popularity due to its modular nature. System designers can pick integrated circuits (ICs), considered as intellectual property (IP), that are produced for specific functionality and fit them together to achieve a specific goal. This leads to a culture of reuse based design. As a result, IP theft has become profitable as well as a threat to IP developers, vendors, and the SoC industry in general, which motivates the IP protection problem [1].

G. Qu (✉) · C. Dunbar · X. Chen
University of Maryland, College Park, MD, USA
e-mail: gangqu@umd.edu

A. Cui
Harbin Institute of Technology Shenzhen Graduate School, Shenzhen, China

© Springer Science+Business Media New York (outside the USA) 2016
C. Wang et al. (eds.), *Digital Fingerprinting*,
DOI 10.1007/978-1-4939-6601-1_6

In such reuse-based IP business models, as well as the related IP protection model, there are two basic types of legal entities involved in an IP transaction: provider (seller, owner) and buyer (user). Another entity, IP intruder, which is illegal, will attempt to infringe upon the legal entities' rights. It was estimated that in 2011 counterfeit circuits make up approximately 1 % of the market with a financial loss of approximately $100 billion worldwide [2]. In addition, the number of reported counterfeiting incidents quadrupled between 2009 and 2011 [3]. Many of these counterfeit devices find their way into mission critical devices for the military and aerospace. These ICs can be of poorer quality and fail quicker than brand new devices from a trusted seller. Therefore, there is an urgent need of developing effective methods to mitigate IP piracy and protect both the IP providers and the IP buyers.

An effective IP protection method should provide an IP owner the ability to determine that an unauthorized use has occurred and then, trace the source of the theft to protect the owner himself and the legal IP users. The well-developed *constraint-based* watermarking technique is effective in helping IP providers to detect their IPs and establish their authorship from illegal copies to discourage piracy and unauthorized IP redistribution [1, 4, 5]. It has proven to be a good complementary tool to law enforcement methods such as patent and copyright. However, watermarking offers little help in protecting IP *buyer's* legal ownership of a given piece of IP. IP buyers desire the protection from being "framed" by other dishonest buyers working in collusion, or by a dishonest IP provider who sells extra copies of the IP and then attempts to blame the buyer. This becomes an insurmountable task if all buyers receive identical copies of the IP.

The idea of watermarking can be extended for fingerprinting to protect IP buyers. Each IP buyer gives the IP provider his digital signature (encrypted using the buyer's public key). The IP provider converts this signature into fingerprinting constraints and integrates them with the original design constraints, as well as the provider's own watermarking constraints. The synthesis tools will then generate a piece of IP that satisfies all the original design constraints and has both the IP provider's watermark and the specific IP buyer's fingerprint embedded. This allows the IP provider to trace individual IP buyers since each IP becomes unique with the buyer's fingerprint. It also protects the buyer in the sense that the IP provider cannot resell this realization of the IP to another buyer since the embedded fingerprint can only be interpreted by the first buyer via his secret key. The difficulty of such symmetric fingerprinting protection is that IP provider most often cannot afford to apply a given watermarking technique with each buyer's signature and repeat the entire design process: creating a large number of different high-quality solutions from scratch has a clear time and cost overhead. Hence, *the challenge is to develop practical fingerprinting protocols that can provide a large number of distinct realization of the same IP with reasonable amortized design effort.*

It is well-known that designers and artists, either intentionally or unintentionally, leave traces or marks or their style in their designed artifacts that can be used to identify whether the artifact is genuine. This is also true for software and IC designs. There are reported IC identification methods based on intrinsic features such as glitches [6] and path delay variations [7]. These techniques, also including the well-studied physical unclonable function (PUF) [8, 9], rely on the uncontrollable variations during fabrication process, which is also believed to be random and unique. They can be used for identification and authentication of IC or IP. However, when an IP or IC is illegally reproduced or overbuilt, the illegal copies will carry their own fabrication variation based fingerprint. This will be different from the fingerprint of the original genuine IP or IC. So they cannot be used directly for the protection of IP and IC.

Fingerprints are the characteristic of an object that is completely unique and incontrovertible so they can be used to identify a particular object from its peers. They have been used for human identification for ages and have been adopted in multimedia for copyright protection of the widely distributed digital data. In the semiconductor and IC industry, the concept of digital fingerprinting was proposed in the late 1990's with the goal of protecting design IP from being misused [10–12]. In this context, digital fingerprints refer to *additional features that are embedded during the design and fabrication process to make each copy of the design unique.* These features can be extracted from the IP or IC to establish the fingerprint for the purposes of identification and protection.

As a quick motivational example, Fig. 1 illustrates what an ideal fingerprint may look like in an IC. Each circled location would be a place where certain small modification could be made without changing the functionality of the circuit and its performance. A 1-bit fingerprint could be embedded with a simple scheme (which is also referred as fingerprinting mechanism, protocol, or technique):

- to embed a 0, do not make the modification
- to embed a 1, make the modification

Such fingerprint information can be easily identified by checking whether the modifications exist or not in the circuit layout.

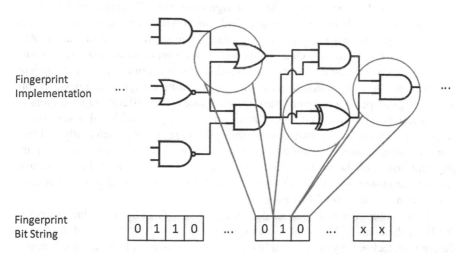

Fig. 1 A simple conceptual fingerprint example

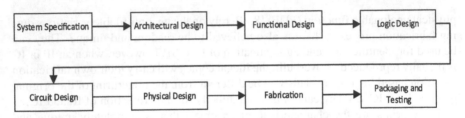

Fig. 2 The typical VLSI design cycle

With the promise of giving each copy of the IC or IP a unique fingerprint, digital fingerprinting has become a hardware security primitive and enabling technique for applications such as IP metering, identifying IP piracy, detecting IC counterfeiting and overbuilding. Early work on IP fingerprinting [10–12] have demonstrated the possibility of creating large amount of functional identical IPs with distinct implementations. However, these techniques are not practical because all fingerprinted design will be different and require different masks for fabrication, which is prohibitively expensive.

To understand this and many other cyber threats in IC design, let us see the traditional VLSI design cycle as shown in Fig. 2. The pre-silicon design phase includes all the steps before the chip fabrication process and the post-silicon phase focuses on the testing and packaging after the silicon is fabricated. The early development of fingerprinting techniques [10–12] are not practical because they generate the fingerprints in the pre-silicon phase, either at logic design, circuit design, or physical design stages. Although each fingerprinted copy will have a rather unique implementation, which is good for fingerprint metrics, this requires a different mask for each copy of the design, which no one can afford given today's cost of mask and fabrication.

In the early days before reuse based design emerged, IC design and fabrication were conducted in-house where people had their own design team and foundries and the design process was strictly controlled. Then starting from the late 1990's, with the new applications such as embedded systems that require a shorter time-to-market window and more sophisticated functionality, it becomes more cost efficient, and perhaps the only option to meet those demanding design constraints, to split these design steps up among different groups, some are in different organizations or even different countries, that specialize in different aspects of VLSI design states. As a simple example, one may develop the system specification internally and then hand that data to another party who designs everything from the architecture to the physical layout of the device. This layout could be given back to the person who created the system specification who in turn, gives it to a foundry, which is most likely from overseas, for fabrication.

At this point two new parties, design house and foundry, have had access to the IP of the creator. The addition of these parties as well as the use of third party design tool, technology library, and IPs to the VLSI design cycle creates a substantial security risk and although the simple example above only uses two additional parties, many more could be added. Logically then, for every party involved, the chance of malicious behavior increases. One risk of the multi-party design cycle is the insertion of hardware Trojan Horses, or simply Trojans, to the design. Trojans can be simple changes to the circuit level design or significant changes to the functional or logical design, with the intention of damaging the circuit, stopping functionality at critical points, or siphoning off data that was meant to be secure.

In addition to the multi-party design cycle issue, the entities that purchase or lease an IP introduce risk as well. Once a design is completed, it can be considered an IP core, and at that point it is vulnerable to theft by duplication. If a group does all of the design work themselves, or with a trusted third party, that the weak points for duplication occur once a client leases a design or buys the design or the physical IC or the IP design is sent to a third party for fabrication. At each point, the third party can simply copy the physical layout of the device and claim it as their own.

In the rest of this chapter, we will first survey the early work on fingerprinting. Then we will elaborate three practical circuit level fingerprinting techniques. The common feature behind these techniques that makes them practical is that they all create fingerprints at post-silicon stage. However, this may also introduce security vulnerabilities because such post-silicon fingerprints will not be as robust and secure as those embedded in the design. We will provide theoretical analysis of such tradeoffs in this chapter and readers can find the experimental validations in [11–14].

2 Digital Fingerprinting for IP Protection

2.1 Background on Fingerprinting

Fingerprints are characteristics of an object which are sufficient enough to distinguish it from other similar objects. Fingerprinting refers to the process of adding fingerprints to an object and recording them, or process of identifying and recording fingerprints that are already intrinsic to the object [15]. The core idea of fingerprinting is to give each user a copy of the object containing a unique fingerprint, which can be used to identify that user.

One of the most accepted models for fingerprinting [15–17] can be described as: In the original object, a set of marks is selected probabilistically, where a *mark* is one bit of information that has two slightly different versions. The distributor can choose one of the two versions of each mark to embed either a 0 or a 1 when the object is sold to a user, and thus construct a binary word which becomes the fingerprint of this user. Two general assumptions on the object to be fingerprinted are:

- *Error-tolerance assumption*: the object should remain useful after introducing small errors or marks, and the user cannot detect the marks from the data redundancy. The more errors that the object can tolerate, the more places we can put these marks.
- *Marking assumption*: two or more users may detect a few marks that differ in their copies, but they cannot change the undetected marks without rendering the object useless.

According to a taxonomy given by Wagner [15], the *statistical fingerprinting* is characterized as: given sufficiently many misused objects to examine, the distributor can gain any desired degree of confidence that he has correctly identified the compromised. The identification is, however, never certain. This is one of the fundamentals for many fingerprinting schemes [16, 17].

2.2 The Need and Challenge of Digital Fingerprinting IPs

As we have pointed out in the previous section, IP vendors have to protect both themselves and their legal customers. The IP ownership needs to be protected to recover the high R&D cost. It can be achieved by law enforcement methods such as patent and copyright. The *constraint-based watermarking* paradigm, which embeds IP provider's signature as additional design constraints during the design and synthesis process to create rather unique implementations of the IP, can also assist to establish the ownership of the IP [1, 4, 5].

It is also crucial to distribute IPs with the same functionality but different appearance to different users, because the problem of determining legality of the ownership will become insurmountable if all users get exact same IP and one of them illegally redistributes the IP. The above fingerprint concept is one promising solution. However, IPs are usually error-sensitive, which violates the *error-tolerance assumption*. Therefore, we cannot directly apply the existing fingerprinting techniques for IP protection.

Another option is to build a unique IP for every legal user by applying the same watermarking technique on users' signatures. Embedding different watermarks will ensure that the resulting IPs will be distinct. This will incur very high overhead design cost and it won't be practical until we find ways to perform it at post-silicon stage. This brings us the challenge of *how to efficiently and effectively create distinct realization of functional identical IPs*, which we refer to as the digital fingerprinting problem. Efficiency can be measured by the time and efforts to create fingerprint copies, while effectiveness will be measured by the easiness to identify the embedded fingerprints and the confidence of the obtained fingerprint.

2.3 Requirements of Digital Fingerprinting

A fingerprint, being the signature of the buyer, should satisfy all the requirements of any effective watermarks, namely, it should provide

high credibility. The fingerprint should be readily detectable in proving legal ownership, and the probability of coincidence should be low.

low overhead. Once the demand for fingerprinted solutions exceeds the number of available good solutions, the solution quality will necessarily degrade. Nevertheless, we seek to minimize the impact of fingerprinting on the quality of the software or design.

resilience. The fingerprint should be difficult or impossible to remove without complete knowledge of the software or design.

transparency. The addition of fingerprints to software and designs should be completely transparent, so that fingerprinting can be used with existing design tools.

part protection. Ideally, a good fingerprint should be distributed all over the software or design in order to identify the buyer from any part of it.

At the same time, the IP protection business model implies that fingerprints have additional mandatory attributes:

collusion-secure. Different users will receive different copies of the solution with their own fingerprints embedded. These fingerprints should be embedded in such a way that it is not only difficult to remove them, but also difficult to forge a new fingerprint from existing ones (i.e., the fingerprinted solutions should be structurally diverse).

short runtime. The (average) run-time for creating a fingerprinted solution should be much less than the run-time for solving the problem from scratch. The complexity of synthesis problem and the need for large quantity of fingerprinted solutions make it impractical to solve the problem from scratch for each individual buyer.

preserving watermarks. Fingerprinting should not diminish the strength of the author's watermark. Ideally, not only should the fingerprinting constraints not conflict with the watermarking constraints, any hint on the watermark from fingerprints should also be prevented as well.

From the above objectives, we extract the following three key requirements for fingerprinting protocols:

(1) A fingerprinting protocol must be capable of generating solutions that are "far away" from each other. If solutions are too similar, it will be difficult for the seller to identify distinct buyers and it will be easy for dishonest buyers to collude. In most problems, there exist generally accepted definitions for distance or similarity between different solutions.
(2) A fingerprinting protocol should be nonintrusive to existing design optimization algorithms, so that it can be easily integrated with existing software tool flows.
(3) The cost of the fingerprinting protocol should be kept as low as possible. Ideally, it should be negligible compared to the original design effort.

Next we review two early fingerprinting approaches that meet these requirements.

2.4   Iterative Fingerprinting Techniques

To maintain reasonable run-time while producing a large number of fingerprinted solutions, it was proposed to exploit the availability of iterative heuristics for difficult optimizations [11]. Notably, these heuristics are applied in an *incremental* fashion to design optimization instances that have been perturbed according to a buyer's signature (or fingerprint).

---

1. Create a watermarked instance I_0 by embedding the IP provider's watermark into the initial instance I;
2. Generate a (watermarked) initial solution S_0 from I_0 by a *from-scratch* optimization;
3. **for** $j = 1$ to n (n is the number of IP buyers)
4.   Create a fingerprinted instance I_j with the j-th buyer's fingerprint F_j added into I_0;
5.   Using S_0 as the initial solution, apply an *incremental* optimization to generate a fingerprinted solution S_j for I_j;

Fig. 3 The generic iterative approach for generating fingerprinted solutions

Figure 3 outlines the proposed approach. Lines 1 and 2 generate an initial watermarked solution S_0 using an (iterative) optimization heuristic in "from-scratch" mode. Then we use this solution as the "seed" to create fingerprinted solutions as follows: Lines 3 and 4 embed the buyer's signature into the design as a fingerprint (e.g., by perturbing the weights of edges in a weighted graph) to yield a fingerprinted instance. This fingerprinted instance is then solved by an *incremental* iterative optimization using S_0 as the initial solution.

The addition of individual user's fingerprint can ensure that the all the fingerprinted solutions will be different. The shortened run-time comes from the fact that in Line 5 we generate a new solution from the existing ones, not from scratch. Moreover, adding fingerprinting constraints changes the *optimization cost surface* and can actually lead to improved solution quality, which is a well-known fact in the metaheuristics literature. This approach has been applied to fingerprint classic iterative optimization algorithms such as those designed to solve the partitioning and standard-cell placement and optimization problems that may not be solved by iterative improvement such as the graph coloring problem [11]. In the following, we show how it can also be adopted to fingerprint solutions to a Boolean satisfiability (SAT) problem, a representative decision problem.

The SAT problem seeks to decide, for a given formula $\mathcal{F}$, whether there exists a truth assignment for the variables that makes the formula true. For a satisfiable formula, a solution is an assignment of 0 (false), 1 (true), or—(don't care) to each of the variables. For example, the following formula

$$\mathcal{F} = (v_1 + v_2')(v_1 + v_3 + v_4')(v_1' + v_2 + v_6')(v_2 + v_3' + v_7)(v_2 + v_4 + v_6)$$
$$(v_3' + v_4 + v_5)(v_4' + v_6' + v_7)(v_5' + v_6 + v_7)$$

is satisfiable with the assignment $\{v_1 = 1, v_2 = 1, v_3 = -, v_4 = 1, v_5 = 0, v_6 = 0, v_7 = 0\}$. We necessarily assume that the given SAT instance is satisfiable and that it has a sufficiently large solution space to accommodate multiple fingerprinted solutions.

1	Solve $\mathcal{F}$ for an initial solution S_0: $\{v_1 = b_1, \cdots, v_n = b_n\}$, where $b_i \in \{0, 1, -\}$;
2	According to the i-th user's fingerprint, select a subset of variables: $V' = \{v_{i_1}, \cdots, v_{i_l}\} \subset V$;
3	Create the fingerprinted formula $\mathcal{F}'$
3.0	$\mathcal{F}' = \mathcal{F}$;
3.1	for $(j = 1, \cdots, l)$
3.2	$\{$ if $(b_{i_j} = 1)$
3.3	$\mathcal{F}' = \mathcal{F}'_{v_{i_j}}$;
3.4	else if $(b_{i_j} = 0)$
3.5	$\mathcal{F}' = \mathcal{F}'_{v'_{i_j}}$;
3.6	else $\mathcal{F}' = \mathcal{F}' \setminus v_{i_j}$;
	$\}$
3.7	$\mathcal{F}' =$ watermarking $(\mathcal{F}',$ user's fingerprints$)$;
4	Solve $\mathcal{F}'$ for an assignment to the variables in $V \setminus V'$, variables that are in V but not in V';
5	Construct the fingerprinted solution for formula $\mathcal{F}$
5.1	for $(j = 1, \cdots, l)$
5.2	$v_{i_j} = b_{i_j}$;
6	Go to step 2 if another fingerprinted solution is needed;

Fig. 4 Pseudocode of the iterative fingerprinting approach for the Boolean satisfiability problem

Iterative improvement techniques cannot be applied to generate new SAT solutions from an existing one. Our fingerprinting goal is to efficiently construct a sequence of distinct solutions from a given solution. We achieve this by iteratively building and solving "new" SAT instances with (much) smaller size. Figure 4 outlines our approach on a formula $\mathcal{F}$ over Boolean variables $V = \{v_1, v_2, \ldots, v_n\}$.

Using the above example, we assume that v_3, v_4, v_5 are selected in step 2. Because in the initial solution, we have $v_3 = -, v_4 = 1, v_5 = 0$, when we construct the new formula $\mathcal{F}'$, we remove all the occurrence of v_3 and v'_3 (according to step 3.6), replace (according to steps 3.2 and 3.3) all the v_4 by 1 (that is, remove any clause that has a v_4, and remove all the v'_4) and all v_5 by 0 (that is, remove all the v_5 and remove any clause that has a v'_5) according to steps 3.4 and 3.5. The last two operations are known as cofactoration. This gives us the following new formula

$$\mathcal{F}' = (v_1 + v'_2)(v_1)(v'_1 + v_2 + v'_6)(v_2 + v_7)(v'_6 + v_7)$$

In step 3.7, assume that we watermark this formula by adding two more clauses based on user's fingerprint, we have

$$\mathcal{F}' = (v_1 + v_2')(v_1)(v_1' + v_2 + v_6')(v_2 + v_7)(v_6' + v_7)(v_1 + v_6 + v_7)(v_2' + v_6)$$

which can be easily solved with one satifiable assignment $\{v_1 = 1, v_2 = 0, v_6 = 0, v_7 = 1\}$. Following step 5, we can construct a new solution to the original formula by adding $v_3 = -, v_4 = 1, v_5 = 0$. Clearly, this assignment $\{v_1 = 1, v_2 = 0, v_3 = -, v_4 = 1, v_5 = 0, v_6 = 0, v_7 = 1\}$ (1) is a solution to the original formula $\mathcal{F}$, (2) is different from the initial solution $\{v_1 = 1, v_2 = 1, v_3 = -, v_4 = 1, v_5 = 0, v_6 = 0, v_7 = 0\}$, and (3) embeds a user fingerprint in the form of keeping the assignment to variables $\{v_3 = -, v_4 = 1, v_5 = 0\}$ and satisfying two additional clauses $(v_1 + v_6 + v_7)(v_2' + v_6)$. In sum, it meets all the requirements for a fingerprinted solution.

Here it is clear that the reduction on run-time is a result of (1) the cofactoration in steps 3.3 and 3.5 as well as in step 3.6 which reduces the size of the (fingerprinted) SAT instance and (2) the preservation of the values for a selected subset of variables which reuses the effort in finding the initial solution.

2.5   Fingerprinting with Constraint-Addition

By careful manipulation of constraints in the design or problem, we can develop digital fingerprinting techniques that have almost zero run-time overhead while generating controllable number of distinct fingerprinted copies. In this section, we illustrate this idea by the example of graph coloring problem.

Given a graph $G(V, E)$ and a positive integer $k \le |V|$, we say that G is k-colorable if we can color the vertices V such that adjacent vertices have different colors. The optimization graph (vertex) coloring problem is to find the minimum number k such that G is k-colorable. This problem is *NP-complete* and many heuristic algorithms have been developed dedicated to this problem (http://dimacs.rutgers.edu/).

For a given coloring scheme to a graph, if we know that one vertex can also be colored by another alternative color, then immediately we can have one more solution to the same GC problem. Furthermore, on knowing k vertices each has a second valid color, we are able to create 2^k different solutions with almost no cost. And these k vertices and their associate colors will serve as the base for the solution space we have.

Figure 5 depicts an example. The idea is to select a vertex, duplicate it by creating a new vertex and connecting it to all the neighbors of the selected vertex. Now the selected vertex can be labeled by either its color or the color of its duplication without violating the rules for GC. To guarantee these two vertices receive different colors, we add an edge in between. In Fig. 5b, vertices A and A' will be labeled by two different colors which can both be used to color A in the original graph in Fig. 5a.

For the same original graph, we show another way to introduce new constraints so we can generate multiple solutions simultaneously. This is based on the observation that in the graph coloring problem, there is no explicit constraint for two vertices that do not have an edge connecting them. Therefore, by coloring a pair of unconnected

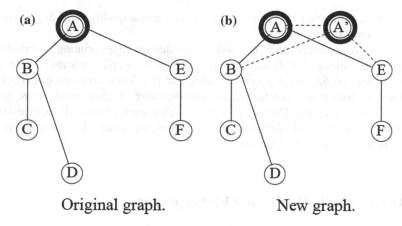

Original graph.   New graph.

Fig. 5 Duplicating vertex (A) to generate various solutions

Fig. 6 Constructing bridge (BE) to generate various solutions

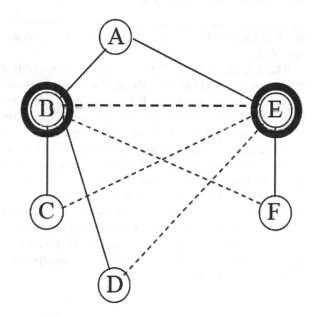

vertices with the same or different colors, we can create different solutions. This can be implemented by selecting a pair of unconnected vertices, connecting one to all the neighbors of the other as well as these two vertices themselves. In Fig. 6, vertices B and E are selected, and when we color the new graph, B and E will have different colors, say *red* and *green*. Now we can build 4 solutions where B and E are colored as *(red, red)*, *(red, green)*, *(green, red)* or *(green, green)*.

In both these two techniques, we add new constraints to the graph. By coloring the new graph only once, we can do simple post-process on the solution to obtain multiple guaranteed distinct solutions. Thus, the run-time overhead in creating fingerprinted copies can be eliminated. However, it is hard to control the quality of the fingerprinted copies obtained by this method.

The iterative fingerprinting and constraint-addition fingerprinting successfully address the challenge for digital fingerprinting: *how to efficiently and effectively create distinct realization of functional identical IPs*. Their common drawback is that they are both pre-silicon techniques and therefore different masks have to be made for chip fabrication. This makes them as well as most of other IP fingerprinting methods impractical. In the following three sections, we present three practical post-silicon IP fingerprinting techniques.

3   Observability Don't Care Fingerprinting

3.1   Illustrative Example

We first use a small example to show the basic ideas behind this fingerprinting approach.

The left circuit in Fig. 7 realizes the function $(AB)(C + D) = F$. When the Y input to the AND is zero, the output F will be zero regardless of the value of X input; however, when Y = 1, F will be determined by the X input. So when we direct signal Y to the AND gate that generates X, as shown in the right of Fig. 7, we can easily verify that this circuit implements the same function F. However, these two circuits are clearly distinct. Moreover, if one makes a copy of any of these circuits, this distinction remains. Thus we can embed one bit fingerprint information by controlling whether X depends on Y.

One key feature of this approach is that the changes we make on the circuit are minute. We can make a connection, as shown on the right circuit in Fig. 7, during routing and placement; then determine whether to keep this connection based on the fingerprint bits at post-silicon phase. This avoids the expensive redesign and fabrication based on a new layout as in the fingerprinting approaches we discussed in the previous section.

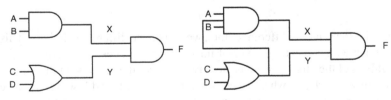

Fig. 7   Two 4-input circuits that implement the same function

3.2 Observability Don't Care Conditions

Observability Don't Cares (ODC) are a concept in Boolean computation. The conditions by which an ODC occurs are when local signal changes cannot be observed at a primary output (see Fig. 7). ODCs can be several layers deep and can cause several different signals to be blocked, depending on the input to the circuit.

Formally, the ODC conditions of a function F with respect to one of its input signal x can be defined as the following Boolean difference:

$$ODG_x = \left(\frac{\partial F}{\partial x}\right)' = (F_x \oplus F_x)' = F_x F_x + F_x' F_{x'}'$$

where F_x is the cofactor of F with respect to variable x obtained by replacing all the x with logic 1 and all the x' with logic 0. Basically, this states that when we have a function F, and a variable x, when the condition ODC_x is satisfied, the value of variable x will not have any impact to the value of the function F.

For example, for a 2-input AND gate, F = xy, we have $ODC_x = y'$ from the above definition. Intuitively, this tells us that when the input y has value zero (to make the ODC true), output F is a constant 0 and input x becomes an ODC.

3.3 Finding Locations for Circuit Modification Based on ODCs

Every logic circuit that is created uses a library of gates that determines the logical relationships that can occur. Most libraries contain gates that create ODCs as defined above, but not every instance of these gates will be able to be modified to accommodate a fingerprint. There are four necessary conditions that must be met for a gate to be considered a fingerprint location and are enumerated in the following definition.

Definition 1 (*Fingerprint location*) A fingerprint location is defined as two or more gates that can be considered for modification for a circuit fingerprint without changing the functionality of the circuit. These gates consist of a single primary gate and one or more gates that generate inputs for the primary gate that meet the following criteria:

1. The primary gate must have at least one input that is not a primary input of the circuit.
2. The primary gate must have at least one input which is the output signal of a fanout free cone (FFC), which means that this signal only goes into the primary gate.
2. The FFC in criterion 2 must have either a gate with non-zero ODC or a single input gate (e.g. an inverter).
4. The primary gate must have a non-zero ODC with respect to one or more of its input signals other than the one from the FFC.

Fig. 8 Generic fingerprint
change based on ODC

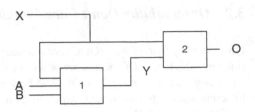

Criterion 1 is necessary for making local minor changes to the circuit (for fingerprinting purpose). Criterion 2 ensures that the changes made to the FFC will not
affect the functionality of the circuit elsewhere. Criteria 3 and 4 provide a possible
signal (in criterion 4) that can be added to a gate in the FFC (in criterion 3). Each
ODC gate, in a circuit is analyzed using Definition 1 and if it satisfies all the criteria
in the definition, it is then considered to be a fingerprint location, a location where
the circuit can be modified to add the fingerprint.

3.4 Determining Potential Fingerprinting Modifications

For each fingerprint location that is found, a modification can be applied to the gate's
inputs. A generic modification for a fingerprint is depicted in Fig. 8.

Figure 8 has two generic gates, represented as boxes 1 and 2, three primary inputs
(X, A, and B), and one primary output (O). Gate 2 represents the primary gate, gate 1
represents the gate within the FFC that generates signal Y, and signal X is independent
of the FFC that generates signal Y. Suppose that signal X satisfies ODC$_Y$, thus we
can add signal X into the FFC of Y, for example gate 1 as shown in Fig. 8, either in its
regular form X or its complement form X'. However, when we make this addition,
we need to guarantee that when signal X takes the value that does not satisfy ODC$_Y$,
it will not change the correct output value Y. In the rest of this section, signal X will
be known as an ODC trigger signal, as defined below.

Definition 2 (*ODC Trigger Signal*) An ODC Trigger signal is a signal that feeds
into a gate, with a non-zero set of ODC conditions, which causes the ODC condition
to activate. In the context of this work it also represents the signal that is used to
modify the input gate to the primary gate for the fingerprint modification.

In order for this to work, the relationship between the signal X, gate 2, and gate 1
must be analyzed so that X only changes gate 1's output, Y, when it also triggers the
ODC, criterion 3 in the definition of a fingerprint location. For every possible pair
of gates that can be considered a fingerprint location, similar to gate 1 and gate 2, a
structural change must be proposed in order to modify that location. This requires a
maximum of n^2 proposed changes, where n is the number of ODCs and single input
gates in a library.

For simple changes like the one in Fig. 7 or those in the motivation example, each location like this can be considered a position to embed one bit in a bit string that represents the fingerprint. For each circuit that is manufactured, this fingerprint location can be either modified 1, or left alone 0. This means that for a circuit for n potential fingerprint locations there are at least 2^n possible fingerprints and n bits of data in the bit string.

3.5 Maintaining Overhead Constraints

The fingerprint modifications proposed can cause a large overhead, relative to the circuit's initial performance. Rerouting paths, increasing the input size to input gates, and introducing new inverters are the cause of the overhead. Two heuristic methods have been considered for reducing this overhead, a reactive method and proactive method.

Of the two methods, the reactive method is easier to implement but is difficult to scale. This method involves taking a fully fingerprinted circuit and by removing one fingerprint modification at a time, analyzing the difference in overhead, whether it be area, delay, power, or something else. The modification that results in the largest change to the overhead is removed and the resulting circuit is tested again. This is done until a certain overhead constraint is met or there are no more modifications to remove.

The proactive method is more difficult to implement, but because it is done as modifications are applied, it scales well with larger circuits. This heuristic requires that each modification is analyzed before being implemented. For area and power, this is simple because any new gates or changes in gates will result in overhead that can be estimated using information about the cells in the library. Delay is more difficult to analyze because not every modification will slow the circuit down. As modifications are added, the critical path may change which changes where new modifications should be considered. The delay can be estimated by determining the slack on each gate and updating the information every time a modification is made, but this can be time consuming for large gates that will have a large number of modifications. For this proactive method, modifications would be added until a certain overhead constraint was met, the opposite of the reactive method.

3.6 Security Analysis

As we have mentioned in the introduction, an IP will be protected by both watermark (to establish the IP's authorship) and fingerprint (to identify each IP buyer). When a suspicious IP is found, the watermark will be first verified to confirm that IP piracy has occurred. Next, the fingerprint needs to be discovered to trace the IP buyer who may be involved in the IP piracy. It is trivial for the IP designer to detect the fingerprint embedded by our proposed approach because the designer can compare the fingerprinted IP with the design that does not have any fingerprint to check whether and what change has occurred in each fingerprint location to obtain the fingerprint.

However, it is infeasible for an attacker to reveal the fingerprint locations from a single copy of the IC. This is because when the fingerprint information is embedded at a fingerprint location, the FFC of the fingerprinted IP will include the signal that is not in the FFC in the original design when the fingerprint location is identified. Consider the left circuit in Fig. 7 of the motivational example, the FFC that generates signal X contains only the 2-input AND gate with A and B as input. When signal Y is added to this AND gate, the FFC will include the 2-input OR gate with C and D as input. This will invalidate this portion of the circuit as a fingerprint location (criterion 4 is violated).

When the attacker has multiple copies of fingerprinted ICs, he can compare the layout of these ICs and identify the fingerprint locations where different fingerprint bits were embedded in these ICs. This collusion attack is a powerful attack for all known fingerprinting methods. Carefully designed fingerprint copy distribution schemes may help [6, 7, 12], but require a large number of fingerprinting copies. As we have demonstrated through experiments [13], the proposed approach has this capability and thus can reduce the damage of collusion attack. In addition, it is also known that as long as the collusion attacker does not remove all the fingerprint information, all the copies that are involved in the collusion can be traced [6, 7, 12].

4   Satisfiability Don't Care Fingerprinting

4.1   Satisfiability Don't Care and Illustrative Example

Satisfiability Don't Cares are a Boolean concept used in circuit design optimization. Considering all the primary input (PI) signals, and the internal signals from each logic gate in a circuit, SDC conditions describe the signal combinations that cannot occur. For example, consider the 2-input NAND gate in Fig. 9 below, $C = NAND(A, B)$, we cannot have $\{A = 1, B = 1, C = 1\}$, $\{A = 0, C = 0\}$, or $\{B = 0, C = 0\}$.

In general, for a signal y generated from logic gate $G(x_1, x_2, \ldots, x_k)$, the SDC at this gate can be computed by the equation

$$SDG = G(\chi_1, \chi_2, \ldots, \chi_k) \oplus y$$

In the example of the above 2-input NAND gate, the SDC conditions can be obtained from this equation as follows:

$$\overline{AB} \oplus C = \overline{AB}\bar{C} + ABC$$

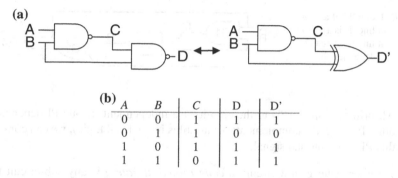

(b)

A	B	C	D	D'
0	0	1	1	1
0	1	1	0	0
1	0	1	1	1
1	1	0	1	1

Fig. 9 SDC modification. **a** Gate replacement. **b** Truth table for both circuits

When some of these signals fan-in to the same gate later in the circuit, the SDC conditions can be used to optimize the design. In our approach, we will use these SDC conditions to embed fingerprints as illustrated in Fig. 9. Clearly we see two different circuits in Fig. 9a where the only difference is at the output logic gate. It is a 2-input NAND on the left circuit while a 2-input XOR fate on the right. However, when we list the truth tables for the two circuits (see the table in Fig. 9b), we find that the two circuits have identical output signals regardless of the input combination. This is because the difference between the NAND gate and the XOR gate only occurs when both input signals B and C are 0. As Fig. 9b shows, this condition is never satisfied. So we can hide one bit of fingerprinting information by deliberately choose which gate we will use to implement the circuit.

4.2 Assumptions for SDC Based Fingerprinting

By locating gates that have SDCs leading into them, which we refer to as *fingerprint locations*, and finding alternative gates, we can modify the circuit by using either the original gate or one of its alternatives at each fingerprint location, to generate different fingerprinted copies. We now analyze and solve the following SDC based fingerprint location problem:

> Given an IP in the form of a gate level netlist, find a set of fingerprint locations, determine the alternative gates at each location, and define a fingerprint embedding scheme to create fingerprinted copies of the IP with any k-bit fingerprint.

Before presenting our solution to the problem, we list the necessary assumptions and define the terminologies.

A1. The given netlist should be sufficiently large to accommodate the k-bit fingerprint.
A2. The given netlist is optimized and does not have internal gates producing constant outputs. Circuits normally can be simplified if we replace constant-valued variables with their value (0 or 1).

Fig. 10 Example of a
dependent line. B is a
dependent line for gate G2
and A is a dependent line for
G4

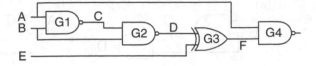

A3. All primary inputs (PI) to the circuits are independent. If one PI depends on
other PIs (e.g. the complementary variables in dual-rail logic), we can consider
this PI as an internal signal.

For a given gate *g* in a circuit, a *cone rooted at gate g* is any sub-circuit that
directly or indirectly produces a fan-in for gate *g*. A *dependent line/fan-in for gate
g* is defined as a signal that directly or indirectly impact two or more of *gate g*'s
fan-ins. For example, in Fig. 10, gates {G3, G4} is a cone rooted at G4 with inputs
{A, D, E}; {G1, G2, G3, G4} is also one with inputs {A, B, E}. A is a dependent
line for G4 and B is a dependent line for G2 (but not for G3 or G4).
A necessary condition for fingerprint locations: a gate must have dependent lines
to be a fingerprint location.

When a gate, say G1 in Fig. 10, does not have any dependent lines, its fan-ins
will be independent and thus all possible fan-in combinations may happen. No SDC
can be found. On the other hand, dependent lines do not guarantee a gate to be a
fingerprint location. Consider the dependent line A for gate G4 in Fig. 10, it is easy
to see that when B = 0, we have F = E', which is independent of A, so all four
combinations of A and F can be fan-in to G4 and thus G4 cannot be a fingerprint
location.

4.3   SDC Based Fingerprinting Technique

Based on the above observations, we propose the following heuristics to find fingerprint locations for k-bit fingerprints:

1.   find a topological order of the gates G_1, G_2, ..., G_n;
2.   for each gate G_i (i=1, 2, ..., n)
3.   { if (G_i has a dependent line)
4.   { find the cone rooted at G_i whose inputs are the dependent line or the
       intermediate lines closest to G_i;
5.   for each combination of G_i's fan-ins that does not happen
6.   { mark G_i as a fingerprint location;
7.   record this fan-in combination;
8.   update the number of fingerprint bits, FP;
9.   if (FP > k)
10.   { i = n+1; break;}
11.   }}
12.   mark G_i's output as PI;}

We search the gates for fingerprint locations following a topological order (Lines 1–2). If a fingerprint location is found, we mark the output of that gate as PI (Line 12). In Line 3, we trace each fan-in of gate G_i back to PIs; whenever we see two fan-ins share the same signal, that signal is a dependent line. Then we construct the core rooted at G_i by backtracking each fan-in of G_i until we find the source of the dependent line or the closest, intermediate or primary, input signals to the cone for G_i that don't include the dependent lines (note here the PIs can either be the PI of the entire circuit of the fan-out of a fingerprint location as we mark in Line 12). Next we simulate all the combinations of input signals to this core and observe whether they can create any SDC at G_i's fan-in (Line 5). If so, we find a new fingerprint location in G_i and update the number of fingerprint bits (FP) we can produce (Lines 6–8). When FP becomes larger than k, the number of bits in the required fingerprint, we force the program to stop (Lines 9–10). The way to update FP depends on how fingerprint will be embedded, which we will discuss next.

Correctness of the heuristics: the heuristics may not find all the fingerprint locations, but the ones it finds as well as the SDC conditions (Line 7) are all valid. This claim states that our heuristics will not report any false fingerprint location or SDC conditions. This ensures that when we do the gate replacement, the function of the original circuit will not be altered, one of the most important requirement for digital fingerprint.

Complexity of the heuristics: this is dominated by the size of the cone rooted at the gate under investigation. In Line 3 (other operations are either $O(1)$ or $O(n)$), we have to solve the Boolean satisfiability to check whether each fan-in combination will occur or simply do an exhaustive search for all the combinations of the inputs to the core (which we choose to implement for this paper). In both cases, the complexity will be exponential to the number of inputs to the core. However, after we consider the fan-outs of fingerprint locations also as PIs, our simulation shows that the average number of inputs to the cone is only 5.24. The heuristics' run time is in seconds for all the benchmarks.

4.4 Fingerprint Embedding Scheme

For each fingerprint location and its SDC conditions, we propose two replacement methods to embed the fingerprint:

R1. Replace the gate at the fingerprint location by another library gate where the two gates have different outputs only on the SDC conditions at the fingerprint location.

R2. Replace the gate at the fingerprint location by a multiplexer.

Figure 9 shows one example of **R1**, where a 2-input NAND gate and a 2-input XOR gate become inter-exchangeable when the input combination 00 is a SDC condition. Suppose that there are p_i different library gates (including G_i) which are can replace gate G_i, by choosing one of them, we can embed $\lfloor \log(p_i) \rfloor$ bits. So we update FP by this amount in Line 8 of our heuristics.

Fig. 11 Multiplexer
replacement technique. *Left*
An unconfigured MUX;
Right A MUX configured to
run as a 2-input NAND gate

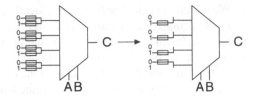

In **R2,** an m-input gate can be replaced with a $2^m \times 1$ multiplexer (MUX). The selection lines of the MUX are tied to the original inputs of the gate and the data inputs are tied to either Vdd or Gnd, to match the patterns to implement the needed gate. Because the $2^m \times 1$ MUX can realize any m-input function, if there are p SDC conditions at gate G_i, we can find 2^p gates as the alternative for G_i, including itself. So we will increase FP by p in Line 8 of our heuristics.

Option **R1** will require that new masks be created for each fingerprint, which is an expensive process. This leads us to prefer option **R2** which gives us the flexibility for post-silicon configuration. With this option we can utilize fuses, or other engineering changes such as the one presented in [18], to implement a fingerprint bit string in a circuit at the post-silicon phase. However this comes at the cost of high design overhead due to the large size and delay of the MUX. Figure 11 illustrates how the fuses will be used to implement the fingerprint.

4.5 Security Analysis

We first briefly discuss fingerprint detection because this is directly related to most attacks. When an adversary can detect the fingerprint, he may have an easier time to remove or change the fingerprint than with no knowledge about the fingerprint.

Fingerprint detection: when we are allowed to open up the chip and view its layout, we can recover the fingerprint by identifying the gate type at each fingerprint location (for **R1**) or checking the configuration at each MUX (for **R2**).

As the authors have shown in [13, 14], there are abundant fingerprint locations in real-life circuits. Therefore we can choose to embed fingerprint bits (or part of it) at gates that are visible to output pins. Then when we inject the SDC conditions to the fingerprint location, we can tell the gate type (and thus the fingerprint bit) from the output values. Consider Fig. 9, if we inject B = 0 and C = 0, if we observe 1 as the value for D, we know the gate is a NAND; otherwise it is a XOR.

Now we consider the following attacking scenario based on the adversary's capabilities.

Simple Removal Attack. The most obvious attack against a fingerprint is to simply remove it. This requires that an adversary knows every location on an IC that our fingerprinting algorithm has modified, and more importantly, a way to remove these fingerprints without affecting the functionality of the original IC. In both **R1** and **R2**, because the fingerprint locations are required to provide the correct functionality of the circuit/IP, simply removing them will destroy the design and make the IP useless.

Simple Modification Attack. An adversary may also attempt to modify, instead of removing, a fingerprint to attempt to distribute additional copies of an IC that were not approved by the original developer. These copies will behave the same way as the original IC but will contain fingerprints that the original developer did not produce. To achieve this, an adversary can attempt to modify the fingerprint locations so that they create an unused bit string.

For **R1**, this is the same as modifying the gate replacement based watermarks, which is known to be hard. For **R2**, the attacker can find the fingerprint locations by looking for the MUXs. He can try to change the configuration of these MUXs, but without fully reverse engineering the design, it will be hard to maintain the correct functionality.

Finally, we mention that our results show that we can easily embed hundreds, or even thousands, of fingerprint bits [20]. So we will have room to choose fingerprints that are relatively far from each other (e.g. in terms of Hamming distance). Then the attacker has to remove a large amount of fingerprint bits to remove the fingerprint.

Collusion Attack. This is an attack when multiple adversaries or an adversary with access to multiple fingerprinted IPs collude by comparing their copies to find the fingerprint locations and the alternatives at each location. This can be used to attack both **R1** and **R2**.

To prevent this, we propose that the fingerprint bit string be chosen using certain encoding scheme (such as error correction or any coding designed for integrity checking) such that these bits will become dependent and have certain pattern, property, or structure. In this way, the colluded bits will fail to have these required pattern/property/structure.

5 Scan Chain Fingerprinting

5.1 Illustrative Example

Figure 12 depicts a 5-stage scan chain where the five scan cells (scan flip flops, or SFF) are labeled as D_1 through D_5 from left to right. It gives testing engineer the ability to put the core under test (CUT) in any desired state (represented as the values of the SFFs) by inputting the values, called test vectors, through the scan in (SI) port; then observe how the core behaves through the scan out (SO) port. Assume that in this case, we have two test vectors $X_1 = 00000$ and $X_2 = 01001$. The corresponding responses (or next states) are $Y_1 = 00000$ and $Y_2 = 10011$.

Our fingerprinting approach takes advantage of the fact that *scan cells can be chained by either the Q-SD or the Q'-SD connection style* [19, 20]. Suppose that we have identified two pairs of SFFs, (D_2, D_3) and (D_4, D_5), as the location to embed the fingerprint. We use the Q-SD connection to embed a bit '0' and the Q'-SD connection as a bit '1' (see Fig. 12). This will allow us to embed any 2-bit fingerprint, "00", "01", "10", or "11", by selecting different connection styles.

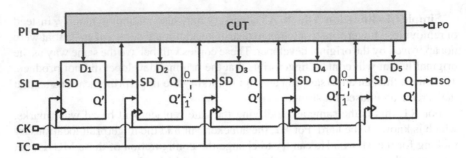

Fig. 12 A 5-bit Scan Chain with the second and fourth connections chosen as the fingerprinting locations. A 2-bit fingerprint can be created by selecting how the flip flops are connected at these two locations

Table 1 Different test vectors and output responses for all 4 different 2-bit fingerprints

f_1f_2	X_1	Y_1	X_2	Y_2
00	00000	00000	01001	10011
01	00001	11110	01000	01101
10	00111	11000	01110	01011
11	00110	00110	01111	10101

Suppose the original design uses Q-SD connection on both locations, that is, it carries the fingerprint "00". To embed fingerprint "01", for example, we will connect the Q' port of D_4 to the SD port of D_5. As a result, when data moves from D_4 to D_5, its value will be flipped. Therefore, we have to change the two test vectors to $X_1 = 00001$ and $X_2 = 01000$ to ensure that the CUT is tested with states 00000 and 01001, respectively. Similarly, the output responses Y_1 and Y_2 will change in a similar fashion. Table 1 lists the two test vectors and their corresponding output responses for all the four possible fingerprinted designs.

To identify each copy of the design, we can simply check the test vector. If the test vector or its output response is different from Table 1, then the design is not genuine.

5.2 Basics on Scan Chain Design

Scan design adds testability to an IC by allowing the system to forego the complex automatic test pattern generation. The main change a scan chain causes to a circuit is to replace the normal D-Flip-Flops with the so-called Scan-Flip-Flops (SFFs). As depicted in Fig. 12, an SFF consists of a normal DFF as well as a multiplexer and two new input signals: scan-data SD and test control TC. The SFFs are chained together by connecting the output port (Q or Q') of one SFF to the SD input of another SFF. The TC signal is used to switch operating modes of the core under test (CUT) between normal and testing. While in the normal operating mode, the SFFs act as the DFFs that the circuit design originally had. In testing mode, test data comes in from the scan input (SI) port, and the test results are supplied to the scan output (SO) port.

In most technology libraries, DFFs contain two outputs: Q and its complement Q'. Both are used by the CUT. Since SFFs are built on top of DFFs, both Q and Q' ports are available for SFFs. This allows two adjacent SFFs to be connected either in the Q-SD style or the Q'-SD style [19].

5.3 Scan Chain Fingerprinting

We utilize the Q-SD and Q'-SD connection styles between SFFs to create a fingerprint for a design in the following steps:

Step 1. Perform the normal scan design to obtain the best possible solution. This normally includes determining (1) a set of test vectors to achieve the best fault coverage; (2) the order of the scan chain, that is, which SFF will be the next for a given SFF; (3) the connection style between each two SFFs.

Step 2. Identify the fingerprint locations. By deliberately choosing whether two adjacent flip-flops have a Q-SD or a Q'-SD connection, we can create a bit of information for the fingerprint. If the design has n flip flops in its scan chain, we can embed any of the 2^n possible n-bit fingerprints. When we only need to k-bit fingerprints (k < n), the problem will be how to select k pairs of SFFs as fingerprint locations to minimize the performance overhead in the fingerprinted copies.

Step 3. Develop fingerprint embedding protocols. This can be as simple as the one in the illustrative example where 0 and 1 are embedded as Q-SD and Q'-SD connection styles. But a good fingerprint embedding protocol should balance (1) low design cost, (2) low or no performance degradation, (3) easy detectability, and (4) high robustness and resilience.

Step 4. Modify the set of test vectors. While fingerprints are in the forms of Q-SD or Q'-SD connection styles, we want to maintain the test vector's fault coverage. Therefore, the set of test vectors have to be updated based on the fingerprint embedded in the design, as shown in the illustrative example.

5.4 Security Analysis

In this section, we first discuss the advantages of the proposed scan chain based fingerprinting technique and then conduct a security analysis on potential attacks, as well as the corresponding countermeasures.

Our approach can easily be implemented by local rewiring to determine a specific connection style of certain pairs of scan cells. Since the change is local, it would successfully avoid the high design overhead introduced by scan chain reordering or rerouting. Therefore, the proposed fingerprinting technique would only incur low overhead in terms of area, power and speed.

Another major change would be that the test vectors that are applied would need to be adjusted for different fingerprinting configurations, in order to maintain high fault coverage. This gives us two ways to detect fingerprints: on one hand, we could physically open up the chip and check connection styles to directly determine the fingerprinting bits; on the other hand, fingerprints can also be extracted from associated test vectors and output responses. It's obvious that the second method, detecting fingerprints from test vectors is non-intrusive and costless, which makes the proposed scheme easy detectable.

Next we analyze various possible attacks on our proposed approach and present corresponding countermeasures to show that the approach is resistant to tampering.

Fingerprint Denial. The most straightforward attack is to simply declare that the existing fingerprint in the IP is merely a coincidence while not making any change on the IC. We could defeat this attack by proving that the probability of coincidence is really low when the length of fingerprint is long enough. In our proposed scheme, it's rational to assume that the connection style at any position is equally likely to be Q-SD or Q'-SD. Thus, the probability that the m bits generated by a non-fingerprinted design match a specific m-bit fingerprint will be $1/2^m$. As a result, we can see that a long fingerprint provides strong authorship proof. More importantly, since the fingerprinted design would inevitably incur a power overhead compared to the optimal design [19], it would make no sense for the designer to choose this specific connection style if it is not used for embedding fingerprinting bits.

Fingerprint Removal. In regards to removability, the result is similar to that in [20]. If an adversary wishes to remove the fingerprint they would need to reverse engineer the device, or have access to a netlist at which point they would need to remove the entire scan-chain. Reverse engineering the entire device and attempting to rebuild a new scan chain in a netlist would both be an extreme cost to the adversary, making it unlikely that they would attempt to remove or redesign the circuit without the scan chain fingerprint.

Fingerprint Modification. In this type of attack, the adversary attempts to alter the fingerprints. We will discuss this type of attack based on two different detection methods, by checking the testing vectors or opening up the chip. In the first case, adversaries could carry out changing the test vectors associated with a certain device, making it difficult or impossible to identify the fingerprint. It only works when we use test vectors to detect fingerprints. It is difficult to perpetrate because adjusting the test vectors only will lead to lower fault coverage of the scan chain. Without the proper test coverage, a circuit may be malfunctioning and the end user may not know. Furthermore, we could detect this attack by observing the mismatch between test vectors and output responses of fake IP.

If we could open up the chip to detect fingerprints, the attacker would turn to modifications on the interior structure of ICs instead of only test vectors. In this case, the attacker could randomly change the connection styles between SFFs such that the IP author is not able to obtain accurate evidence to establish his ownership.

To prevent this, we could implement data integrity when embedding fingerprints to make the fingerprint bits become dependent. As a result, the fingerprints encoded by authorized parties would have a certain pattern, property, or structure. If the attacker arbitrarily changes the fingerprint bits, the design would definitely fail to meet this requirement and thus be detected.

Another major attack for fingerprinting methods is collusion attack. This is when the attacker has access to multiple copies of fingerprinted ICs, he can compare the layout of these ICs and find the differences in these copies to expose a lot of fingerprinting locations. Data integrity is also used to prevent the attackers from arbitrarily changing the connection styles in these fingerprinting locations.

6   Conclusion

Fingerprinting is one of the most powerful and efficient methods to discourage illegal distribution. A fingerprinted IP will not directly prevent misuse of the IP, but will allow the IP provider to detect the source of the redistributed IP and therefore trace the traitor. The key problem related to the use of fingerprinting for IP protection is the tradeoff between collusion resilience and the run-time overhead to generate large number of distinct IP instances. In this chapter, we provide a comprehensive review of the existing research on digital fingerprinting for IP protection. We analyze the needs and basic requirements for digital fingerprint. We present two generic approaches that can be used to create fingerprinted copies of IP at many of the pre-silicon design and synthesis stages. This demonstrates that multiple (and many) distinct copies of IP can be generated with short run-time. However, these approaches are not practical because the IPs they create require different masks for fabrication. Therefore, we further report several practical digital fingerprinting methods at post-silicon stage. For each of these methods, we show the key idea with illustrative examples, elaborate the technical details, perform security analysis on potential attacks and propose corresponding countermeasures.

Acknowledgments This work is supported in part by Army Research Office under grant W911NF 1210416 and W911NF1510289, and by AFOSR MURI under award number FA9550-14-1-0351.

References

1. Qu, G., Potkonjak, M.: Intellectual Property Protection in VLSI Designs: Theory and Practice. Kluwer Academic Publishers, ISBN 1-4020-7320-8, January 2003
2. Guin, U., Huang, K., DiMase, D., Carulli Jr., J.M., Tehranipoor, M., Makris, Y.: Counterfeit integrated circuits: a rising threat in the global semiconductor supply chain. Proc. IEEE **102**(8), 1207–1228 (2014)
3. IHS Technology: Reports of counterfeit parts quadruple since 2009, challenging US defense industry and national security. https://technology.ihs.com/389481/. Accessed 14 Feb 2012
4. Qu, G., Yuan, L.: Secure hardware IPs by digital watermark. In Introduction to hardware security and trust, pp. 123–142. Springer, ISBN 978-1-4419-8079-3 (2012)

5. Kahng, A.B., Lach, J., Magione-Smith, W.H., Mantik, S. Markov, I.L., Potkonjak, M., Tucker, P., Wang, H., Wolfe, G.: Watermarking techniques for intellectual property protection. In: 35th Design Automation Conference Proceedings, pp. 776–781 (1998)

6. Patel, H.J., Crouch, J.W., Kim, Y.C., Kim, T.C.: Creating a unique digital fingerprint using existing combinational logic. In: IEEE International Symposium on Circuits and Systems, Taipei (2009)

7. Jin, Y., Makris, Y.: Hardware Trojan detection using path delay fingerpring. In: IEEE International Workshop on Hardware-Oriented Security and Trust. Anaheim, CA (2008)

8. Pappu, R., Recht, B., Taylor, J., Gershenfeld, N.: Physical one-way functions. Science **297**(5589), 2026–2030 (2002)

9. Zhang, J., Qu, G., Lv, Y., Zhou, Q.: A survey on silicon PUFs and recent advances in ring oscillator PUFs. J. Comput. Sci. Technol. **29**(4), 664–678 (2014). doi:10.1007/s11390-014-1458-1

10. Lach, J., Mangione-Smith, W.H., Potkonjak, M.: FPGA fingerprinti-ng techniques for protecting intellectual property. Proc. CI-CC (1998)

11. Caldwell, A.E., et.al.: Effective iterative techniques for fingerprin- ting design IP. In: Proceedings of the 36th Annual ACM/IEEE Design A-utomation Conference, New York, NY (1999)

12. Qu, G., Potkonjak, M.: Fingerprinting intellectual property using co-nstraint-addtion. In: Proceedings of the 37th Annual ACM/IEEE Design Automation Conference, New York, NY (2000)

13. Dunbar, C., Qu, G.: A practical circuit fingerprinting method utilizing observability don't care conditions. In: Design Automation Conference (DAC'15), June 2015

14. Dunbar, C., Qu, G.: Satisfiability don't care condition based circuit fingerprinting techniques. 20th Asia and South Pacific Design Automation Conference (ASPDAC'15), pp. 815–820, January 2015

15. Wagner, N.R.: Fingerprinting. In: IEEE Computer Society Proceedings of the 1983 Symposium on Security and Privacy, pp. 18–22 (1983)

16. Biehl, I., Meyer, B.: Protocols for collusion-secure asymmetric fingerprinting. In: Reischuk, Morvan (eds.) STACS'97 Proceedings of 14th Annual Symposium on Theoretical Aspect of Computer Science, pp. 399–412. Springer (1997)

17. Boneh, D., Shaw, J.: Collusion-secure fingerprinting for digital data. In: Coppersmith (ed.) Advances in Cryptology—CRYPTO'95, Proceedings of 15th Annual International Cryptology Conference, pp. 452–465. Springer (1995)

18. Chang, K., Markov, I.L., Bertacco, V.: Automating post-silicon debugging and repair. In: IEEE/ACM Intl Conference on Computer Aided Design, San Jose, CA (2007)

19. Gupta, S., Vaish, T., Chattopadhyay, S.: Flip-flop chaining architecture for power-effcient scan during test application. In: Proceedings of Asia Test Symposium, pp. 410–413. Kolkata, India (2005)

20. Cui, A., Qu, G., Zhang, Y.: Dynamic Watermarking on Scan Design for Hard IP Protection with Ultra-low Overhead. IEEE Trans. Inf. Foren. Secur. **10**(11), 2298–2313 (2015). doi:10.1109/TIFS.2015.2455338

Operating System Fingerprinting

Jonathan Gurary, Ye Zhu, Riccardo Bettati and Yong Guan

Abstract Operating system fingerprinting, helps IT administrators to perform vulnerability assessment and internal auditing in securing their networked systems. Meanwhile, it is, oftentimes, the first step to launch security attacks to a targeted system or service online, thereby enables an adversary to tailor attacks by exploiting known vulnerabilities of the target system(s). In this chapter, we focus on major approaches in fingerprinting techniques at operating system level. We examine the instantiations of the OS fingerprinting concepts, and discuss the details of their design and implementation to demonstrate the complexity and limitations. In particular, we present a case study on OS identification against smartphones that use encrypted traffic. We consider the security of these schemes in term of effectiveness, and raise challenges that future OS fingerprinting research must address to be useful for practical digital forensic investigations.

1 Overview of Operating System Fingerprinting

The purpose of operating system fingerprinting can vary ranging from being as a tool for internal auditing or external vulnerability assessment, detecting unauthorized devices in a network, or tracking hosts' operating system deployment status, to tailoring offensive exploits.

J. Gurary · Y. Zhu
Cleveland State University, Cleveland, OH 44115, USA
e-mail: j.gurary@vikes.csuohio.edu

Y. Zhu
e-mail: y.zhu61@csuohio.edu

R. Bettati
Texas A&M University, College Station, TX 77840, USA
e-mail: bettati@cs.tamu.edu

Y. Guan (✉)
Iowa State University, Ames, IA 50011, USA
e-mail: guan@iastate.edu

© Springer Science+Business Media New York (outside the USA) 2016
C. Wang et al. (eds.), *Digital Fingerprinting*,
DOI 10.1007/978-1-4939-6601-1_7

Just like a human fingerprint's unique pattern (i.e., positions and shapes of ridge endings, bifurcations, and dots) that serves to identify an individual in the real physical world, an Operating System (OS) has unique characteristics in its own design as well as its communication implementation variations. By analyzing protocol flags, option fields, and payload in the packets a device sends to the network, one can make useful and relatively accurate guesses about the OS of the host that sent those packets (*a.k.a*, operating system fingerprinting).

Operating system fingerprinting can generally be done using two complimentary, approaches: *Active* scanning approaches actively send carefully-crafted queries to hosts, while *passive* analysis examines the captured network traffic, with the same purpose of identifying the OS on the host being analyzed. Active scanning includes the use of automated or semi-automated use of tools such as nmap, and performs manual analysis of the response from these hosts. Active scanning generally allows more precise estimation about the OS on each host, but its use is often limited due to overhead, privacy, and other legal or policy constraints. On the contrary, passive OS fingerprinting does not send specially-crafted probe messages to a host being analyzed. Instead, it only examines values of fields in the TCP/IP packet header from the passively-collected network packets. For the same reason, sometimes, passive fingerprinting may not be as accurate as active fingerprinting.

The requirements of operating system fingerprinting include:

- Accuracy: Type 1 and 2 errors in term of falsely detected OS.
- Firewall and IDS neutrality: OS fingerprinting should not be disturbed by, nor disturb existing firewalls and IDS in networked IT systems.
- Politeness: OS fingerprinting should not create overly-large volume of network traffic, nor cause harm to networked IT systems.
- Adaptiveness and extensibility: OS fingerprinting should be adaptive and easily extensible to new or update of OSes.
- Complexity: OS fingerprinting can minimize the time and other complexity such as space requirement.

2 Major Operating System Fingerprinting Techniques

In this section, we review existing OS fingerprinting approaches, reconnaissance through traffic analysis, and analysis of smartphone traffic.

2.1 OS Fingerprinting

A multitude of approaches to traffic-based fingerprinting, both passive and active, have been proposed. In passive fingerprinting the observer monitors traffic from the target to detect a pattern, while in active fingerprinting the observer may stimulate the target by sending its own requests and so cause the target to display a particular behavior for the observer to monitor.

Fingerprinting can be used for beneficial and malicious purposes. Many professionals in network management consider fingerprinting a valuable tool, allowing them to adjust their services based on the OS of the user. A common issue is maintaining networks that allow Bring Your Own Device (BYOD) policies, i.e. the user can bring a device, such as a mobile phone or laptop, into the network. By enabling the network to detect the type and OS of the device, security and connectivity can be simplified for network administrators. In the security field fingerprinting is considered a type of *reconnaissance*: the attacker uses fingerprinting to determine the nature of the victim's system and plans an attack according to its vulnerabilities.

2.1.1 Passive Fingerprinting

Passive fingerprinting does not interfere with traffic to or from the target. There are only a few situations where passive fingerprinting is possible:

1. The victim connects to the attacker, and the attacker wants to determine what sort of system is connecting to them. Sometimes this can involve tricking the victim into connecting to the attacker in some way.
2. The attacker connects to the victim in an innocuous way, for example by visiting a web site hosted on the victim's server. The traffic is not altered from normal traffic to the victim in order to avoid detection, thus we consider this a passive approach even though packets are being sent from the attacker.
3. The attacker sits between the victim and the destination server to intercept their traffic on the wire. This can include capturing traffic from the target's WiFi connection or sniffing for traffic on the target's gateway.

Network analysis tools such as p0f, developed as a part of the Honeynet Project [32], fingerprint the OS by checking TCP signatures. These tools generally examine the TCP SYN packet. For a pair of computers to establish a TCP connection, they must first perform a TCP handshake across the network. To start the handshaking protocol, the client sends a SYN packet to the server. It contains the client's desired TCP settings in the header, for example the window size and Time-to-Live (TTL). Using signatures in the SYN packet's header, tools such as p0f can build a classification system that determines which OS is generating the SYN packet.

Here we discuss the most common TCP signatures used in fingerprinting SYN packets.

- Two commonly used TCP signatures are the TTL and the TCP window size as discussed in [27].

  - TTL is often OS specific, for example many Unix OSes use a TTL of 64, while most versions of Windows use a TTL of 128. Many different OSes share the same window size so TTL is seldom enough by itself.
  - Window size can change between different OS releases. Windows XP uses a TCP window size of 65535, while Windows 7 uses a size of 8192.

- Two additional TCP signatures, the Don't Fragment (DF) bit and the Type of Service (ToS) flags, also vary between different OSes and OS releases by the same manufacturer.

  – Older operating systems seldom use the DF bit. A handful of older OSes, for example SCO and OpenBSD, do not use the DF flag.
  – The ToS flag is typically 0 during the SYN exchange, but some OSes set ToS to another value. Several versions of FreeBSD, OpenBSD, AIX set the ToS flag to minimize delay (16) instead of 0.

- Some tools examine the Selective Acknowledgement (SackOk), No-Operation (NOP), and End of Option List (EOL) options, as well as Window Scale value and Maximum Segment Size (MSS).

  – Most Linux and Windows releases set the SackOk flag, while many MAC, Cisco IOS, and Solaris releases do not set SackOk.
  – Taleck [36] presents a table with different ways NOP options can be padded onto TCP options.
  – EOL can be used as padding, and thus depends on other options.
  – Most newer OSes implement window scaling, however older OSes (such as pre-2000 Windows releases) do not.
  – MSS specifies the maximum packet size the host can receive in one segment. This value is determined by the OS and varies by release. Novell uses a MSS of 1368, and FreeBSD uses a MSS of 512.

Further common fingerprinting values can be found at [34] or by studying the pOf database.

Sometimes, it is possible for the attacker to obtain the SYN-ACP response from the server as well as the SYN, or perhaps the attacker is only able to get the SYN-ACP. This may be the case when fingerprinting a device that seldom initiates TCP connections but often receives them, for example a printer. A SYN-ACP packet does not necessarily have the same information as the ACP, since the server likely has its own TCP settings and choose certain parts of the packet differently (e.g. the DF or NOP bits). However, a server's reply to a SYN packet often varies depending on the SYN packet's settings (and by extension, the sender's OS). Thus it is possible for an attacker to create a database of SYN-ACP responses, covering the responses to various OSes, and use these to fingerprint the sender. The database required to accurately fingerprint an OS in this manner would be significantly larger than using the SYN packets.

Taleck [36] implements a TCP SYN mapping tool to identify 42 different operating systems based on many of the options described above. Bevels [6] uses signatures collected by the pOf community to train a classifier and perform passive finger-printing. Other passive fingerprinting tools similar to pOf include DISCO [39] and Eternal.

Timescales are also frequently used to examine traffic. Kohl et al. [22] presents a technique for determining the system time clock skew from TCP timescales, and using this information to determine the OS. Operating Systems can send their packets in specific patterns or bursts, and this too can be used to identify the OS.

Tollman [23] proposes to fingerprint the OS based on the implementation of the DEP protocol, as different computer OSes support different combinations of DEP options. For example, most Windows OSes need to look up their Netball servers, while most MAC OSes are not interested in these options. Several proprietary services such as Infolds [20] utilize DEP fingerprinting to help network managers identify devices on their network. Since DEP messages are broadcast through the local network, it is easy for an attacker (or network administrator) to identify devices on the local network by connecting to the network and listening in.

ICBM messages can also be used for fingerprinting, as demonstrated in [3]. For example, the IP level TTL for ICBM Echo replies on most Windows OSes is 128, while many Unix distributions use a IP TTL of 255. In addition to header data, ICBM messages can also contain important identification information in the reply. Windows 2000 zeros out the ToS field in its ICBM Echo reply when sent an Echo request with a non-zero ToS, a unique behavior that only a few relatively unpopular other OSes share (namely Novell Network and Ultra).

A number of methods to identify the computer OS by inspecting application layer data in traffic, such as server banners in HTTP, SSH and FTP as well as HTTP client User-Agent strings, are also discussed in [27].

Many passive fingerprinting methods can be overcome by simple modifications to the OS and network settings. TCP options can be changed to obfuscate the OS, for example changing the TCP window size of a Windows XP PC to 8192 in order to mask as Windows 7. Changing OS settings is not ideal, and probably inaccessible to most users. Most consumer firewalls disallow ICBM Echo requests by default, and many modern firewalls block ICBM timescales as well. Furthermore, a large percentage of Internet users are behind NAT devices, where it is difficult to tell how many unique devices are behind each NAT device. In 2002, Armitage [4] estimated that 17–25 % of Internet users access the Internet through a NAT-enabled gateway, router, or firewall. This number is likely much higher today. Accessing a victim's local area network can be difficult.

2.1.2 Active Fingerprinting

Active fingerprinting involves sending packets to the victim in order to determine their OS and other system information. Since fingerprinting is primarily a "reconnaissance" mission, detection can result in the network administrator discovering the potential for an attack before it occurs.

The most popular tool for active fingerprinting is the nmap program [28]. Nmap has several useful features to fingerprint a system:

1. **Port Scanning**: Nmap finds open ports on the target network. Generally speaking, avoiding detection is not a goal of the nmap program. There are several ways in which nmap can find open ports:

   - **TCP SYN scan**: Nmap sends a SYN packet to ports on the victim's network until it receives a response, indicating the port is open. This method is very fast, potentially scanning thousands of ports per second, but can be detected by a well configured Intrusion Detection System (IDS).
   - **TCP scan**: This method is used when the attacker's OS does not allow them to create raw packets. Nmap asks the OS to initiate a TCP connection to ports on the victim's system. In addition to being significantly slower than the SYN scan, this method is more likely to be detected as it actually completes the TCP connection.
   - **UDP scan**: Scanning for UDP ports is complicated. Open ports do not have to send any response, since there is no connection set up as there is in TCP. Closed ports generally send back an ICBM port unreachable error, but most hosts will only send a certain number of ICBM port unreachable messages in a given timeframe. Nmap slows down the rate at which ports are scanned automatically when it determines packets are being dropped.
   - **SCTP scan**: SCTP is a new protocol that combines features from TCP and UDP. Like TCP, SCTP initiates connections by handshaking. An INIT packet is sent to targeted ports on the victim's network. An INIT-ACP response indicates an open port, while an ABORT, ICBM-unreachable, or a series of timeouts is considered a closed port.
   - **TCP NULL, FIN, and Xmas scan**: These scans all utilize loopholes in TCP defined in the official TCP Request for Comments (RFC). A null scan sends a TCP packet with a flag header of 0, a FIN scan sets only the FIN bit, and an Xmas scan sets the FIN, PSH, and URG flags. When receiving these ill-constructed packets a system configured properly according to TCP RFC will send a Reset (RST) packet if the port is closed and no response if the port is open. Most major operating systems send a RST packet regardless, and are thus immune to this attack.
   - **ACP scan**: To determine if certain ports are filtered, nmap sends ACP packets to target ports on the victim's network. Open or closed ports return an RST, while filtered ports will not respond or send an ICBM error.
   - **TCP Window scan**: An extension of the ACP scan, this method also examines the TCP Window field of the RST response. Some systems use a positive window size for open ports and a size of zero for closed ports.

2. **Host Discovery**: A local network can be allocated thousands or even millions of IP addresses, but use only a tiny fraction of them. Nmap determines which IP addresses map to real hosts. By default, nmap sends a ICBM Echo request, a TCP SYN on port 443, a TCP ACP on port 80, and an ICBM Timestamp request to determine which hosts reply.

3. **Version Detection**: Certain ports generally map to certain services, for example SMTP mail servers often listen on port 25. Nmap maintains a list of which services map to which ports, and is also able to probe open ports to see what service is running on them based on patterns in its database.

4. **OS Detection**: Perhaps the best known feature of namp, OS detection sends a series of TCP and UDP packets to the victim and compares the responses against a database of over 2,500 (mostly community generated) known OS fingerprints. The following probes are sent to open ports on the target's network:

   - A series of six TCP SYN packets are sent to the target 100ms apart. The window scale, MSS, NOP, timestamp, SACKOK, EOL, and window field are set to specific quantities. More detailed information about these settings can be found in [28].
   - Two ICBM Echo requests are sent to the target.
   - A TCP explicit congestion notification (ECN) is sent to the target. This is a special TCP SYN packet that sets certain congestion control flags.
   - An additional six TCP packets are sent with a variety of unique settings. For example, a TCP null packet with no flags set, several TCP ACP packets, and a TCP SYN packet addressed to a closed port.
   - A UDP packet is sent to a closed port on the target.

In addition to examining headers in responses from the target, as described previously, namp studies timing data from the responses to fingerprint the OS. The responses to the initial six TCP SYN packets are studied for their initial sequence number (ISN). Some operating systems increment the ISN in predictable ways, for example incrementing it by a multiple of 64,000 for each new connection. First, namp calculates the difference between probe responses, i.e. subtracting ISN1 from ISN2, for a total of five values. Namp then calculates the greatest common divisor of the *differences* between the six TCP SYN responses to determine if there is a pattern to ISN choice. Nmap also uses these differences to calculate the ISN counter rate (ISR). The differences are divided by the time elapsed in seconds, and the average of these values is recorded. With these two values, nmap can also attempt to predict what the target's next assigned ISN will be.

Various other network scanning tools, such as Zmap [12], use active fingerprinting to remotely collect information about nodes connected to the Internet. Some tools, such as SinFP [5] combine active and passive approaches to fingerprinting. In SinFP, the attacker actively probes the server with TCP SYN packets or intercepts TCP SYN + ACP responses passively. Kohl et al. [22] uses ICBM Timestamp requests actively aimed at the target to identify their system time clock skew and further to determine their OS. Arackaparambil et al. [2] expand upon this method further and propose an attack that spoofs the clock skew of a real system. This is similar to work by [1] in using ICBM timescales to estimate network-internal delays.

Various countermeasures have been proposed that are designed to defeat OS fingerprinting. Smart et al. [35] developed a TCP/IP stack fingerprint scrubber to defend against active and passive OS fingerprinting attacks based on the TCP/IP stack.

The scrubber sanitizes packets from a group of hosts at both the network and transport layers to block fingerprinting scans. These sanitized packets will not reveal OS information.

Blocking certain traffic, for example ICBM Echo requests, can help thwart tools such as nmap, however this is not a practical approach for servers that need to answer all sorts of traffic. Systems can also be configured not to respond to malformed or unique packets such as a null TCP packet or a stray ACP. As with passive fingerprinting, it is also possible to modify network settings to alter a system's response from the norm, however not all network settings can be modified by the user and this is an impractical approach for most users.

Lastly, we note that all these approaches require access to the packet headers or packet content. As a result, these methods are largely ineffective when applied to intercepted encrypted traffic.

2.2 Reconnaissance Through Packet-Content Agnostic Traffic Analysis

Packet-content agnostic analysis refers to fingerprinting when packet headers and payload cannot be read due to some sort of encryption. Various reconnaissance approaches through packet-content agnostic traffic analysis have been proposed, and some of the approaches are studied in the context of privacy breaches.

Website Fingerprinting: Herrmann et al. [18] developed a method for website fingerprinting with traffic encrypted and anonymized by Tor. The method uses common text mining approaches on frequency distributions of packet sizes. The method is reported to be capable of identifying 300,000 real-world traffic traces with 97 % accuracy using a sample of 775 sites.

Panchenko et al. [31] discussed the effectiveness of website fingerprinting attacks on anonymity networks. Their approaches can increase the detection accuracy from 3 to 55 % on Tor traffic and from 20 to 80 % on JAP traffic. Their experiments on a real-world data set can achieve an accuracy of 73 %. The countermeasure applying camouflage to hamper the fingerprinting attack was proposed in [31] and the countermeasure is able to decrease the accuracy to as low as 3 %.

A website detection attack that could be executed from a remote location was proposed in [15]. The attack first estimates the load inside a victim's router queue by sending regularly spaced probe packets and then measuring their round trip time. Based on this estimation of the load, any of the website fingerprinting methods described above can be used. Cai et al. [9] attempted to defeat countermeasures proposed to website fingerprinting, more specifically HTTPOS and randomized pipelining over Tor. Their method used packet size vectors from encrypted traffic and the Damper-Levenshtein algorithm to detect which web pages the traffic was associated with. They were able to achieve website fingerprinting accuracy as high as 90 % against some countermeasures with a sample set of 100 websites.

Liberatore and Levine [25] proposed traffic analysis on encrypted HTTP streams to infer the source of a web page retrieved in encrypted HTTP streams. A profile of each known website is created in advance. The traffic analysis identifies the source by comparing observed traffic with established profiles with classified algorithms. They used a sample size of 2,000 websites with 400,000 traffic traces.

Inferring Users' Online Activities Through Traffic Analysis: Zhang et al. [42] use short traces of encrypted traffic on IEEE 802.11 wireless local area networks (WLAN) to infer activities of a specific user (e.g. web browsing, file downloading, or video streaming). Their experiments include traffic traces from web browsing, online chatting, online gaming, file downloading, and video conversations. They developed a learning hierarchical classification system to discover web activities that were associated with a traffic trace. They performed their experiments in a home environment, a university campus, and on a public network. They were able to infer the user's activities with 80 % accuracy using 5 s of traffic and 90 % accuracy with 1 min of traffic.

Hidden Services: Hidden services are used in anonymity networks like Tor to resist censorship and attacks like a denial of service attack. verlier and Syverson [30] proposed attacks to reveal the location of a hidden server in the Tor network. Using one corrupt Tor node they were able to locate a hidden server in minutes. They then proposed changes to the Tor network in order to resist their attacks.

A very similar effort in [7] investigates the flaws in the Tor network and its hidden services. Three practical cases including a botnet with hidden services for command and control channels, a hidden service used to sell drugs, and the DuckDuckGo search engine are used for evaluation. Their method involves first gaining control of the descriptors of a hidden service and then performing a traffic correlation attack on the hidden service. Zander and Murdoch [41] aim to improve their clock-skew measurement technique for revealing hidden services. Their original method [26] correlates clock-skew changes during time of high load. They noticed two areas of noise, network jitter and timestamp quantization error, and aim to reduce the latter by synchronizing measurements to the clock ticks. They were able to reduce the timestamp quantization error and increase their accuracy by two magnitudes.

2.3 Analysis of Smartphone Traffic

Smartphone traffic has been analyzed for various purposes. In [37] Tzagkarakis et al. proposed to use the Singular Spectrum Analysis to characterize network load in a large WLAN. This is beneficial to monitor the load and to place access points accordingly. Their findings can help design large-scale WLANs that can be used by smartphones in large public areas.

Chen et al. [11] studied the network performance of smartphones in a university-wide WLAN. They analyzed 2.9 TB of data collected over three days and were able to gather interesting insights on TCP and application behavior of smartphones and their effect on performance.

Huang et al. [19] proposed a methodology for comparing application performance based on 3G communications. Their study shows how YouTube buffering techniques vary across smartphone OSes.

2.4 Analysis of Encrypted Traffic

The fingerprinting and traffic analysis attacks above are based on information in packet headers and payload data. Since using encrypted traffic is becoming more popular to ensure privacy our experiments focus only on encrypted traffic (i.e. the only available information is packet timing and size). There has been a lot of other work on attacks based on encrypted traffic. Wright et al. [40] aimed to classify network traffic using only packet timing, size and direction. They wanted to classify the traffic so that network security monitors could still enforce security policies with encrypted traffic. Their classification accuracy was as high as 90%. In [38] Wang et al. proposed a watermark-based approach to correlation attacks on attacker stepping stones. They were able to show through their experiments that their active attacks perform better than passive correlation timing attacks and also require fewer packets. In Zhu et al. [43] aimed to show the security threats created by the silence suppression feature (i.e. packets are not sent unless speech is detected) of online speech communications. They show that talk patterns can then be recovered by only looking at the packet timing. They proposed packet timing traffic analysis attacks on encrypted speech communication using different codecs. They were able to detect speakers of encrypted speech communications with high accuracy with only 15 min of traffic timing data. Bissias et al. aimed to identify the source of encrypted HTTP traffic streams in [8]. Their initial results were as low as 23% accuracy but they were able to achieve 100% accuracy with only three guesses. These experiments show that traffic analysis attacks on encrypted traffic using packet timing can be and are very successful.

3   Case Study: Smartphone OS Reconnaissance

In this section, we present a case study on the identification of operating systems (OS) of smartphones that communicate using encrypted traffic [33].

Mobile devices such as Smartphones have become the dominant communication and computing devices in our daily life since 2009. This has been evidenced by (a) the number of mobile devices sold each year has exceeded the total of desktop and laptop computers, (b) mobile devices allow nearly ubiquitous Internet access through communication capabilities such as WiFi, 3G, 4G, and in the next couple of years, 5G networks, (c) the user-friendly interfaces supports touch and gesture based input, and (d) a huge number of mobile apps being developed and used have revolutionized the ways of living and work for billion of online users. With the increasing reliance on smartphones, users are increasingly using them to share sensitive data via social network apps. Smartphones are also adopted in business and military environments [16] because of their portability and constant network access. As a result, smartphone security is of great importance nowadays.

For the same reason, we have seen more and more serious security attacks against mobile platform and apps running on them. Smartphone reconnaissance, usually the first step of security attacks [13], is aimed at collecting information on a target. In order to launch an effective attack on a particular smartphone an attacker usually needs to tailor the attack to the target smartphone's platform. This in turn requires that the attacker be able to identify the operating system running on the target smartphone. Once the attacker knows the target OS, he or she becomes able to exploit known vulnerabilities both of the smartphone OS and of the applications and services running on the OS. The most readily obtainable information that enables OS identification is the wireless traffic generated by the target smartphone. Since more and more smartphone traffic is encrypted to protect the confidentiality of the wireless communications [14], the OS identification must not rely on either the content of packets or packet headers.

The ability to identify smartphone OSes can enable many applications, some of which are benign, however, many others are not (i.e., they are malicious in nature): (1) As a smartphone owner or a smartphone defense designer, we would like to know how susceptible a particular OS platform is to identification based on encrypted traffic. (2) OS identification can enable content providers, including websites, to tailor the content for different applications running on smartphones in different OSes. (3) The OS identification in conjunction with application identification enables network operators, especially mobile network operators, to predict the bandwidth requirements from a smartphone so that the network operators can better allocate resources to match expected bandwidth requirements.

When the traffic is encrypted, the observer cannot access packet content, and his or her ability to monitor the traffic is limited to the timing of the packets. Observations indicate, however, that different OSes still cause the smartphone to generate traffic with different timing. Differences in timing footprints are caused by differences in OS implementations (e.g. CPU scheduling, TCP/IP protocol stack), and by differences in resource management (e.g. memory management or power management). Similarly, differences in applications caused by the OS differences (e.g. audio/video codecs available for multimedia communications) become visible in the timing footprint of sent packets as well.

We will describe how differences in OSes can be identified by analyzing the timing traces of the generated traffic in the frequency domain. Frequency domain analysis is a classical tool to analyze temporal signals [29], including the timing behavior of traffic in our project, by converting signals from the time domain to the frequency domain.

The main challenge in OS identification with the frequency analysis comes from the fact that the frequency spectrum contains many *noise frequency components*, i.e., frequency components that are not caused by the OS features, but rather by application or user behavior. The noise frequency components can also be caused by network dynamics (such as network congestion and round trip time), and traffic content (such as periodicity in the video content when streaming a video clip). In this work, we name the frequency components that are helpful for OS identification, i.e., the frequency components caused by OS features, as the *characteristic frequency components*. The effectiveness of any frequency-domain based identification clearly depends on its ability to filter out noise and retain the *characteristic frequency components*.

Once the frequency spectrum of a device has been collected, it must be matched against training data, that is the spectrum of interest needs to be correlated with the spectrum generated by a known smartphone OS. The complexity of the correlation grows with the number of retained frequency components, so careful attention must be given to the selection of the latter. In this section, we will show the approaches to identify characteristic frequency components allow for efficient and accurate identification of smartphone OSes. Our major contributions in this case study are summarized as follows: (1) The identification algorithm using the frequency spectrum of packet timing captures the differences in smartphone OSes. Correlation is used to match the spectrum of interest to the spectra generated by known smartphone OSes. Noise frequency components are removed to improve identification accuracy. (2) We evaluate the OS identification algorithm with extensive empirical experiments, which are based on over 489 GB of smartphone traffic collected over 3 months to show that the proposed algorithm can identify smartphone OSes with very high accuracy with only small amounts of smartphone traffic. (3) We extend the OS identification algorithms to remotely identify the *applications* running on smartphones in different OSes. The identification accuracy can be achieved with as little as 30 s of smartphone traffic. According to our best knowledge, this is the first attempt to extract characteristic frequency components from frequency spectra for identification. A traffic flow has lots of frequency components caused by various factors such as OS features, network dynamics, and traffic content. The extraction enables a new series of identification applications to possibly identify each factor.

This section is organized as follows: The system and threat models are presented in Sect. 3.1. We explain the rationale behind the proposed identification approach and describe the details of the smartphone OS identification algorithm in Sect. 3.2. In Sect. 3.3, we evaluate the smartphone OS identification algorithm against a large volume of traffic data.

3.1   System and Threat Model

3.1.1   System Model

Our goal is to identify smartphone operation systems (OS) when the smartphone communicates using encrypted traffic. The capability of OS identification is needed: First, the identification of the OS and running applications during a reconnaissance step enables an informed and targeted attack. The attack can exploit known vulnerabilities and select a vector that is specific to the OS and the applications. On the other hand, defending against attacks benefits from an understanding about how effective such a reconnaissance can be.

We are particularly interested in the identification based on WiFi traffic (as opposed to 3G, for example) for three reasons: First, although current smartphones have various communication capabilities, such as WiFi, 3G, or even 4G, nearly every smartphone on the market is capable of WiFi communication. Next, the majority of traffic from smartphones is sent through WiFi [10] partly because of its low cost and relatively high bandwidth. Finally, WiFi based passive attacks are easy to stage. A drive-by or walk-by detection of the smartphone OS is therefore very easy to stage.

3.1.2   Threat Model

In this work, we assume a passive adversary who is able to capture packets exchanged by a smartphone of interest that uses encryption for its communication. This reflects the increasing popularity of encryption tools available for smartphones [17]. The encryption used by such tools disables access to packet content and renders traffic analysis based on packet content ineffective. In summary, we assume that the adversary has the following capabilities: (1) The adversary is able to eavesdrop on WiFi communications from the target smartphones and collect encrypted traffic for the identification. (2) The adversary is able to collect traffic from known smartphone OSes and analyze the traffic for future identification. (3) We assume a passive adversary. That is, the adversary is not allowed to add, delete, delay, or modify existing traffic for OS identification. (4) The traffic traces, including the traffic traces collected for training on known smartphone OSes and the traffic traces of interest for identification by the adversary, may be collected independently. In other words, the traffic traces may be collected in different network sessions and possibly on different WiFi networks.

Other attack scenarios can be very easily taken into consideration. For example one can envision a scenario where the observer does not have access to the wireless link, but rather collects data on the wired part of the path downstream. In this section, we focus on data collection on the wireless link.

3.2 Identifying Smartphone Operating Systems

In this section, we present approaches to identify smartphone operating systems based on the threat model described above. We begin this section with an introduction of the rationale behind the identification approach. We then describe the details of the identification algorithms.

3.2.1 Rationale

OS identification through encrypted traffic is possible because of implementation differences and differing resource management policies among smartphone OSes. These differences include:

Differences in OS implementations: Different smartphone OSes may have different kernels, different CPU scheduling, and different implementations of the TCP/IP protocol stack. These differences in the OS implementations can cause the timing behavior of traffic to differ from one smartphone OS to another.

Differences in Resource Control: Smartphones are resource-constrained devices. Largely due to their small form factor, smartphones have limited CPU processing capability, limited memory, and limited battery lifetime. To better utilize these resources, smartphone OSes adopt a number of policies for resource control. For example, different smartphone OSes may have different power management policies.

Differences in Applications: Because of the differences across OSes, the same application for different smartphone OSes may be implemented differently. For example, different OSes support different combinations of audio and video codecs used for multimedia communications. Obviously, different codecs used for multimedia communications will very likely generate network traffic differently. Another example is YouTube: In [19], iPhone is reported to first download a portion of video at a high rate, pause for a while, and then continue downloading. The Android phone reported in [19] periodically downloads small chunks of YouTube video every 10 s.

The differences described above will obviously give rise to different timing behaviors for the traffic generated by different smartphone OSes. These differences in the timing behavior can be easily captured in the frequency domain. A typical spectrum of YouTube video streaming on Android OS is shown in Fig. 1b: We observe that the YouTube traffic flow has many significant frequency components, some of which are coincidental, while others are associated with the YouTube buffering strategy on the Android OS. Others again may be associated with specific OS policies. To show the correspondence, we draw the time domain signal of the YouTube traffic flow in Fig. 2a. We can easily observe the periodic nature of the buffering in the figure. By checking the data, we confirm that some periodic buffering happens every 250 s. For verification, we zoom in the corresponding frequency range of Fig. 1b and the zoomed-in portion is shown in Fig. 2b. We note the peak at the frequency of 0.004 Hz, which corresponds to the buffering period of 250 s. Thus, the frequency

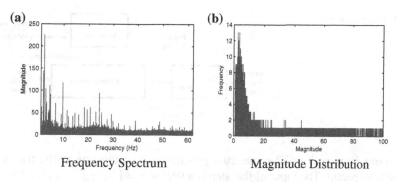

Fig. 1 Sample frequency spectrum and its magnitude distribution (The spectrum is based on 50 min of YouTube streaming traffic on Android v2.3 OS with an 8 ms sample interval.)

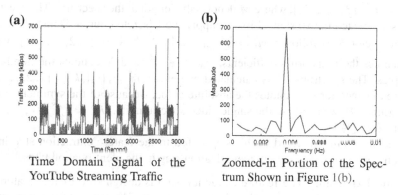

Fig. 2 Correspondence between the periodicities in a time domain signal and the characteristic frequency component in the spectrum

component corresponding to the buffering is helpful in OS identification. We call such frequency components *characteristic frequency components*. In Fig. 1b, we observe a large number of *noise frequency components* as well, which in turn are caused by network dynamics such as round trip time and the video content. These noise frequency components are not caused by OS features, and they are therefore not helpful for OS identification. Obviously, removing the *noise frequency components* will very likely improve the identification performance.

3.2.2 Identification Algorithm

The identification can be divided into two phases as shown in Fig. 3: *training phase* and *identification phase*. The training phase consists of two steps: *spectrum generation* step, followed by the *feature extraction* step. The identification phase uses the same *spectrum generation* step, followed by the *OS identification* step. We describe the details of each step below.

Fig. 3 Identification
framework

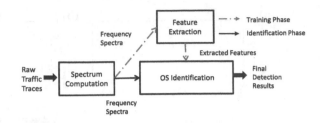

Spectrum Generation: The spectrum generation step converts traffic traces into frequency spectra. The input of this step is a vector $S = [s_1, s_2, \ldots, s_N]$, where s_i is the number of bytes received during the ith sample interval of length T, and N is the number of samples. The output of this step is the corresponding frequency spectrum $F^S = [f_1^S, f_2^S, \ldots, f_M^S]$, where M denotes the length of the spectrum. The spectrum F^S is calculated in two steps. First we apply the Discrete Fourier Transform (DFT) to the vector S as follows: $y_k = \sum_{j=1}^{N} s_j \omega_N^{(j-1)(k-1)}, k = [1, 2, \ldots, M]$, where y_k denotes the transform coefficients, $\omega_N = e^{-\frac{2\pi i}{N}}$, and N denotes the number of samples. The spectrum F^S is calculated as below: $f_k^S = |y_k|, k = [1, 2, \ldots, M]$ where the operator $|\cdot|$ denotes the absolute value. Because of the symmetry of the spectrum [29], we only use the single-sided spectrum, i.e., $F^S = [f_1^S, f_2^S, \ldots, f_L^S]$ where $L = \lfloor \frac{M}{2} \rfloor + 1$.

The spectrum generated in this step is fed to the feature extraction step in the training phase or fed to the OS identification step in the identification phase.

Feature Extraction: The feature extraction step is designed to extract features in the frequency spectra generated in the previous step. The inputs to the step are the frequency spectra of *labeled traces* that we use for training. The outputs are the features that are selected for the identification step.

The step is designed to improve the identification performance by removing *noise frequency components*, which are not helpful for OS identification, from the spectrum. As shown in Figs. 1b and 2, a traffic flow may contain many frequency components. These include *characteristic frequency components*, such as components caused by the OS's power management, as well as *noise frequency components*, such as those components caused by network round-trip time, network congestion, and other effects that are due to network dynamics. Obviously, removing the noise frequency components can improve identification performance.

Ideally, each frequency component should be evaluated to decide whether it is helpful for OS identification. Unfortunately, the computational cost to identify the optimal combination of frequency components to include in the feature set is prohibitive. To make this approach practical, we apply a genetic algorithm to decide which frequency component should be kept for OS identification.

Whether a frequency component is helpful for OS identification is decided during the training phase, based on the labeled traces. The feature extraction step first divides the labeled traces into two sets: Set_U and Set_V. Instead of exhaustively searching over all the possible combinations of candidate frequency components, we formulate

Table 1 Specifications of smartphones used

Phone	OS	CPU	RAM
HTC Desire HD	Android v2.3	1 GHz Scorpion	768 MB
Samsung Galaxy S4	Android v4.4	1.6 GHz 4-core Cortex-A15	2 GB
iPhone 4S	iOS 5	1 GHz 2-Core Cortex-A9	512 MB
iPhone 5S	iOS 8	1.3 GHz 2-core Cyclone	1 GB
Nokia Lumia N8	Symbian 3	680 MHz ARM 11	256 MB
Nokia Lumia 900	Win Phone 7.5	1.4 GHz Scorpion	512 MB

the search as a 0–1 optimization problem: The objective function to be optimized is the portion of correctly identified labeled traces in Set_V. The variables of the optimization problem are binary numbers, which indicate whether the corresponding frequency component is selected or not. We represent the binary variables as a vector $B_{selected} = [b_1, b_2, \ldots, b_L]$, where the binary variable b_i indicates whether the ith frequency component is selected to be part of the feature-extracted spectrum. We use a genetic algorithm to solve the optimization problem. This approach is more efficient than exhaustive search, at the cost of possibly finding a local maximum and so leading to a less effective identification. The pseudo code of the algorithm is shown in Algorithm 1 in Appendix A (Table 1).

OS Identification: This step identifies the OS based on two inputs: (1) F^x, the spectrum generated from the trace of interest, denoted as Trace x, and (2) the feature selection from the feature extraction step in the training phase. The output is the identification result.

The OS identification step will first apply the feature selection decided in the feature extraction step to F^x, the spectrum generated from the trace of interest. We denote the feature extracted spectrum as F'^x. The selected spectral features of the test trace will be compared with the spectral features in the labeled traces of each smartphone OS by correlation. In the following, we denote the pth labeled trace of smartphone OS A as A_p, its spectrum as F^{A_p}, and its feature-extracted spectrum as F'^{A_p}. The correlation between the two feature-extracted spectra F'^x and F'^{A_p} is calculated as follows: $corr(F'^x, F'^{A_p}) = \dfrac{\sum_{k=1}^{L} (f_k'^x - \overline{F'^x})(f_k'^{A_p} - \overline{F'^{A_p}})}{\sqrt{\sum_{k=1}^{L} (f_k'^x - \overline{F'^x})^2 \sum_{k=1}^{L} (f_k'^{A_p} - \overline{F'^{A_p}})^2}}$, where $\overline{F'^x} = \frac{1}{L}\sum_{k=1}^{L} f_k'^x$ and $\overline{F'^{A_p}} = \frac{1}{L}\sum_{k=1}^{L} f_k'^{A_p}$.

The OS type is determined by maximizing the average of all correlations of the feature-extracted spectra $F'^{A_1}, F'^{A_2}, \ldots, F'^{A_{P_A}}$ of the P_A labeled traces of smartphone OS A against the feature-extracted spectrum F'^x of the trace of interest x. Formally, the OS type is determined as follows:

OS Type $= \text{argmax}_{A \in \mathcal{A}} \frac{1}{P_A} \sum_{i=1}^{P_A} corr(F'^x, F'^{A_p})$, where $\mathcal{A}$ is the set of all the smartphone OSes under consideration.

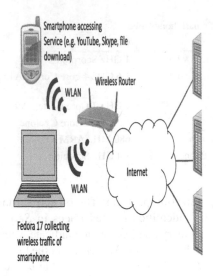

Fig. 4 Data collection setup

3.3 Empirical Evaluation

In this section, we evaluate the identification performance of the proposed identification algorithms. The evaluation is based on 489 GB of smartphone traffic collected over more than three months on different smartphone OSes.

3.3.1 Experiment Setup

The experiment setup is shown in Fig. 4. The smartphones with different OSes are used to watch different YouTube streaming videos, download files with the HTTP protocol from different webs sites, and make video calls with Skype. If multitasking is supported in a smartphone OS, we also use the smartphone for video streaming, file downloading, and Skype video calls at the same time. The wireless traffic from the smartphone is collected by an HP dc7800 computer. The data collection is through a Linksys Compact Wireless USB adapter (WUSB54GC) installed on the computer. The wireless access points used in the experiments include both the wireless router in our research lab and wireless access points managed by the university.[1]

The smartphone OSes included in our experiments are Apple's iOS, Google's Android OS, Windows Phone OS, and Nokia Symbian OS. For each possible combination of the smartphone OS and the application, at least 30 traffic traces of 50 min each are collected.

---

[1] In a different scenario, the data-collecting machine may be monitoring the traffic on the wired portion of the traffic path. The scenario chosen for our experiments is representative of a drive-by or walk-by attack.

3.3.2 Performance Metrics

The identification performance is measured with the following three performance metrics: (1) *identification rate* defined as the ratio of successful identifications to the number of attempts, (2) *false negative rate* defined as the proportion of traces generated by smartphone OS, say OS A, identified as traces generated by other smartphone OSes, and (3) *false positive rate* defined as the proportion of the traces generated by other smartphone OSes identified as traces generated by smartphone OS A.

Information about false positives and false negatives can provide more detailed performance information than the identification rate since the false positive rate and false negative rate are specific to each type of smartphone OS. On the other hand the identification rate, averaged across all the smartphone OSes, can show us the overall identification performance.

3.3.3 Length of Traffic Traces

Our first experiments focus on the length of the traffic traces used for the OS identification. The traffic used in the OS identification includes YouTube video streaming traffic, file downloading traffic, Skype traffic, and combined traffic. The combined traffic is collected by running YouTube video streaming, file downloading, and Skype video calls simultaneously on the OSes that support multitasking. We call the four type of traffic *YouTube*, *Download*, *Skype*, and *Combined* respectively in the rest of the chapter.

The sample interval used in this set of experiments is of length 8 ms. For each type of traffic and each smartphone OS, we collected 30 traces. We used 20 of these traces as labeled traces and the rest 10 traces as test traces. The experiment results are obtained with 1000 random combinations of the 20 labeled traces and 10 test traces. The experiment results of the four proposed algorithms are shown in Fig. 5.

Fig. 5 Identification performance with traces of different length

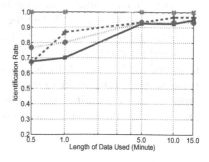

Fig. 6 Smartphone OS
minor version identification
based on Skype traffic
(Sample interval: 8 ms)

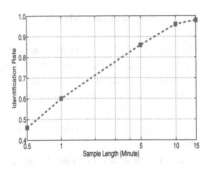

We observe that the identification rates are very high, even for short traces of observed traffic. Compared to the 25 % identification rate of a random identifier, the algorithm in most cases display rates of around 70 % for short traces (30 s) and around 90 % and above for long traces (5 min or more). For combination traffic, the identification rate can reach 100 % with only 30 s of traffic.

3.3.4 Identification of Minor Versions of Smartphone OSes

In this set of experiments, we investigate the possibility of identifying minor versions of smartphone OSes. More specifically we plan to identify the two iPhone OSes (iOS 5 and iOS 8) and the two Android Smartphone OSes (Android v2.3 and Android v4.4). So instead of classifying iOS 5 and iOS 8 as iOS and classifying Android v2.3 and Android v4.4 as Android OS, the identification algorithm is tested to classify a trace of interest as generated by any of the following OSes: Android v2.3, Android v4.4, iOS 5, iOS 8, Symbian, and Windows.

Figure 6 shows the identification performance of the algorithm on Skype traffic. As shown in Fig. 6, the identification rate can reach 98 % on 15-min-long traffic traces. The corresponding false alarm rates on 15-min-long traces are all below 10 %. However our experiment results on YouTube traffic show that the false negative rate of identifying Android v2.3 with the algorithm is larger than 50 % for 15-min-long traces, meaning that a large percentage of traces generated by Android v2.3 are identified incorrectly. Our data also shows that most of Android v2.3 traces were identified as Android v4.4 traces. We believe the differences in the identification performance are due to the higher power consumption and CPU usage of Skype. In other words, the identification of minor versions of smartphone OSes will be more effective when the resource consumption is high.

Table 2 Empirical running times (Traffic Length: 15 min, sample interval: 8 ms, computer configuration: HP Z220, Intel Core i7-3770@3.4 GHz CPU, 8 GB memory)

Training (minute)		Identification (second)	
YouTube	Skype	YouTube	Skype
977.63	1682.24	0.0683	0.0320

3.3.5 Running Time

Table 2 shows the empirical running time of the training phase and the identification phase. It can be observed that the identification takes less than 0.7 s. It means the identification is very efficient and feasible once the training is finished.

4 Summary and Future Directions

In this chapter, we discuss the major operating system fingerprinting techniques, and present and evaluate a case study on smartphone OS fingerprinting based on the frequency-domain analysis algorithm. Through the experimental evaluation, we illustrates how susceptible smartphones are against passive attacks that aim at inferring OS of a target smartphone, despite that the phone using encrypted communication. Our extensive experiments showed that the identification accuracy can reach 100 % with only 30 s of smartphone traffic.

As a future direction, OS fingerprinting work need to be adaptive to future OSes in a variety of system and application domains, such as mobile platform, wearable devices, Internet of Things, etc. Also, there is an immediate need to call for scientific foundation, and measurable metrics and methodologies to evaluate the effectiveness of OS fingerprinting and the limitations thereof.

Preventing OS fingerprinting is only necessary in those cases where malicious reconnaissance is a concern. But also consider the situation where someone's device is already on your network and wishes not to be found, though he has tried and blended in with the rest of the devices on your network, a research for developing effective countermeasures that focus on the possible options and behaviors to watch for about OS fingerprinting is in immediate need. Some possible directions in developing countermeasures against this type of attack include, for example, the OS can mask its timing footprint by randomizing/disturbing the timing of outgoing packets. Perturbing the timing behavior of outgoing packets may have unwanted effects on applications and interactions of users across the network. However, this has to be done carefully for latency sensitive applications, because any perturbing of the timing may lead to a reduction of timing slack, which makes it the more difficult (or even infeasible) to satisfy end-to-end timing requirements. Similarly, it has been shown that such perturbation of timings on TCP packets can cause visible secondary timing footprints caused by end-to-end TCP dynamics and so may be counter-productive.

Appendix A: Detailed Descriptions of Algorithms

Function 1: Feature Extraction

Input: F^{A_p} : The pth spectrum generated by smartphone OS A. P_A denotes the number of traces available for smartphone OS A, and L the number of frequency components

Output: F'^{A_p} : The pth feature-extracted spectrum of smartphone OS A,

$B_{selected}=[b_1, b_2, \ldots, b_L]$: spectrum selection vector where the binary bit b_i indicate whether the ith frequency component is selected

$B_{selected}$ = ga(fitfun, Set_U, Set_V);

```
// We use ga to represent any genetic algorithm and ga
   accepts the definition of the fitness function fitfun and
   outputs values of the variables (in our case the vector
   Bselected) resulting the maximum of the fitness function. The
   fitness function fitfun is defined in Function 2.
```

foreach *spectrum in the input* **do**
    for $i \leftarrow 1$ **to** L **do**
        if $B_i == 1$ **then**
            include the ith frequency component of F^{A_p} in the feature-extracted spectrum F'^{A_p};
        end
    end
end

Function 2: Fitness Function (*fitfun*)

Input: $B_{selected} = [b_1, b_2, \ldots, b_L]$: spectrum selection vector, Set_U: one set of labeled traces, Set_V: set of the remaining labeled traces

Output: $Rate_{Identification}$: Identification Rate

foreach *spectrum F in Set_U* **do**
    for $i \leftarrow 1$ **to** L **do**
        if $b_i == 1$ **then**
            include the ith frequency component of F in the feature-extracted spectrum;
        end
    end
end

foreach *spectrum F in Set_U* **do**
    include the corresponding feature-extracted spectrum F' into F'^{Set_U};
end

success=0;

foreach *spectrum F in Set_V* **do**
    $OStype = OS\ Identification(F'^{Set_U}, F, B_{selected})$;
    if $OStype == u$ **then**
        $success = success + 1$;
    end
end

$Rate_{Identification} = \frac{success}{number\ of\ traces\ in\ Set_V}$;

Acknowledgments This work draws in part from [21, 24, 33]. We would like to thank our co-authors of those works, including Riccardo Bettati, Yong Guan, Jonathan Gurary, Kenneth Johnson, Jeff Kramer, Rudy Libertini, Nicholas Ruffing, and Ye Zhu, as well as reviewers of those original papers who provided us with valuable feedback. This work is supported in part by the U.S. National Science Foundation under grants CNS-1338105, CNS-1343141 and CNS-1527579.

References

1. Anagnostakis, K.G., Greenwald, M., Ryger, R.S.: Cing: measuring network-internal delays using only existing infrastructure. In: INFOCOM 2003. Twenty-Second Annual Joint Conference of the IEEE Computer and Communications. IEEE Societies, vol. 3, pp. 2112–2121. IEEE (2003)
2. Arackaparambil, C., Bratus, S., Shubina, A., Kotz, D.: On the reliability of wireless fingerprinting using clock skews. In: Proceedings of the Third ACM Conference on Wireless Network Security, pp. 169–174. ACM (2010)
3. Arkin, O.: Icmp usage in scanning. Black Hat Briefings (2000)
4. Armitage, G.J.: Inferring the extent of network address port translation at public/private internet boundaries. In: Centre for Advanced Internet Architectures, Swinburne University of Technology, Melbourne, Australia, Tech. Rep. A **20712** (2002)
5. Auffret, P.: Sinfp, unification of active and passive operating system fingerprinting. J. Comput. Virol. **6**(3), 197–205 (2010)
6. Beverly, R.: A robust classifier for passive tcp/ip fingerprinting. In: Passive and Active Network Measurement, pp. 158–167. Springer (2004)
7. Biryukov, A., Pustogarov, I., Weinmann, R.P.: Trawling for tor hidden services: detection, measurement, deanonymization In: Proceedings of IEEE Symposium on Security and Privacy (2013)
8. Bissias, G., Liberatore, M., Jensen, D., Levine, B.: Privacy vulnerabilities in encrypted http streams. In: Danezis, G., Martin, D. (eds.) Privacy Enhancing Technologies, Lecture Notes in Computer Science, vol. 3856, pp. 1–11. Springer, Berlin, Heidelberg (2006). doi:10.1007/11767831_1
9. Cai, X., Zhang, X., Joshi, B., Johnson, R.: Touching from a distance: website fingerprinting attacks and defenses. In: Proceedings of the 19th ACM Conference on Computer and Communications Security (CCS 2012) (2012)
10. Charts, M.: Wifi mobile phone traffic grows. http://www.marketingcharts.com/wp/direct/wifi-mobile-phone-traffic-grows-19604/ (2011)
11. Chen, X., Jin, R., Suh, K., Wang, B., Wei, W.: Network performance of smart mobile handhelds in a university campus wifi network. In: Proceedings of the 2012 ACM Conference on Internet Measurement Conference, pp. 315–328. ACM, New York, NY, USA (2012). doi:10.1145/2398776.2398809
12. Durumeric, Z., Wustrow, E., Halderman, J.A.: Zmap. http://zmap.io/
13. Engebretson, P.: The basics of hacking and penetration testing: ethical hacking and penetration testing made easy. Syngress the basics (2011)
14. Gayle, D.: This is a secure line: the groundbreaking encryption app that will scramble your calls and messages. http://www.dailymail.co.uk/sciencetech/article-2274597/How-foil-eavesdroppers-The-smartphone-encryption-app-promises-make-communications-private-again.html (2013)
15. Gong, X., Borisov, N., Kiyavash, N., Schear, N.: Website detection using remote traffic analysis. In: Proceedings of the 12th Privacy Enhancing Technologies Symposium (PETS 2012). Springer (2012)
16. Greenemeier, L.: Cloud warriors: U.S. army intelligence to arm field ops with hardened network and smartphones. http://www.scientificamerican.com/article.cfm?id=us-army-intelligence-cloud-smartphone (2013)

17. Grimes, S.: App to provide military-level encryption for smartphones. http://www.ksl.com/? nid=1014&sid=22513938 (2012)
18. Herrmann, D., Wendolsky, R., Federrath, H.: Website fingerprinting: attacking popular privacy enhancing technologies with the multinomial naïve-bayes classifier. In: Proceedings of the 2009 ACM Workshop on Cloud Computing Security, pp. 31–42 (2009). http://doi.acm.org/10. 1145/1655008.1655013
19. Huang, J., Xu, Q., Tiwana, B., Mao, Z.M., Zhang, M., Bahl, P.: Anatomizing application performance differences on smartphones. In: Proceedings of the 8th International Conference on Mobile Systems, Applications, and Services, MobiSys '10, pp. 165–178 (2010). doi:10. 1145/1814433.1814452
20. InfoBlox: Infoblox dhcp fingerprinting. https://www.infoblox.com/sites/infobloxcom/files/ resources/infoblox-note-dhcp-fingerprinting.pdf/
21. Johnson, K.: Windows 8 forensics: journey through the impact of the recovery artifacts in windows 8. MS thesis, Lowa State University (2013)
22. Kohno, T., Broido, A., Claffy, K.C.: Remote physical device fingerprinting. IEEE Trans. Dependable Secur. Comput. 2(2), 93–108 (2005)
23. Kollmann, E.: Chatter on the wire: a look at extensive network traffic and what it can mean to network security. http://chatteronthewire.org/download/OS%20Fingerprint.pdf (2005)
24. Kramer, J.: Droidspotter: a forensic tool for android location data collection and analysis. MS thesis, Lowa State University (2013)
25. Liberatore, M., Levine, B.N.: Inferring the source of encrypted HTTP connections. In: Proceedings of the 13th ACM Conference on Computer and Communications Security, pp. 255–263 (2006)
26. Murdoch, S.J.: Hot or not: revealing hidden services by their clock skew. In: Proceedings of CCS 2006 (2006)
27. Netresec.com: Passive os fingerprinting. http://www.netresec.com/?page=Blog&month= 2011-11&post=Passive-OS-Fingerprinting (2011)
28. Nmap.org: Nmap network scanning. http://nmap.org/book/osdetect.html
29. Oppenheim, A.V., Willsky, A.S., Nawab, S.H.: Signals & Systems, 2nd edn. Prentice-Hall Inc., Upper Saddle River, NJ, USA (1996)
30. Øverlier, L., Syverson, P.: Locating hidden servers. In: Proceedings of the 2006 IEEE Symposium on Security and Privacy. IEEE CS (2006)
31. Panchenko, A., Niessen, L., Zinnen, A., Engel, T.: Website fingerprinting in onion routing based anonymization networks. In: Proceedings of the Workshop on Privacy in the Electronic Society (WPES 2011). ACM (2011)
32. Project, H.: Know your enemy: passive fingerprinting. http://old.honeynet.org/papers/finger/ (2002)
33. Ruffing, N., Zhu, Y., Libertini, R., Guan, Y., Bettati, R.: Smartphone reconnaissance: operating system identification. In: 2016 13th IEEE Annual Consumer Communications Networking Conference (CCNC), pp. 1086–1091 (2016). doi:10.1109/CCNC.2016.7444941
34. Sanders, C.: Practical Packet Analysis: Using Wireshark to Solve Real-World Network Problems. No Starch Press (2011)
35. Smart, M., Malan, G.R., Jahanian, F.: Defeating tcp/ip stack fingerprinting. In: Proceedings of the 9th Conference on USENIX Security Symposium, SSYM'00, vol. 9, pp. 17–17. USENIX Association, Berkeley, CA, USA (2000). http://dl.acm.org/citation.cfm?id=1251306.1251323
36. Taleck, G.: Ambiguity resolution via passive os fingerprinting. In: Recent Advances in Intrusion Detection, pp. 192–206. Springer (2003)
37. Tzgkarakis, G., Papadopouli, M., Tsakalides, P.: Singular spectrum analysis of traffic workload in a large-scale wireless lan. In: Proceedings of the 10th ACM Symposium on Modeling, Analysis, and Simulation of Wireless and Mobile Systems, MSWiM '07, pp. 99–108. ACM, New York, NY, USA (2007). doi:10.1145/1298126.1298146
38. Wang, X., Reeves, D.: Robust correlation of encrypted attack traffic through stepping stones by flow watermarking. IEEE Trans. Dependable Secur. Comput. 8(3), 434–449 (2011). doi:10. 1109/TDSC.2010.35

39. Wood, P.: Disco: the passive ip discovery tool. http://www.altmode.com/disco/
40. Wright, C.V., Monrose, F., Masson, G.M.: On inferring application protocol behaviors in encrypted network traffic. J. Mach. Learn. Res. **7**, 2745–2769 (2006). http://dl.acm.org/citation.cfm?id=1248547.1248647
41. Zander, S., Murdoch, S.J.: An improved clock-skew measurement technique for revealing hidden services. In: Proceedings of the 17th USENIX Security Symposium (2008)
42. Zhang, F., He, W., Liu, X., Bridges, P.G.: Inferring users' online activities through traffic analysis. In: Proceedings of the Fourth ACM Conference on Wireless Network Security, WiSec '11, pp. 59–70. ACM, New York, NY, USA (2011). doi:10.1145/1998412.1998425
43. Zhu, Y., Lu, Y., Vikram, A.: On privacy of encrypted speech communications. IEEE Trans. Dependable Secur. Comput. **9**(4), 470–481 (2012). doi:10.1109/TDSC.2011.56

Secure and Trustworthy Provenance Collection for Digital Forensics

Adam Bates, Devin J. Pohly and Kevin R. B. Butler

Abstract Data provenance refers to the establishment of a chain of custody for information that can describe its generation and all subsequent modifications that have led to its current state. Such information can be invaluable for a forensics investigator. The first step to being able to make use of provenance for forensics purposes is to be able to ensure that it is collected in a secure and trustworthy fashion. However, the collection process along raises several significant challenges. In this chapter, we discuss past approaches to provenance collection from application to operating system level, and promote the notion of a *provenance monitor* to assure the complete collection of data. We examine two instantiations of the provenance monitor concept through the Hi-Fi and Linux Provenance Module systems, discussing the details of their design and implementation to demonstrate the complexity of collecting full provenance information. We consider the security of these schemes and raise challenges that future provenance systems must address to be maximally useful for practical forensic use.

1 Introduction

Successful forensics investigations rely on the trustworthiness of data that is retrieved. As a result, the ability to retrieve trustworthy logs and other information that explains where information was generated can be critical to successful inquiries. Such artifacts go part of the way, but not all of the way, towards answering the following question:

A. Bates (✉)
University of Illinois at Urbana-Champaign, Urbana, IL 61801, USA
e-mail: batesa@illinois.edu

D.J. Pohly
Pennsylvania State University, University Park, State College, PA 16801, USA
e-mail: djpohly@cse.psu.edu

K.R.B. Butler
University of Florida, Gainesville, FL 32611, USA
e-mail: butler@cise.ufl.edu

© Springer Science+Business Media New York (outside the USA) 2016
C. Wang et al. (eds.), *Digital Fingerprinting*,
DOI 10.1007/978-1-4939-6601-1_8

141

how can we be assured that the chain of custody for data from the time it was originated until it arrived in its current state is both secure and trustworthy?

Data *provenance* provides a compelling means of providing answers to this challenging problem. The term *provenance* comes from the art world, where it refers to the ability to trace all activities related to an piece of art, in order to establish that is genuine. An example of this usage is with Jan van Eyck's Arnolfini portrait, currently hanging in the National Gallery of London. The provenance of this celebrated portrait can be traced back almost 600 years to its completion in 1432, with metadata in the form of markings associated with its owners painted on the painting's protective shutters helping to establish the hands through which it has passed over the centuries [23].

More recently, data provenance has become a desired feature in the computing world. From its initial deployment in the database community [17] to a more recent focus to its proposed use as an operating systems feature [42], data provenance provides a broad new capability for reasoning about the genesis and subsequent modification of data. In contrast to the current computing paradigm where interactions between system components are largely opaque, data provenance allows users to track, and understand how a piece of data came to exist in its current state. The realization of provenance-aware systems will fundamentally redefine how computing systems are secured and monitored, and will provide important new capabilities to the forensics community. Ensuring its efficacy in a computer system, though, is an extremely challenging problem, to the extent that the Department of Homeland Security has included provenance as one of its Hard Problems in Computing [14]. Ensuring that information is collected in a trustworthy fashion is the first problem that needs to be solved in order to assure the security of provenance. Without adequate protections in place, adversaries can target the collection mechanisms to destroy or tamper with provenance metadata, calling the trustworthiness of data into question or using it in a malicious fashion.

This book chapter focuses on how to ensure the secure and trustworthy collection of data provenance within computing systems. We will discuss past approaches to provenance collection and where and why those fall short, and discuss how taking a systems security approach to defining trustworthy provenance collection can provide a system that fulfills the qualities necessary for a secure implementation. We will then discuss approaches from the research community that have attempted to ensure the fine-grained secure collection of provenance, as well as our own work in this area to provide a platform for deploying secure provenance collection as an operating system service.

2   Provenance-Aware Systems

Data provenance provides the ability to describe the history of a data object, including the conditions that led to its creation and the actions that delivered it to its present state. The potential applications for this kind of information are virtually limitless;

provenance is of use in any scenario where a context-sensitive decision needs to be made about a piece of data. Specifically, provenance can be used to answer a variety of historical questions about the data it describes. Such questions include, but are not limited to, *"What processes and datasets were used to generate this data?"* and *"In what environment was the data produced?"* Conversely, provenance can also answer questions about the successors of a piece of data, such as *"What objects on the system were derived from this object?"*

A necessary prerequisite to the use of data provenance is its reliable capture and management, which is facilitated by provenance-aware software systems. Provenance capture mechanisms can be deployed at various layers of system operation, including applications, middleware, and operating systems. They can broadly be grouped into two categories: *disclosed* and *automatic*. In disclosed systems, provenance is recorded based on manual annotations created by the operator, while in automatic systems, software is instrumented to automatically generate and record lineage information.

2.1 Disclosed Provenance-Aware Systems

The earliest efforts in provenance tracking arose from the scientific processing and database management communities. While the potential use cases for data provenance have broadened in scope over time, early investigators aims were to maintain virtual data descriptions that would allow them to explain data processing results and re-constitute those results in the event of their deletion. One of the earliest efforts in this space was Chimera [17], which provided a virtual data management system that allowed for tracking the derivations of data through computational procedures. Chimera is made up of a *virtual data catalog* that represents computation procedures used to derive data and a *virtual data language interpreter* for constructing and querying the catalog. It uses transformation procedures (i.e., processes) as its integral unit; its database is made up of *transformations* that represent executable programs and *derivations* that represent invocations of transformations. All other information (e.g., input files, output files, execution environment) are a subfield in the process' entry.

The Earth Science System Workbench, used for processing satellite imagery, also offered support for provenance annotations [18], as did the Collaboratory for the Multi-scale Chemical Sciences [46] and the Kepler system [41]. Specification-based approaches, which generated data provenance based on process documentation [40] also appeared in the literature at this time. Chimera and other early systems relied on manual annotations or inferences from other metadata as sources for data provenance, and are therefore referred to as *disclosed* provenance-aware systems.

2.2 Automatic Provenance-Aware Systems

Automatic provenance-aware systems can be further divided into several categories based on software layer at which provenance collection occurs. We now consider past proposals for provenance at different operational layers, and identify the opportunities and challenges of each approach. We focus in this discussion on applications operating system mechanisms to support provenance.

2.2.1 Automatic Provenance in Operating Systems

Capturing data provenance at the operating system layer offers a broad perspective into system activities, providing insight into all applications running on the host. Muniswamy-Reddy et al.'s Provenance-Aware Storage System (PASS) instruments the VFS layer of the Linux kernel to automatically collect, maintain, and provide search for data provenance [42]. PASS defines provenance as a description of the execution history that produced a persistent object (file). Provenance records are attribute/value pairs that are referenced by a unique pond number. PASS provenance is facilitate a variety of useful tasks, including script generation and document reproduction, detecting system changes, intrusion detection, retrieving compile-time flags, build debugging, and understanding system dependencies. One limitation of the PASS system is that the model for provenance collection was fixed, and did not provide a means of extending the system with additional provenance attributes or alternate storage models.

Gehani and Tariq present SPADE in response to requests for coarser-grained information and the the ability to experiment with different provenance attributes, novel storage and indexing models, and handling provenance from diverse sources [21]. SPADE is a java-based daemon that offers provenance *reporter* modules for Windows, Linux, OSX, and Android. The reporters are based on a variety of methods of inference, including polling of basic user space utilities (e.g., *ps* for process info, *lsof* for network info), audit log systems (e.g., Window's ETW, OSX's BSM), and interposition via user space file systems like FUSE. Due to its modular design, SPADE can be easily extended to support additional provenance streams.

Both the PASS and SPADE systems facilitate provenance collection through ad hoc instrumentation or polling efforts, making it difficult to provide any assurance of the *completeness* of the provenance that they collect. In fact, there are several examples of how these systems fail to provide adequate tracking for explicit data flows through a system. As SPADE records provenance in part through periodic polling of system utilities, there exists the potential for race conditions in which short-lived processes or messages could be successfully created between polling intervals. By observing the VFS layer, PASS provides support for non-persistent data, such as network sockets which are represented by a system file; however, it fails to track a variety of forms of interprocess communication, such as signals or shared memory, which provides a covert channel for communicating applications.

2.2.2 Automatic Provenance in Middleware

The earliest disclosed provenance-aware systems were proposed for middleware, such as Chimera [17] and the Earth Science System Workbench [18]. Today, automatic provenance-aware middleware continues to be one of the most widespread and impactful forms of provenance capability. Tools such as VisTrails [54], which tracks the provenance of scientific visualizations, have established themselves as viable platforms in scientific computing communities. By instrumenting a common computing platform within a community, such as a database management system or scientific computing engine, provenance-aware middleware provides easy access to semantically rich, domain specific provenance metadata.

Propagating lineage information as datasets are fused and transformed is one of the strongest motivations for provenance capabilities. Chiticariu et al.'s DBNotes provides a "post-It note" system for relational data in which annotations are propagated based on lineage [12]. DBNotes provides a SQL extension (pSQL) that allows one to specify how provenance annotations should propagate through a SQL query. pSQL also allows annotations to be queried inline with other relational data. DBNotes also has a visualization feature that demonstrates the *journey* taken by a piece of data through various databases and transformation steps. In related work, Holland et al. [26, 43] present PQL, another query model for data provenance provides a semistructured data and query model for the graph-centric nature of provenance. By extending the Lowel query language to support bidirectional edge traversal and more expressive attributes, PQL compares favorably due to alternate models for provenance querying as relational languages cannot efficiently encode graphs, nor can tree-based structures like XML.

While both of these systems require users to adopt a new query language, Glavic and Alonso [22] present PERM (Provenance Extension of the Relational Model), a system that uses query rewriting to annotate result tuples with provenance information, permitting provenance to be queried, stored, and optimized using standard relational database techniques without impacting normal database operations. Given a query q, Perm creates q^+ that produces the same result as q but extended with additional attributes. Through using standard relational models, PERM offers support for more sophisticated queries than other provenance-aware databases, and outperforms the Trio system by at least a factor of 30.

2.2.3 Automatic Provenance in Applications

Manual instrumentation of applications offers concise and semantically rich data provenance. Several development libraries have appeared in the literature to aid in instrumentation efforts, providing a standardized API through which to emit data provenance. Muniswamy-Reddy et al.'s *Disclosed Provenance API (DPAPI)* [43] and Macko and Seltzer's *Core Provenance Library (CPL)* [37] provide portable, multi-lingual libraries that application programmers could use to disclose provenance by defining provenance objects and describing the flows between those objects. CPL offers the advantages of avoiding version disconnect between files that are seemingly distinct to the operating system but are actually ancestors, integration between different provenance-aware applications due to a look-up function in the API, and reconciling different notions of provenance in a unified format.

DPAPI is a component of the PASSv2 project [43]. It's intended purpose is to create provenance-aware applications whose provenance can be layered on top of information collected by the PASS system, allowing system operators to reason holistically about activities at multiple system layers. Several exemplar applications for provenance layering as part of this effort: Kepler, Lynx, and a set of general-purpose Python wrappers. Similarly, the SPADE system offers support for provenance layering by exposing a named pipe and generic domain-specific language for application layer provenance disclosure [21].

Other work has sought out alternate deployment model to create provenance-aware applications at a lower cost and without developer cooperation. Hassan et al. present Sprov, a modified version of the `stdio` library that captures provenance for file I/O system calls at the application layer. By replacing the `glibc` library with the modified version, Sprov is able to record file provenance for all dynamically linked applications on the system. This system also provides integrity for provenance records through the introduction of a tamper-evident *provenance chain* primitive. By cryptographically binding time-ordered sequences of provenance records together for a given document, Sprov is able to prevent undetected rewrites of the document's history.

Recent efforts have also attempted to reconstitute application workflow provenance through analysis of system layer audit logs, requiring only minimally invasive and automated transformation of the monitored application. A significant consequence of provenance tracking at the operating system layer is *dependency explosion*—for long-lived processes, each new output from an application must conservatively be assumed to have been derived from all prior inputs, creating *false provenance*. The BEEP systems resolves this problem through analysis and transformation of binary executables [32]. Leveraging the insight that most long-lived processes are made up of an initialization phase, main work loop, and tear-down phase, BEEP procedurally identifies the main work loop in order to decompose the process into autonomous units of work. After this *execution partitioning (EP)* step, the system audit log can then be analyzed to build causal provenance graphs for the monitored applications. Ma et al. go on to adapt these techniques Windows and other proprietary software [35], where EP can be performed by perform regular expression analysis of audit logs in order to identify autonomous units of work. The LogGC system extends BEEP by introducing a garbage collection filtering mechanism to improve the forensic clarity of the causal graphs [33]; for example, if a process creates and makes use of a short-lived temporary file that no other process ever reads, this node contains no semantic value in the causal graph, and can therefore be pruned. These techniques should be able to be applied in tandem with Chapman et al.'s provenance factorization techniques that find common subtrees and manipulate them to reduce the provenance size [11]. Although these systems do not modify the operating system, by operating at the system call or audit logs levels, Sprov, LogGC, and BEEP provide provenance at a similar granularity to that of provenance-aware operating systems; they offer only limited insight into application layer semantics.

3   Ensuring the Trustworthiness of Provenance

Data provenance has proven to be of tremendous value in addressing a variety of security challenges. Provenance is most commonly employed as a forensic tool for performing offline event attribution. Pohly et al. [48], Ma et al. [36], and Lee et al. [32, 33] all demonstrate that their provenance-aware systems can be used to diagnose system intrusions such as malware and data exfiltration. Jones et al. [28] propose a technique to use provenance to aid in determining potential sources of information leaks. When a removable storage device or network connection is opened by a provenance-aware host, a "ghost object" is created representing the device. Files which are read by the user during the session are added as inputs to the ghost object. The ghost object is annotated with information to make it later identifiable, including device ID, user ID, process ID, and remote network information. If a leak occurs, the ghost objects (i.e.,"transient provenance") can be used to limit the list of potential culprits.

In other work, data provenance has been shown to be a promising means of enforcing and verifying the realtime security of computer systems. Provenance-based access control schemes (PBAC) have been presented that leverage richer contextual information than traditional MAC labels [44, 45, 47]. By inspecting the ancestry of a data object, it is possibly to dynamically infer its present security context before applying an access control rule. A provenance-based approach provides a general method for handling arbitrary data fusions, obviating the need to exhaustively enumerate transitions between security contexts. Provenance has similarly been considered in mechanisms for facilitating regulatory compliance. Aldeco-Pérez and Moreau present a methodology for incorporating provenance into applications during their design such that they satisfy the auditing requirements of the UK Data Protection Act [1]. Bates et al. consider the challenges of managing data provenance between cloud deployments [2], and present a general distributed mechanism for the enforcement of regulatory policies such as ITAR [60] and HIPAA [10].

3.1   Security Challenges to Provenance Collection

Unfortunately, while the above work has shown that provenance is an invaluable capability when securing systems, less attention has been given to *securing* provenance-aware systems. Provenance itself is a ripe attack vector; adversaries may seek to tamper with provenance to hide evidence of their misdeeds, or to subvert another system component that uses provenance as an input. In light of this realization, it becomes clear that the integrity, authenticity, and completeness of provenance must be guaranteed before it can be put to use.

When provenance collection occurs in user-space, either through software or middleware, an implicit decision is made to fully trust user space applications. However, in a malicious environment, there is likely to be exploitable software bugs in provenance-aware applications that handle untrusted inputs. An attacker in control of a compromised application could instruct it to disclose false provenance about its activities, or simply disable the mechanism responsible for provenance collection altogether. Examples of such vulnerabilities abound in the systems surveyed above. An attacker with root privilege could terminate the SPADE collection daemon [21] or modify environment variables to prevent Sprov from being linked [24]. In spite of the fact that BEEP and LogGC are intended to aid in Advanced Persistent Threat (APT) detection, a compromised application could violate BEEP's EP assumptions in order to cast doubt onto other system users [32, 33]. Due to the confinement problem that persists in commodity operating systems [31], extraordinary lengths would need to be taken to harden these systems from attack. As a result, the provenance collected by these mechanisms is only suitable for benign operating environments.

Capturing data provenance within the operating system is a more promising direction for secure data provenance under a realistic threat model. While PASS was designed for benign environments [8], its approach of instrumenting the kernel for provenance collection creates an opportunity to insulate the provenance capture agent from the dangers of user space. Hardening the kernel against attack, while a difficult problem, can be achieved through use of Mandatory Access Control (MAC) mechanisms and other trusted computing techniques. Unfortunately, as PASS instruments the VFS layer [42], it is unable to monitor a variety of explicit data flows within the system, such as shared memory and other forms of interprocess communication. Moreover, PASSv2, which supports layered provenance, does not have a defense against the untrustworthy provenance-aware applications discussed above. The efficient ProTracer system suffers from many of the same problems. While it records provenance outside of the file system, its instrumentation of the kernel is ad hoc and unverified, making it possible that explicit data flows are left unmonitored [36]. ProTracer also places trust in user space applications during a training phase that provides EP; like BEEP, this assumption could be violated by an active attacker, injecting uncertainty into the provenance record.

In response to these issues, and to facilitate data provenance's use in other security-critical tasks, concurrent work in 2010 began to advocate for the union of data provenance and trusted computing. Lyle and Martin [34] argue that trusted computing is useful and immediately applicable to the provenance domain. They sketch a service-oriented architecture that uses Trusted Platform Module (TPM) attestations to track the provenance of jobs in a smart grid. When a node receives a job, it hashes the job into one of the TPM's Platform Configuration Registers (PCRs) and extends the PCR with the hased result upon finishing the job. It then sends a full attestation up to and including the job result to a provenance store. This allows the grid to later produce a non-repudiable assertion of the software and hardware stack that produced the result.

However, Lyle and Martin's proposal did not describe a complete provenance-aware operating system, as provenance proofs did not describe configuration files, environment variables, generated code, and load information, nor can this system explain *who* accessed a piece of data.

3.2   The Provenance Monitor Concept

To address the challenges discussed above, McDaniel et al. [38] developed the concept of a *provenance monitor*, where provenance authorities accept host-level provenance data from validated monitors to assemble a trustworthy provenance record. Subsequent users of the data obtain a provenance record that identifies not only the inputs, systems, and applications leading to a data item, but also evidence of the identity and validity of the recording instruments that observed its evolution. At the host level, the provenance monitor acts as the recording instrument that observes the operation of a system and securely records each data manipulation. The concept for a provenance monitor is based on the *reference monitor* proposed by Anderson (cite), which has become a cornerstone for evaluating systems security. The two concepts share the following three fundamental properties.

The host level provenance monitor should enforce the classic reference monitor guarantees of complete mediation of relevant operations, tamper-proofness of the monitor itself, and basic verification of correct operation. For the purpose of the provenance monitor, we define these as follows.

- **Complete Mediation**. A provenance monitor should *mediate* all provenance-relevant operations, whatever these may be for a given application. In other words, there should be no way by which the provenance monitor can be bypassed if an event is provenance-sensitive.
- **Tamperproof**. The provenance monitor must be isolated from the subjects operating on provenance-enhanced data, e.g. the OS kernel or storage device, and there should be no means by which the monitor can be modified or disabled by the activities of users on a system.
- **Verifiable**. Finally, the provenance monitor should be designed to allow for simple verification of its behavior, and optimally should be subject to formal verification to assure its trustworthy operation.

The provenance monitor provides powerful guarantees for the secure and trustworthy collection of provenance. However, while the idea is seemingly simple in concept, its execution requires considerable design and implementation considerations. As we have seen above, a large amount of provenance related proposals, while pushing forth novel functionality and advancing the state of research, do not pass the provenance monitor criteria. Complete mediation and tamperproofness cannot be guaranteed if the mechanisms used to collect provenance are subject to compromise, and collecting sufficiently fine-grained provenance to ensure complete mediation is a challenge unaddressed by other systems discussed. The next two sections discuss recent attempts to satisfy the provenance monitor concept and detail the challenges and design decisions made to assure a practical and functional collection system.

4 High-Fidelity Whole Systems Provenance

As we described in the previous section, for a data provenance system to provide the holistic view of system operation required for such forensic applications, it must be complete and faithful to actual events. This property, which we call "fidelity," is necessary for drawing valid conclusions about system security. A missing entry in the provenance record could sever an important information flow, while a spurious entry could falsely implicate an innocuous process. The provenance monitor concept provides a strong conceptual framework for achieving trustworthy proenance collection. In particular, this mechanism must provide complete mediation for events which should appear in the record.

Forensic investigation requires a definition of provenance which is broader than just file metadata. What is needed is a record of *whole-system provenance* which retains actions of processes, IPC mechanisms, and even the kernel. These "transient" system objects can be meaningful even without being an ancestor of any "persistent" object. The command-and-control daemon on Alice's server, for example, was significant because it was a *descendant* of the compromised process. If the provenance system had deemed it unworthy of inclusion in the record, she could not have traced the outgoing connections to the compromise.

To address these issues, Pohly et al. developed the Hi-Fi provenance system, designed to collect high-fidelity whole-system provenance. Hi-Fi was the first provenance system to collect a *complete* provenance record from early kernel initialization through system shutdown. Unlike existing provenance systems, it accounts for all kernel actions as well as application actions. Hi-Fi also collects *socket provenance*, creating a system-level provenance record that spans multiple hosts.

4.1 Design of Hi-Fi

Hi-Fi consists of three components: the provenance collector, the provenance log, and the provenance handler. An important difference between Hi-Fi and previous work is that rather than collecting events at the file system level, Hi-Fi ensures complete mediation by collecting events as a Linux Security Module (LSM) (cite). Because the collector is an LSM, it resides below the application layer in the operating system's kernel space, and is notified whenever a kernel object access is about to take place. When invoked, the collector constructs an entry describing the action and writes it to the provenance log. The log is a buffer which presents these entries to userspace as a file. The provenance handler can then access this file using the standard file API, process it, and store the provenance record. The handler used in our experiments simply copies the log data to a file on disk, but it is possible to implement a custom handler for any purpose, such as post-processing, graphical analysis, or storage on a remote host.

Such a construction allows for a far more robust adversarial model. Hi-Fi maintains the fidelity of provenance collection regardless of any compromise of the OS user space by an adversary. This is a strictly stronger guarantee than those provided by any previous system-level provenance collection system. Compromises are possible against the kernel, but other techniques for protecting kernel integrity, including disk-level versioning [57] or a strong write-once read-many (WORM) storage system [55], can mitigate the effects of such compromises. Because provenance never changes after being written, a storage system with strong WORM guarantees is particularly well-suited to this task. For socket provenance, Hi-Fi guarantees that incoming data will be recorded accurately; to prevent on-the-wire tampering by an adversary, standard end-to-end protection such as IPsec should be used.

The responsibility of the provenance handler is to interpret, process, and store the provenance data after it is collected, and it should be flexible enough to support different needs. Hi-Fi decouples provenance handling from the collection process, allowing the handler to be implemented according to the system's needs.

For the purposes of recording provenance, each object which can appear in the log must be assigned an identifier which is unique for the lifetime of that object. Some objects, such as inodes, are already assigned a suitable identifier by the kernel. Others, such as sockets, require special treatment. For the rest, Hi-Fi generates a *provid*, a small integer which is reserved for the object until it is destroyed. These provids are managed in the same way as process identifiers to ensure that two objects cannot simultaneously have the same provid.

4.2 Handling of System-Level Objects

Collecting system-level provenance requires a clear model of system-level objects. For each object, Hi-Fi must first describe how data flows into, out of, and through it. Next, the LSM hooks for mediating data-manipulating objects must be identified (as listed in Table 1), or new hooks are placed if existing ones are insufficient.

Each entry in the provenance log describes a single action on a kernel object. This includes the type of action, the subject, the object, and any appropriate context.

The data-flow model includes transferring data between multiple systems or multiple boots of a system. Hi-fi must therefore identify each boot separately. To ensure that these identifiers do not collide, a random UUID is created at boot time, which is written to the provenance log so that subsequent events can be associated with the system on which they occur.

Within a Linux system, the only actors are processes (including threads), and the kernel. These actors store and manipulate data in their respective address spaces, and we treat them as black boxes for the purpose of provenance collection. Most data

Table 1 LSM hooks used to collect provenance in Hi-Fi

Kernel object	LSM hook
Inode	`inode_init_security`
	`inode_free_security`
	`inode_link`
	`inode_unlink`
	`inode_rename`
	`inode_setattr`
	`inode_readlink`
	`inode_permission`
Open file	`file_mmap`
	`file_permission`
Program	`bprm_check_security`
	`bprm_committing_creds`
Credential	`cred_prepare`
	`cred_free`
	`cred_transfer`
	`task_fix_setuid`
Socket	`socket_sendmsg`
	`socket_post_recvmsg`
	`socket_sock_rcv_skb`
	`socket_dgram_append`
	`socket_dgram_post_recv`
	`unix_may_send`
Message queue	`msg_queue_msgsnd`
	`msg_queue_msgrcv`
Shared memory	`shm_shmat`

flows between processes use one of the objects described in subsequent sections. However, several actions are specific to processes: forking, program execution, and changing subjective credentials.

Since LSM is designed to include kernel actions, it does not represent actors using a PID or `task_struct` structure. Instead, LSM hooks receive a `cred` structure, which holds the user and group credentials associated with a process or kernel action. Whenever a process is forked or new credentials are applied, a new credential structure is created, allowing us to use these structures to represent individual system actors. As there is no identifier associated with these `cred` structures, we generate a provid to identify them.

Regular files are the simplest and most common means of storing data and sharing it between processes. Data enters a file when a process writes to it, and a copy of this data leaves the file when a process reads from it. Both reads and writes are mediated by a single LSM hook, which identifies the the actor, the open file descriptor, and whether the action is a read or a write. Logging file operations is then straightforward.

Choosing identifiers for files, however, requires considering that files differ from other system objects in that they are persistent, not only across reboots of a single system, but also across systems (like a file on a portable USB drive). Because of this, it must be possible to uniquely identify a file independent of any running system. In this case, already-existing identifiers can be used rather than generating new ones. Each file has an inode number which is unique within its filesystem, which can be combined with a UUID that identifies the filesystem itself to obtain a suitable identifier that will not change for the lifetime of the file. UUIDs are generated for most filesystems at creation.

Files can also be mapped into one or more processes' address spaces, where they are used directly through memory accesses. This differs significantly from normal reading and writing in that the kernel does not mediate accesses once the mapping is established. Hi-Fi only records the mapping when it occurs, along with the requested access mode (read, write, or both). This does not affect the notion of complete mediation if it is assumed that flows via memory-mapped files take place whenever possible.

Shared memory segments are managed and interpreted in the same way. POSIX shared memory is implemented using memory mapping, so it behaves as described above. XSI shared memory, though managed using different system calls and mediated by a different LSM hook, also behaves the same way, so our model treats them identically. In fact, since shared memory segments are implemented as files in a temporary filesystem, their identifiers can be chosen in the same way as file identifiers.

The remaining objects have stream or message semantics, and they are accessed sequentially. In these objects, data is stored in a queue by the writer and retrieved by the reader. The simplest such object is the pipe, or FIFO. Pipes have stream semantics and, like files, they are accessed using the read and write system calls. Since a pipe can have multiple writers or readers, it cannot be directly represented as a flow from one process to another. Instead, flow is split into two parts, modeling the data queue as an independent file-like object. In this way, a pipe behaves like a sequentially-accessed regular file. In fact, since named pipes are inodes within a regular filesystem, and unnamed pipes are inodes in the kernel's "pipefs" pseudo-filesystem, pipe identifiers can be chosed similarly to files.

Message queues are similar to pipes, with two major semantic differences: the data is organized into discrete messages instead of a single stream, and these messages can be delivered in a different order than that in which they are sent. However, because LSM handles messages individually, a unique identifier can be created for each, allowing reliable identification of which process receives the message regardless of the order in which the messages are dequeued. Since individual messages have no natural identifier, a provid is generated for each.

Sockets are the most complex form of inter-process communication handled by Hi-Fi but can be modeled very simply. As with pipes, a socket's receive queue can be represented an intermediary file between the sender and receiver. Sending data merely requires writing to this queue, and receiving data is reading from it. The details of network transfer are hidden by the socket abstraction. Stream sockets provide the simplest semantics with respect to data flow: they behave identically to pipes. Since stream sockets are necessarily connection-mode, all of the data sent over a stream socket will arrive in the same receive queue. Message-oriented sockets, on the other hand, do not necessarily have the same guarantees. They may be connection-mode or connectionless, reliable or unreliable, ordered or unordered. Each packet therefore needs a separate identifier, since it is unclear at which endpoint the message will arrive.

Socket identifiers must be chosen carefully. An identifier must never be re-used since since a datagram can have an arbitrarily long lifetime. The identifier should also be associated with the originating host. Associating messages with a per-boot UUID addresses these requirements. By combining this UUID with an atomic counter, a sufficiently large number of identifiers can be generated.

4.3   Hi-Fi Implementation

Provenance Logging. As noted in Sect. 2, provenance collection has been noted to generate a large volume of data. Because of this, an efficient and reliable mechanism for making large quantities of kernel data available to user space is necessary. Other systems have accomplished this by using an expanded `printk` buffer [52], writing directly to on-disk log files [43], or using FUSE [56]. Each of these approaches has drawbacks, so Hi-Fi instead uses a Linux kernel object known as a *relay,* which is designed specifically to address this problem [63].

A relay is a kernel ring buffer made up of a set of preallocated sub-buffers. Once the relay has been initialized, the collector writes provenance data to it using the `relay_write` function. This data will appear in userspace as a regular file, which can be read by the provenance handler. Since the relay is backed by a buffer, it retains provenance data even when the handler is not running, as is the case during boot, or if the handler crashes and must be restarted. Since the number and size of the sub-buffers in the relay are specified when it is created, the relay has a fixed size. Although the collector can act accordingly if it is about to overwrite provenance which has not yet been processed by the handler, a better solution is allowing the relay's size parameters to be specified at boot time.

Early Boot Provenance. The Linux kernel's boot-time initialization process consists of setting up a number of subsystems in sequence. One of these subsystems is the VFS subsystem, which is responsible for managing filesystem operations and the kernel's in-memory filesystem caches. These caches are allocated as a part of VFS initialization. They are then used to cache filesystem information from disk, as well as to implement memory-backed "pseudo-filesystems" such as those used for pipes, anonymous memory mappings, temporary files, and relays.

The security subsystem, which loads and registers an LSM, is another part of this start-up sequence. This subsystem is initialized as early as possible, so that boot events are also subject to LSM mediation. In fact, the LSM is initialized *before* the VFS, which has a peculiar consequence for the relay we use to implement the provenance log. Since filesystem caches have not yet been allocated, the relay cannot be created when the LSM is initialized, which violated Hi-Fi's goal of fidelity. In response, Hi-Fi separates relay creation from the rest of the module's initialization and registers it as a callback in the kernel's generic `initcall` system. This allows it to be delayed until after the core subsystems such as VFS have been initialized. In the meantime, provenance data is stored in a small temporary buffer. Inspection of this early boot provenance reveals that a one-kilobyte buffer is sufficiently large to hold the provenance generated by the kernel during this period. Once the relay is created, temporary boot-provenance buffer is flushed of its contents and freed.

OS Integration. One important aspect of Hi-Fi's design is that the provenance handler must be kept running to consume provenance data as it is written to the log. Since the relay is backed by a buffer, it can retain a certain amount of data if the handler is inactive or happens to crash. It is important, though, that the handler is restarted in this case. Fortunately, this is a feature provided by the operating system's `init` process. By editing the configuration in `/etc/inittab`, we can specify that the handler should be started automatically at boot, as well as respawned if it should ever crash.

Provenance must also be collected and retained for as much of the operating system's shutdown process as possible. At shutdown time, the `init` process takes control of the system and executes a series of actions from a shutdown script. This script asks processes to terminate, forcefully terminates those which do not exit gracefully, unmounts filesystems, and eventually powers the system off. Since the provenance handler is a regular user space process, it is subject to this shutdown procedure as well. However, there is no particular order in which processes are terminated during the shutdown sequence, so it is possible that another process may outlive the handler and perform actions which generate provenance data.

In response, Hi-Fi handles the shutdown process similarly to a system crash. The provenance handler must be restarted, and this is accomplished by modifying the shutdown script to re-execute the handler after all other processes have been terminated before filesystems are unmounted. This special case requires a "one-shot" mode in the handler which, instead of forking to the background, exits after handling the data currently in the log. This allows it to handle any remaining shutdown provenance, then returns control to `init` to complete the shutdown process.

Bootstrapping Filesystem Provenance. Intuitively, a complete provenance record contains enough information to recreate the structure of an entire filesystem. This requires three things: a list of inodes, filesystem metadata for each inode, and a list of hard links (filenames) for each inode. Hi-Fi includes a hook corresponding to each of these items, to ensure all information appears in the provenance record starting from an empty filesystem. However, this is difficult to do in practice, as items may have been used elsewhere or provenance may be collected on an existing, populated filesystem. Furthermore, it is actually impossible to start with an empty filesystem. Without a root inode, which is created by the corresponding `mkfs` program, a filesystem cannot even be mounted. Unfortunately, mkfs does this by writing directly to a block device file, which does not generate the expected provenance data.

Therefore, provenance must be bootstrapped on a populated filesystem. To have a complete record for each file, a creation event for any pre-existing inodes must be generated. Hi-Fi implements a utility called pbang (for "provenance Big Bang") which does this by traversing the filesystem tree. For each new inode it encounters, it outputs an allocation entry for the inode, a metadata entry containing its attributes, and a link entry containing its filename and directory. For previously encountered inodes, it only outputs a new link entry. All of these entries are written to a file to complete the provenance record. A new filesystem is normally created using mkfs, then made provenance-aware by executing pbang immediately afterward.

Opaque Provenance. Early versions of Hi-Fi generated continuous streams of provenance even when no data was to be collected. Inspection of the provenance record showed that this data described the actions of the provenance handler itself. The handler would call the read function to retrieve data from the provenance log, which then triggered the file_permission LSM hook. The collector would record this action in the log, where the handler would again read it, triggering file_permission, and so on, creating a large amount of "feedback" in the provenance record. While technically correct behavior, this floods the provenance record with data which does not provide any additional insight into the system's operation. One option for solving this problem is to make the handler completely exempt from provenance collection. However, this could interfere with filesystem reconstruction. Instead, the handler is *provenance-opaque*, treated as a black box which only generates provenance data if it makes any significant changes to the filesystem.

To achieve this Hi-Fi informs the LSM which process is the provenance handler, by leveraging the LSM framework's integration with extended filesystem attributes. The provenance handler program is identified by setting an attribute called security.hifi. The "security" attribute namespace, which is reserved for attributes used by security modules, is protected from tampering by malicious users. When the program is executed, the bprm_check_security hook examines this property for the value "opaque" and sets a flag in the process's credentials indicating that it should be treated accordingly. In order to allow the handler to create new processes without reintroducing the original problem—for instance, if the handler is a shell script—this flag is propagated to any new credentials that the process creates.

Socket Provenance. Network socket behavior is designed to be both transparent and incrementally deployable. To allow interoperability with existing non-provenanced hosts, packet identifiers are placed in the IP Options header field. Two Netfilter hooks process packets at the network layer. The outgoing hook labels each packet with the correct identifier just before it encounters a routing decision, and the incoming hook reads this label just after the receiver decides the packet should be handled locally. Note that even packets sent to the loopback address will encounter both of these hooks.

In designing the log entries for socket provenance, Hi-Fi aims to make the reconstruction of information flows from multiple system logs as simple as possible. When the sender and receiver are on the same host, these entries should behave the same as reads and writes. When they are on different hosts, the only added requirement should be a partial ordering placing each send before all of its corresponding receives. Lamport clocks [30] would satisfy this requirement. However, the `socket_recvmsg` hook, which was designed for access control, executes before a process attempts to receive a message. This may occur before the corresponding `socket_sendmsg` hook is executed. To solve this, a `socket_post_recvmsg` hook is placed after the message arrives and before it is returned to the receiver; this hook generates the entry for receiving a message.

Support for TCP and UDP sockets is necessary to demonstrate provenance for both connection-mode and connectionless sockets, as well as both stream and message-oriented sockets. Support for the other protocols and pseudo-protocols in the Linux IP stack, such as SCTP, ping, and raw sockets, can be implemented using similar techniques. For example, SCTP is a sequential packet protocol, which has connection-mode and message semantics.

TCP Sockets. TCP and other connection-mode sockets are complicated in that a connection involves three different sockets: the client socket, the listening server socket, and the server socket for an accepted connection. The first two are created in the same way as any other socket on the system: using the `socket` function, which calls the `socket_create` and `socket_post_create` LSM hooks. However, sockets for an accepted connection on the server side are created by a different sequence of events. When a listening socket receives a connection request, it creates a "mini-socket" instead of a full socket to handle the request. If the client completes the handshake, a new child socket is cloned from the listening socket, and the relevant information from the mini-socket (including our IP options) is copied into the child. In terms of LSM hooks, the `inet_conn_request` hook is called when a mini-socket is created, and the `inet_csk_clone` hook is called when it is converted into a full socket. On the client side, the `inet_conn_established` hook is called when the SYN+ACK packet is received from the server.

Hi-Fi must treat the TCP handshake with care, since there are two different sockets participating on the server side. A unique identifier is created for the mini-socket in the `inet_conn_request` hook, and this identifier is later copied directly into the child socket. The client must then be certain to remember the correct identifier, namely, the one associated with the child socket. The first packet that the client receives (the SYN+ACK) will carry the IP options from the listening parent socket. To keep this from overriding the child socket, the `inet_conn_established` hook clears the saved identifier so that it is later replaced by the correct one.

UDP Sockets. Since UDP sockets are connectionless, we an LSM hook must assign a different identifier to each datagram. In addition, this hook must run in process context to record the identifier of the process which is sending or receiving. The only existing LSM socket hook with datagram granularity is the `sock_rcv_skb` hook, but it is run as part of an interrupt when a datagram arrives, not in process context. The remaining LSM hooks are placed with socket granularity; therefore, two additional hooks are placed to mediate datagram communication. If the file descriptor of the receiving socket is shared between processes, they can all receive the same datagram by using the MSG_PEEK flag. In fact, multiple processes can also contribute data when *sending* a single datagram by using the MSG_MORE flag or the UDP_CORK socket option. Because of this, placing send and receive hooks for UDP is a very subtle task.

Since each datagram is considered to be an independent entity, the crucial points to mediate are the addition of data to the datagram and the reading of data from it. The Linux IP implementation includes a function which is called from process context to append data to an outgoing socket buffer. This function is called each time a process adds data to a corked datagram, as well as in the normal case where a single process constructs a datagram and immediately sends it. This makes it an ideal candidate for the placement of the send hook, which we call socket_dgram_append. Since this hook is placed in network-layer code, it can be applied to any message-oriented protocol and not just UDP.

The receive hook is placed in protocol-agnostic code, for similar flexibility. The core networking code provides a function which retrieves the next datagram from a socket's receive queue. UDP and other message-oriented protocols use this function when receiving, and it is called once for each process that receives a given datagram. This is an ideal location for the message-oriented receive hook, so the socket_dgram_post_recv hook is placed in this function.

4.4   Limitations of Hi-Fi

Hi-Fi represents a significant step forward in provenance collection, being the first system to consider design with regard to the provenance monitor concept. The complexity of design and implmentation attest to the goals of complete mediation of provenance. However, it fails to address other security challenges identified in this chapter.

Hi-Fi does not completely satisfy the provenance monitor concept; enabling Hi-Fi blocks the installation of other LSM's, such as SELinux or Tomoyo, effectively preventing the installation of a mandatory access control (MAC) policy that could otherwise be used to protect the kernel. This leaves the entire system, including Hi-Fi's trusted computing base, vulnerable to attack, and Hi-Fi is therefore not tamperproof. Hi-Fi is also vulnerable to network attacks. Hi-Fi embeds an identifier into each IP packet transmitted by the host, which the recipient host to later use the identify to query the sender for the provenance of the packet. However, because these identifiers are not cryptographically secured, an attacker in the network can strip the provenance identifiers off of packets in transit, violating the forensic validity of Hi-Fi's provenance in distributed environments. Finally, Hi-Fi does not provide support for provenance-aware applications. Provenance layering is vital to obtaining a comprehensive view of system activity; however, rather than providing an insecure disclosure mechanism like PASSv2 [43], Hi-Fi does not offer layering support at all, meaning that its provenance is not complete in its observations of relevant operations.

5 Linux Provenance Modules

As we have shown in this chapter, the application of data provenance is presently of enormous interest at different scopes and levels in a variety of disparate communities including scientific data processing, databases, software development, storage [42, 52], operating systems [48], access controls [44, 47], and distributed systems [2, 65, 66]. In spite of many proposed models and frameworks, mainstream operating systems still lack support for provenance collection and reporting. This may be due to the fact that the community has yet to reach a consensus on how to best prototype new provenance proposals, leading to redundant efforts, slower development, and a lack of adoptability. Moreover, each of these proposals has conceptualized provenance in different ways, indicating that a one-size-fits-all solution to provenance collection is unlikely to meet the needs of all of these audiences

Exacerbating this problem is that, due to a lack of better alternatives, researchers often choose to implement their provenance-aware systems by overloading other system components [42, 48]. Unfortunately, this introduces further security and interoperability problems; in order to enable provenance-aware systems, users currently need to disable their MAC policy [48], instrument applications [24, 66], gamble on experimental storage formats [42], or sacrifice other critical system functionality. These issues point to a pressing need for a dedicated platform for provenance development.

The **Linux Provenance Modules (LPM)** project [5] is an attempt to unify the operational needs of the disparate provenance communities through the design and implementation of a generalized framework for the development of automated, whole-system provenance collection on the Linux operating system. LPM extends and generalizes the Hi-Fi approach to kernel layer provenance collection with consideration for a variety of automated provenance systems that have been proposed in the literature. The framework is designed in such a way to allow for experimentation with new provenance collection mechanisms, and permits interoperability with other security mechanisms.

5.1 Augmenting Whole-System Provenance

The LPM project provides an explicit definition for the term *whole-system provenance* introduced in the Hi-Fi work that is broad enough to accommodate the needs of a variety of existing provenance projects. To arrive at a definition, four past proposals were inspected that collect broadly scoped provenance: SPADE [21], LineageFS [52], PASS [42], and Hi-Fi [48]. **SPADE** provenance is structured around primitive operations of system activities with data inputs and outputs. It instruments file and process system calls, and associates each call to a process ID (PID), user identifier, and network address. **LineageFS** uses a similar definition, associating process IDs with the file descriptors that the process reads and writes. **PASS** associates a process's output with references to all input files and the command line and process environment of the process; it also appends out-of-band knowledge such as OS and hardware descriptions, and random number generator seeds, if provided. In each of these systems, networking and IPC activity is primarily reflected in the provenance record through manipulation of the underlying file descriptors. **Hi-Fi** takes an even broader approach to provenance, treating non-persistent objects such as memory, IPC, and network packets as principal objects.

In all instances, provenance-aware systems are exclusively concerned with operations on *controlled data types*, which are identified by Zhang et al. as files, inodes, superblocks, socket buffers, IPC messages, IPC message queue, semaphores, and shared memory [64]. Because controlled data types represent a superset of the objects tracked by system layer provenance mechanisms, LPM defines whole-system provenance as *a complete description of agents (users, groups) controlling activities (processes) interacting with controlled data types during system execution.*

We also determine that beyond the reference monitor-inspired properties that comprise the provenance monitor concept, two additional goals are necessary to support whole-system provenance.

- **Authenticated Channel**. In distributed environments, provenance-aware systems must provide a means of assuring authenticity and integrity of provenance as it is communicated over open networks [2, 38, 48, 66]. LPM does not seek to provide a complete distributed provenance solution, but we wish to provide the required building blocks within the host for such a system to exist. LPM must therefore be able to monitor every network message that is sent or received by the host, and reliably explain these messages to other provenance-aware hosts in the network.
- **Attested Disclosure**. Layered provenance, where additional metadata is disclosed from higher operational layers, is a desirable feature in provenance-aware systems, as applications are able to report workflow semantics that are invisible to the operating system [43]. LPM must provide a gateway for upgrading low integrity user space disclosures before logging them in the high integrity provenance record. This is consistent with the Clark-Wilson Integrity model for upgrading or discarding low integrity inputs [13].

5.2 Threat Model

LPM is designed to securely collect provenance in the face of an adversary that has gained remote access to a provenance-aware host or network. Once inside the system, the attacker may attempt to remove provenance records, insert spurious information into those records, or find gaps in the provenance monitor's ability to record information flows. A network attacker may also attempt to forge or strip provenance from data in transit. Because captured provenance can be put to use in other applications, the adversary's goal may even be to target the provenance monitor itself. The implications and methods of such an attack are domain-specific. For example:

- **Scientific Computing**: An adversary may wish to manipulate provenance in order to commit fraud, or to inject uncertainty into records to trigger a "Climategate"-like controversy [50].
- **Access Control**: When used to mediate access decisions [2, 44, 45, 47], an attacker could tamper with provenance in order to gain unauthorized access, or to perform a denial-of-service attack on other users by artificially escalating the security level of data objects.
- **Networks**: Provenance metadata can also be associated with packets in order to better understand network events in distributed systems [3, 65, 66]. Coordinating multiple compromised hosts, an attacker may attempt to send *unauthenticated* messages to avoid provenance generation and to perform data exfiltration.

LPM defines a provenance trusted computing base (TCB) to be the kernel mechanisms, provenance recorder, and storage back-ends responsible for the collection and management of provenance. *Provenance-aware applications are not considered part of the TCB.*

5.3 Design of LPM

An overview of the LPM architecture is shown in Fig. 1. The LPM patch places a set of *provenance hooks* around the kernel; a *provenance module* then registers

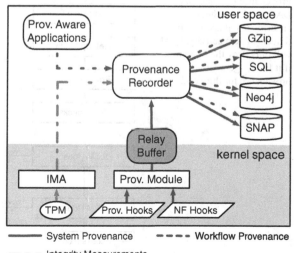

Fig. 1 Diagram of the LPM Framework. Kernel hooks report provenance to a recorder in userspace, which uses one of several storage back-ends. The recorder is also responsible for evaluating the integrity of workflow provenance prior to storing it

to control these hooks, and also registers several Netfilter hooks; the module then observes system events and transmits information via a relay buffer to a *provenance recorder* in user space that interfaces with a datastore. The recorder also accepts disclosed provenance from applications after verifying their correctness using the Integrity Measurements Architecture (IMA) [51].

5.3.1 Provenance Hooks

The LPM patch introduces a set of hook functions in the Linux kernel. These hooks behave similarly to the LSM framework's security hooks in that they facilitate modularity, and default to taking no action unless a module is enabled. Each provenance hook is placed directly beneath a corresponding security hook. The return value of the security hook is checked prior to calling the provenance hook, thus assuring that the requested activity has been authorized prior to provenance capture. A workflow for the hook architecture is depicted in Fig. 2. The LPM patch places over 170 provenance hooks, one for each of the LSM authorization hooks. In addition to the hooks that correspond to existing security hooks, LPM also supports a hook introduced by Hi-Fi that is necessary to preserve Lamport timestamps on network messages [30].

5.3.2 Netfilter Hooks

LPM uses Netfilter hooks to implement a cryptographic message commitment protocol. In Hi-Fi, provenance-aware hosts communicated by embedding a provenance

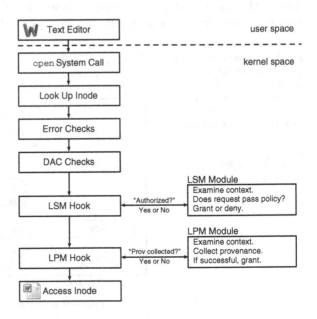

Fig. 2 Hook Architecture for the open system call. Provenance is collected *after* DAC and LSM checks, ensuring that it accurately reflects system activity. LPM will only deny the operation if it fails to generate provenance for the event

sequence number in the IP options field [49] of each outbound packet. This approach allowed Hi-Fi to communicate as normal with hosts that were not provenance-aware, but unfortunately was not secure against a network adversary. In LPM, provenance sequence numbers are replaced with Digital Signature Algorithm (DSA) signatures, which are space-efficient enough to embed in the IP Options field. LPM implements full DSA support in the Linux kernel by creating signing routines to use with the existing DSA verification function. DSA signing and verification occurs in the Net-Filter `inet_local_out` and `inet_local_in` hooks. In `inet_local_out`, LPM signs over the immutable fields of the IP header, as well as the IP payload. In `inet_local_in`, LPM checks for the presence of a signature, then verifies the signature against a configurable list of public keys. If the signature fails, the packet is dropped before it reaches the recipient application, thus ensuring that there are no breaks in the continuity of the provenance log. The key store for provenance-aware hosts is obtained by a PKI and transmitted to the kernel during the boot process by writing to `securityfs`. LPM registers the Netfilter hooks with the highest priority levels, such that signing occurs just before transmission (i.e., after all other IPTables operations), and signature verification occurs just after the packet enters the interface (i.e., before all other IPTables operations).

5.3.3 Workflow Provenance

To support layered provenance while preserving our security goals, LPM requires a means of evaluating the integrity of user space provenance disclosures. To accomplish this, LPM Provenance Recorders make use of the Linux Integrity Measurement Architecture (IMA) [51]. IMA computes a cryptographic hash of each binary before execution, extends the measurement into a TPM Platform Control Register (PCR), and stores the measurement in kernel memory. This set of measurements can be used by the Recorder to make a decision about the integrity of the a Provenance-Aware Application (PAA) prior to accepting the disclosed provenance. When a PAA wishes to disclose provenance, it opens a new UNIX domain socket to send the provenance data to the Provenance Recorder. The Recorder uses its own UNIX domain socket to recover the process's pid, then uses the `/proc` filesystem to find the full path of the binary, then uses this information to look up the PAA in the IMA measurement list. The disclosed provenance is recorded only if the signature of PAA matches a known-good cryptographic hash.

A demonstration of this functionality is shown in Fig. 3 for the popular ImageMagick utility.[1] ImageMagick contains a batch conversion tool for image reformatting, `mogrify`. Shown in Fig. 3, `mogrify` reads and writes multiple files during execution, leading to an *overtainting* problem—at the kernel layer, LPM is forced to conservatively assume that all outputs were derived from all inputs, creating false dependencies in the provenance record. To address this, we extended the Provmon protocol to support a new message, `provmsg_imagemagick_convert`, which

---

[1] See http://www.imagemagick.org.

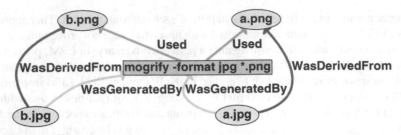

Fig. 3 A provenance graph of image conversion. Here, workflow provenance (*WasDerivedFrom*) encodes a relationship that more accurately identifies the output files' dependencies compared to only using kernel layer observations (*Used*, *WasGeneratedBy*)

links an input file directly to its output file. When the recorder receives this message, it first checks the list of IMA measurements to confirm that ImageMagick is in a good state. If successful, it then annotates the existing provenance graph, connecting the appropriate input and output objects with *WasDerivedFrom* relationships. LPM presents a minimally modified version of ImageMagick that upports layered provenance at no additional cost over other provenance-aware systems [21, 42], and does so in a manner that provides assurance of the integrity of the provenance log.

5.4 Deploying LPM

We now demonstrate how we used LPM in the deployment of a secure provenance-aware system. We configured LPM to run on a physical machine with a Trusted Platform Module (TPM). The TPM provides a root of trust that allows for a measured boot of the system. The TPM also provides the basis for remote attestations to prove that LPM was in a known hardware and software configuration. The BIOS's core root of trust for measurement (CRTM) bootstraps a series of code measurements prior to the execution of each platform component. Once booted, the kernel then measures the code for user space components (e.g., provenance recorder) before launching them, through the use of the Linux Integrity Measurement Architecture (IMA) [51]. The result is then extended into TPM PCRs, which forms a verifiable chain of trust that shows the integrity of the system via a digital signature over the measurements. A remote verifier can use this chain to determine the current state of the system using TPM attestation.

We configured the system with Intel's Trusted Boot, which provides a secure boot mechanism, preventing system from booting into the environment where critical components (e.g., the BIOS, boot loader and the kernel) are modified. Intel tboot relies on the Intel TXT extensions to provide a secure execution environment. Additionally, we compiled support for IMA into the provenance-aware kernel, which is necessary in order for the LPM Recorder to be able to measure the integrity of provenance-aware applications.

After booting into the provenance-aware kernel, the runtime integrity of the TCB must also be assured. To protect the runtime integrity of the kernel, we deploy a Mandatory Access Control (MAC) policy, as implemented by Linux Security Modules. On our prototype deployments, we enabled SELinux's MLS policy, the security of which was formally modeled by Hicks et al. [25]. Refining the SELinux policy to prevent Access Vector Cache (AVC) denials on LPM components required minimal effort; the only denial we encountered was when using the PostgreSQL recorder, which was quickly remedied with the `audit2allow` tool. Preserving the integrity of LPM's user space components, such as the provenance recorder, was as simple as creating a new policy module. We created a policy module to protect the LPM recorder and storage back-end using the `sepolicy` utility. Uncompiled, the policy module was only 135 lines.

6   Analyzing the Security of Provenance Monitors

In this section, we briefly consider metrics for evaluating the provenance monitor solutions that we have discussed in this chapter, specifically Hi-Fi and LPM. We consider their evaluative metrics from both a coverage and performance perspective.

6.1   Completeness Analysis of Hi-Fi

Hi-Fi demonstrated that malware could be observed throughout a variety of elements of a malicious worm's life-cycle. For brevity, we do not discuss full simulation results, which are further discussed in [48].

6.1.1   Recording Malicious Behavior

Our first task is to show that the data collected by Hi-Fi is of sufficient fidelity to be used in a security context. We focus our investigation on detecting the activity of network-borne malware. A typical worm consists of several parts. First, an exploit allows it to execute code on a remote host. This code can be a dropper, which serves to retrieve and execute the desired payload, or it can be the payload itself. A payload can then consist of any number of different actions to perform on an infected system, such as exfiltrating data or installing a backdoor. Finally, the malware spreads to other hosts and begins the cycle again.

For our experiment, we chose to implement a malware generator which would allow us to test different droppers and payloads quickly and safely. The generator is similar in design to the Metasploit Framework [39], in that you can choose an exploit, dropper, and payload to create a custom attack. However, our tool also includes a set of choices for generating malware which automatically spreads from one host to another; this allows us to demonstrate what socket provenance can record about the flow of information between systems. The malware behaviors that we implement and test are drawn from Symantec's technical descriptions of actual Linux malware [58].

To collect provenance data, we prepare three virtual machines on a common subnet, all of which are running Hi-Fi. The attacker generates the malware on machine A and infects machine B by exploiting an insecure network daemon. The malware then spreads automatically from machine B to machine C. For each of the malicious behaviors we wish to test, we generate a corresponding piece of malware on machine A and launch it. Once C has been infected, we retrieve the provenance logs from all three machines for examination.

Each malware behavior that we test appears in some form in the provenance record. In each case, after filtering the log to view only the vulnerable daemon and its descendants, the behavior is clear enough to be found by manual inspection. Below we describe each behavior and how it appears in the provenance record.

6.1.2 Persistence and Stealth

Frequently, the first action a piece of malware takes is to ensure that it will continue to run for as long as possible. In order to persist after the host is restarted, the malware must write itself to disk in such a way that it will be run when the system boots. The most straightforward way to do this on a Linux system is to infect one of the startup scripts run by the `init` process. Our simulated malware has the ability to modify `rc.local`, as the Kaiten trojan does. This shows up clearly in the provenance log:

```
[6fe] write B:/etc/rc.local
```

In this case, the process with provid $0 \times 6fe$ has modified `rc.local` on B's root filesystem. Persistent malware can also add cron jobs or infect system binaries to ensure that it is executed again after a reboot. Examples of this behavior are found in the Sorso and Adore worms. In our experiment, these behaviors result in similar log entries:

```
[701] write B:/bin/ps
```

for an infected binary, and

```
[710] write B:/var/spool/cron/root.new
[710] link B:/var/spool/cron/root.new to
             B:/var/spool/cron/root
[710] unlink B:/var/spool/cron/root.new
```

for an added cron job.

Some malware is even more clever in its approach to persistence. The Svat virus, for instance, creates a new C header file and places it early in the default include path. By doing this, it affects the code of any program which is subsequently compiled on that machine. We include this behavior in our experiment as well, and it appears simply as:

```
[707] write B:/usr/local/include/stdio.h
```

6.1.3   Remote Control

Once the malware has established itself as a persistent part of the system, the next step is to execute a payload. This commonly includes installing a backdoor which allows the attacker to control the system remotely. The simplest way to do this is to create a new root-level user on the system, which the attacker can then use to log in. Because of the way UNIX-like operating systems store their account databases, this is done by creating a new user with a UID of 0, making it equivalent to the root user. This is what the Zab trojan does, and when we implement this behavior, it is clear to see that the account databases are being modified:

```
[706] link (new) to B:/etc/passwd+
[706] write B:/etc/passwd+
[706] link B:/etc/passwd+ to B:/etc/passwd
[706] unlink B:/etc/passwd+
[706] link (new) to B:/etc/shadow+
[706] write B:/etc/shadow+
[706] link B:/etc/shadow+ to B:/etc/shadow
[706] unlink B:/etc/shadow+
```

A similar backdoor technique is to open a port which listens for connections and provides the attacker with a remote shell. This approach is used by many pieces of malware, including the Plupii and Millen worms. Our experiment shows that the provenance record includes the shell's network communication as well as the attacker's activity:

```
[744] exec B:/bin/bash -i
[744] socksend B:173
[744] sockrecv unknown
[744] socksend B:173
[751] exec B:/bin/cat /etc/shadow
[751] read B:/etc/shadow
[751] socksend B:173
[744] socksend B:173
[744] sockrecv unknown
[744] socksend B:173
[744] link (new) to B:/testfile
[744] write B:/testfile
```

Here, the attacker uses the remote shell to view /etc/shadow and to write a new file in the root directory. Since the attacker's system is unlikely to be running a trusted instance of Hi-Fi, we see "unknown" socket entries, which indicate data received from an unprovenanced host. Remote shells can also be implemented as "reverse shells," which connect from the infected host back to the attacker. Our tests on a reverse shell, such as the one in the Jac.8759 virus, show results identical to a normal shell.

6.1.4   Exfiltration

Another common payload activity is data exfiltration, where the malware reads information from a file containing password hashes, credit card numbers, or other sensitive information and sends this information to the attacker. Our simulation for this behavior reads the /etc/shadow file and forwards it in one of two ways. In the first test, we upload the file to a web server using HTTP, and in the second, we write it directly to a remote port. Both methods result in the same log entries:

```
[85f]  read B:/etc/shadow
[85f]  socksend B:1ae
```

Emailing the information to the attacker, as is done by the Adore worm, would create a similar record.

6.1.5   Spread

Our experiment also models three different mechanisms used by malware to spread to newly infected hosts. The first and simplest is used when the entire payload can be sent using the initial exploit. In this case, there does not need to be a separate dropper, and the resulting provenance log is the following (indentation is used to distinguish the two hosts):

```
[807]  read A:/home/evil/payload
[807]  socksend A:153
    [684]  sockrecv A:153
    [684]  write B:/tmp/payload
```

The payload is then executed, and the malicious behavior it implements appears in subsequent log entries.

Another mechanism, used by the Plupii and Sorso worms, is to fetch the payload from a remote web server. We assume the web server is unprovenanced, so the log once again contains "unknown" entries:

```
[7ff]  read A:/home/evil/dropper
[7ff]  socksend A:15b
    [685]  sockrecv A:15b
    [685]  write B:/tmp/dropper
    [6ef]  socksend B:149
    [6ef]  sockrecv unknown
    [6ef]  write B:/tmp/payload
```

If the web server were a provenanced host, this log would contain host and socket IDs in the sockrecv entry corresponding to a socksend on the server.

Finally, to illustrate the spread of malware across several hosts, we tested a "relay" dropper which uses a randomly-chosen port to transfer the payload from each infected host to the next. The combined log of our three hosts shows this process:

```
[83f] read A:/home/evil/dropper
[83f] socksend A:159
    [691] sockrecv A:159
    [691] write B:/tmp/dropper
    [6f5] exec B:/tmp/dropper
[844] read A:/home/evil/payload
[844] socksend A:15b
    [6fc] sockrecv A:15b
    [6fc] write B:/tmp/payload
    [74e] read B:/tmp/dropper
    [74e] socksend B:169
        [682] sockrecv B:169
        [682] write C:/tmp/dropper
        [6e6] exec C:/tmp/dropper
    [750] read B:/tmp/payload
    [750] socksend B:16b
        [6ed] sockrecv B:16b
        [6ed] write C:/tmp/payload
```

Here we can see the attacker transferring both the dropper and the payload to the first victim using two different sockets. This victim then sends the dropper and the payload to the next host in the same fashion.

6.2   Security Analysis of LPM

We now turn our focus to LPM, which provides additional features for demonstraitng the provenance monitor concept beyond what Hi-Fi enforces. We demonstrate that LPM meets all of the required security goals for trustworthy whole-system provenance. In this analysis, we consider an LPM deployment on a physical machine that was enabled with the Provmon module, which mirrors the functionality of Hi-Fi.

Complete. We defined whole-system provenance as a complete description of agents (users, groups) controlling activities (processes) interacting with controlled data types during system execution (Sect. 5.1). LPM attempts to track these system objects through the placement of provenance hooks (Sect. 5.3.1), which directly follow each LSM authorization hook. The LSM's complete mediation property has been formally verified [15, 64]; in other words, there is an authorization hook prior to every security-sensitive operation. Because every interaction with a controlled data type is considered security-sensitive, we know that a provenance hook resides on all control paths to the provenance-sensitive operations. LPM is therefore capable of collecting complete provenance on the host.

It is important to note that, as a consequence of placing provenance hooks beneath authorization hooks, LPM is unable to record failed access attempts. However, inserting the provenance layer beneath the security layer ensures accuracy of the provenance record. Moreover, failed authorizations are a different kind of metadata than provenance because they do not describe processed data; this information is better handled at the security layer, e.g., by the SELinux Access Vector Cache (AVC) Log.

Tamperproof. The runtime integrity of the LPM trusted computing base is assured via the SELinux MLS policy, and we have written a policy module that protects the LPM user space components. Therefore, the only way to disable LPM would be to reboot the system into a different kernel; this action can be disallowed through secure boot techniques and is detectable by remote hosts via TPM attestation.

Verifiable. While we have not conducted an independent formal verification of LPM, our argument for its correctness is as follows. A provenance hook follows each LSM authorization hook in the kernel. The correctness of LSM hook placement has been verified through both static and dynamic analysis techniques [15, 19, 27]. Because an authorization hook exists on the path of every sensitive operation to controlled data types, and LPM introduces a provenance hook behind each authorization hook, LPM inherits LSM's formal assurance of complete mediation over controlled data types. This is sufficient to ensure that LPM can collect the provenance of every sensitive operation on controlled data types in the kernel (i.e., whole-system provenance).

Authenticated Channel. Through use of Netfilter hooks [59], LPM embeds a DSA signature in every outbound network packet. Signing occurs immediately prior to transmission, and verification occurs immediately after reception, making it impossible for an adversary-controlled application running in user space to interfere. For both transmission and reception, the signature is invisible to user space. Signatures are removed from the packets before delivery, and LPM feigns ignorance that the options field has been set if `get_options` is called. Hence, LPM can enforce that all applications participate in the commitment protocol.

Prior to implementing our own message commitment protocol in the kernel, we investigated a variety of existing secure protocols. The integrity and authenticity of provenance identifiers could also be protected via IPsec [29], SSL tunneling,[2] or other forms of encapsulation [3, 66]. We elected to move forward with our approach because (1) it ensures the monitoring of all processes and network events, including non-IP packets, (2) it does not change the number of packets sent or received, ensuring that our provenance mechanism is minimally invasive to the rest of the Linux network stack, and (3) it preserves compatibility with non-LPM hosts. An alternative to DSA signing would be HMAC [6], which offers better performance but requires pairwise keying and sacrifices the non-repudiation policy; BLS, which approaches the theoretical maximum security parameter per byte of signature [7]; or online/offline signature schemes [9, 16, 20, 53].

Authenticated Disclosures. We make use of IMA to protect the channel between LPM and provenance-aware applications wishing to disclose provenance. IMA is able

---

[2]See http://docs.oracle.com/cd/E23823_01/html/816-5175/kssl-5.html.

to prove to the provenance recorder that the application was unmodified at the time it was loaded into memory, at which point the recorder can accept the provenance disclosure into the official record. If the application is known to be correct (e.g., through formal verification), this is sufficient to establish the runtime integrity of the application. However, if the application is compromised after execution, this approach is unable to protect against provenance forgery.

A separate consideration for all of the above security properties are Denial of Service (DoS) attacks. *DoS attacks on LPM do not break its security properties*. If an attacker launches a resource exhaustion attack in order to prevent provenance from being collected, all kernel operations will be disallowed and the host will cease to function. If a network attacker tampers with a packet's provenance identifier, the packet will not be delivered to the recipient application. In all cases, the provenance record remains an accurate reflection of system events.

7 Current and Future Challenges to Provenance for Forensics

In this chapter, we have discussed the provenance monitor approach to secure and trustworthy collection of data provenance, which can be an extraordinary source of metadata for forensics investigators. The ability to use provenance for this goal is predicated on its complete collection in an environment that cannot be tampered. As we discussed through our exploration of the Hi-Fi and Linux Provenance Modules system, the goals of a provenance monitor can be seen as a superset of reference monitor goals because of the need for integration of layers and the notion of attested disclosure, which are properties unique to the provenance environment.

A common limitation shared by provenance collection systems, including not only Hi-Fi and LPM but also proposals such as SPADE and PASS, is that provenance collection at the operating system layer demands large amounts of storage. For example, in short-lived benchmark trials, each of these systems generated gigabytes of provenance over the course of just a few minutes [21, 42]. There are some promising methods of reducing the costs of collection. Ma et al.'s ProTracer system offers dramatic improvement in storage cost by making use of a hybrid audit-taint model for provenance collection [36]. ProTracer only flushes new provenance records to disk when system writes occur (e.g., file write, packet transmission); on system reads, ProTracer propagates a taint label between kernel objects in memory. By leveraging this approach along with other garbage collection techniques [32, 33], ProTracer reduces the burden of provenance storage to just tens of megabytes per day. Additionally, Bates et al. [4] considered that much of the provenance collected by high-fidelity systems is simply *uninteresting*; in other words, it is the collection of data that does not provide new information essential to system reconstruction or forensic analysis, for example. By focusing on information deemed important through its inclusion in the system's trusted computing base as inferred by its mandatory access policy, it is possible to identify the subset of processes and applications critical to enforcing the system's security goals. By focusing on these systems, the amount of data that needs to be collected can be reduced by over 90 %. Such an approach can be complementary to other proposals for data transformation to assure the efficient storage of provenance metadata [11] and the use of techniques such as provenance deduplication [61, 62].

Extending provenance beyond a single host to distributed systems also poses a considerable challenge. In distributed environments, provenance-aware hosts must attest the integrity of one another before sharing provenance metadata [34], or in layered provenance systems where there is no means to attest provenance disclosures [43]. Kernel-based provenance mechanisms [42, 48] and sketches for trusted provenance architectures [34, 38] fall short of providing a fully provenance-aware system for distributed, malicious environments. Complicating matters further, data provenance is conceptualized in dramatically different ways throughout the literature, such that any solution to provenance security would need to be general enough to support the needs of a variety of diverse communities. Extending provenance monitors into these environments can provide a wealth of new information to the forensics investigator but must be carefully designed and implemented.

While we focus on the collection of provenance in this chapter, it is also important to be able to efficiently query the provenance once it is Provenance queries regarding transitive causes/effects of a *single* system state or event can be answered by a recursive procedure that retrieves relevant portions of a provenance graph [66, 67]. While such queries are useful in many applications, e.g., to find root causes of a detected policy violation, further research is necessary into efficient query languages to allow system operators to perform more complex queries that can identify user-specified subgraphs from the collected provenance in a manner that is easily usable and that facilitate inference of analytics.

To conclude, provenance represents a powerful new means for gathering data about a system for a forensics investigator. Being able to establish the context within which data was created and generating a chain of custody describing how the data came to take its current form can provide vast new capabilities. However, as the systems discussed in this chapter demonstrate, ensuring that provenance is securely collected is a challenging task. Future systems can build from existing work to addresses the challenges we outlined above in order to bring the promises of provenance to practical reality.

Acknowledgments This work draws in part from [5, 38, 48]. We would like to thank our co-authors of those works, including Patrick McDaniel, Thomas Moyer, Stephen McLaughlin, Erez Zadok, Marianne Winslett, and Radu Sion, as well as reviewers of those original papers who provided us with valuable feedback. This work is supported in part by the U.S. National Science Foundation under grants CNS-1540216, CNS-1540217, and CNS-1540128.

References

1. Aldeco-Pérez, R., Moreau, L.: Provenance-based auditing of private data use. In: Proceedings of the 2008 International Conference on Visions of Computer Science: BCS International Academic Conference. VoCS'08, pp. 141–152. British Computer Society, Swinton, UK (2008)
2. Bates, A., Mood, B., Valafar, M., Butler, K.: Towards secure provenance-based access control in cloud environments. In: Proceedings of the 3rd ACM Conference on Data and Application Security and Privacy, CODASPY '13, pp. 277–284. ACM, New York, NY, USA (2013). doi:10.1145/2435349.2435389
3. Bates, A., Butler, K., Haeberlen, A., Sherr, M., Zhou, W.: Let SDN be your eyes: secure forensics in data center networks. In: NDSS Workshop on Security of Emerging Network Technologies, SENT (2014)
4. Bates, A., Butler, K.R.B., Moyer, T.: Take only what you need: leveraging mandatory access control policy to reduce provenance storage costs. In: Proceedings of the 7th International Workshop on Theory and Practice of Provenance, TaPP'15 (2015)
5. Bates, A., Tian, D., Butler, K.R.B., Moyer, T.: Trustworthy whole-system provenance for the linux kernel. In: Proceedings of the 2015 USENIX Security Symposium (Security'15). Washington, DC, USA (2015)
6. Bellare, M., Canetti, R., Krawczyk, H.: Keyed hash functions and message authentication. In: Proceedings of Crypto'96, *LNCS*, vol. 1109, pp. 1–15 (1996)
7. Boneh, D., Lynn, B., Shacham, H.: Short signatures from the weil pairing. In: Boyd, C. (ed.) Advances in Cryptology—ASIACRYPT (2001)
8. Carata, L., Akoush, S., Balakrishnan, N., Bytheway, T., Sohan, R., Seltzer, M., Hopper, A.: A primer on provenance. Commun. ACM 57(5), 52–60 (2014). doi:10.1145/2596628. http://doi.acm.org/10.1145/2596628
9. Catalano, D., Di Raimondo, M., Fiore, D., Gennaro, R.: Off line/On-line signatures: theoretical aspects and experimental results. In: PKC'08: Proceedings of the Practice and Theory in Public Key Cryptography. 11th International Conference on Public Key Cryptography, pp. 101–120. Springer, Berlin, Heidelberg (2008)
10. Centers for Medicare & Medicaid Services: The health insurance portability and accountability act of 1996 (HIPAA). http://www.cms.hhs.gov/hipaa/ (1996)
11. Chapman, A., Jagadish, H., Ramanan, P.: Efficient provenance storage. In: Proceedings of the 2008 ACM Special Interest Group on Management of Data Conference, SIGMOD'08 (2008)
12. Chiticariu, L., Tan, W.C., Vijayvargiya, G.: DBNotes: a post-it system for relational databases based on provenance. In: Proceedings of the 2005 ACM SIGMOD International Conference on Management of Data, SIGMOD'05 (2005)
13. Clark, D.D., Wilson, D.R.: A comparison of commercial and military computer security policies. In: Proceedings of the IEEE Symposium on Security and Privacy. Oakland, CA, USA (1987)
14. Department of Homeland Security: A Roadmap for Cybersecurity Research (2009)
15. Edwards, A., Jaeger, T., Zhang, X.: Runtime verification of authorization hook placement for the linux security modules framework. In: Proceedings of the 9th ACM Conference on Computer and Communications Security, CCS'02 (2002)
16. Even, S., Goldreich, O., Micali, S.: On-line/off-line digital signatures. In: Proceedings on Advances in Cryptology, CRYPTO '89, pp. 263–275. Springer, New York, USA (1989). http://portal.acm.org/citation.cfm?id=118209.118233
17. Foster, I.T., Vöckler, J.S., Wilde, M., Zhao, Y.: Chimera: AVirtual data system for representing, querying, and automating data derivation. In: Proceedings of the 14th Conference on Scientific and Statistical Database Management, SSDBM'02 (2002)
18. Frew, J., Bose, R.: Earth system science workbench: a data management infrastructure for earth science products. In: Proceedings of the 13th International Conference on Scientific and Statistical Database Management, pp. 180–189. IEEE Computer Society (2001)

19. Ganapathy, V., Jaeger, T., Jha, S.: Automatic placement of authorization hooks in the linux security modules framework. In: Proceedings of the 12th ACM Conference on Computer and Communications Security, CCS '05, pp. 330–339. ACM, New York, USA (2005). doi:10.1145/1102120.1102164

20. Gao, C.Z., Yao, Z.A.: A further improved online/offline signature scheme. Fundam. Inf. **91**, 523–532 (2009). http://portal.acm.org/citation.cfm?id=1551775.1551780

21. Gehani, A., Tariq, D.: SPADE: support for provenance auditing in distributed environments. In: Proceedings of the 13th International Middleware Conference, Middleware '12 (2012)

22. Glavic, B., Alonso, G.: Perm: processing provenance and data on the same data model through query rewriting. In: Proceedings of the 25th IEEE International Conference on Data Engineering, ICDE '09 (2009)

23. Hall, E.: The Arnolfini Betrothal: Medieval Marriage and the Enigma of Van Eyck's Double Portrait. University of California Press, Berekely, CA (1994)

24. Hasan, R., Sion, R., Winslett, M.: The case of the fake picasso: preventing history forgery with secure provenance. In: Proceedings of the 7th USENIX Conference on File and Storage Technologies (FAST'09), FAST'09. San Francisco, CA, USA (2009)

25. Hicks, B., Rueda, S., St.Clair, L., Jaeger, T., McDaniel, P.: A logical specification and analysis for SELinux MLS policy. ACM Trans. Inf. Syst. Secur. **13**(3), 26:1–26:31 (2010). doi:10.1145/1805874.1805982

26. Holland, D.A., Bruan, U., Maclean, D., Muniswamy-Reddy, K.K., Seltzer, M.I.: Choosing a data model and query language for provenance. In: Proceedings of the 2nd International Provenance and Annotation Workshop, IPAW'08 (2008)

27. Jaeger, T., Edwards, A., Zhang, X.: Consistency analysis of authorization hook placement in the linux security modules framework. ACM Trans. Inf. Syst. Secur. **7**(2), 175–205 (2004). doi:10.1145/996943.996944

28. Jones, S.N., Strong, C.R., Long, D.D.E., Miller, E.L.: Tracking emigrant data via transient provenance. In: 3rd Workshop on the Theory and Practice of Provenance, TAPP'11 (2011)

29. Kent, S., Atkinson, R.: RFC 2406: IP Encapsulating Security Payload (ESP) (1998)

30. Lamport, L.: Time, clocks, and the ordering of events in a distributed system. Commun. ACM **21**(7), 558–565 (1978). doi:10.1145/359545.359563

31. Lampson, B.W.: A note on the confinement problem. Commun. ACM **16**(10), 613–615 (1973)

32. Lee, K.H., Zhang, X., Xu, D.: High accuracy attack provenance via binary-based execution partition. In: Proceedings of the 20th ISOC Network and Distributed System Security Symposium, NDSS (2013)

33. Lee, K.H., Zhang, X., Xu, D.: LogGC: garbage collecting audit log. In: Proceedings of the 2013 ACM Conference on Computer and Communications Security, CCS (2013)

34. Lyle, J., Martin, A.: Trusted computing and provenance: better together. In: 2nd Workshop on the Theory and Practice of Provenance, TaPP'10 (2010)

35. Ma, S., Lee, K.H., Kim, C.H., Rhee, J., Zhang, X., Xu, D.: Accurate, low cost and instrumentation-free security audit logging for windows. In: Proceedings of the 31st Annual Computer Security Applications Conference, ACSAC 2015, pp. 401–410. ACM (2015). 22. doi:10.1145/2818000.2818039

36. Ma, S., Zhang, X., Xu, D.: ProTracer: towards practical provenance tracing by alternating between logging and tainting. In: Proceedings of the 23rd ISOC Network and Distributed System Security Symposium, NDSS (2016)

37. Macko, P., Seltzer, M.: A general-purpose provenance library. In: 4th Workshop on the Theory and Practice of Provenance, TaPP'12 (2012)

38. McDaniel, P., Butler, K., McLaughlin, S., Sion, R., Zadok, E., Winslett, M.: Towards a secure and efficient system for end-to-end provenance. In: Proceedings of the 2nd conference on Theory and practice of provenance. USENIX Association, San Jose, CA, USA (2010)

39. Metasploit Project. http://www.metasploit.com

40. Moreau, L., Groth, P., Miles, S., Vazquez-Salceda, J., Ibbotson, J., Jiang, S., Munroe, S., Rana, O., Schreiber, A., Tan, V., Varga, L.: The provenance of electronic data. Commun. ACM **51**(4), 52–58 (2008). http://doi.acm.org/10.1145/1330311.1330323

41. Mouallem, P., Barreto, R., Klasky, S., Podhorszki, N., Vouk, M.: Tracking files in the kepler provenance framework. In: SSDBM 2009: Proceedings of the 21st International Conference on Scientific and Statistical Database Management (2009)
42. Muniswamy-Reddy, K.K., Holland, D.A., Braun, U., Seltzer, M.: Provenance-aware storage systems. In: Proceedings of the Annual Conference on USENIX '06 Annual Technical Conference, Proceedings of the 2006 Conference on USENIX Annual Technical Conference (2006)
43. Muniswamy-Reddy, K.K., Braun, U., Holland, D.A., Macko, P., Maclean, D., Margo, D., Seltzer, M., Smogor, R.: Layering in provenance systems. In: Proceedings of the 2009 Conference on USENIX Annual Technical Conference, ATC'09 (2009)
44. Nguyen, D., Park, J., Sandhu, R.: Dependency path patterns as the foundation of access control in provenance-aware systems. In: Proceedings of the 4th USENIX Conference on Theory and Practice of Provenance. TaPP'12, p. 4. USENIX Association, Berkeley, CA, USA (2012)
45. Ni, Q., Xu, S., Bertino, E., Sandhu, R., Han, W.: An access control language for a general provenance model. In: Secure Data Management (2009)
46. Pancerella, C., Hewson, J., Koegler, W., Leahy, D., Lee, M., Rahn, L., Yang, C., Myers, J.D., Didier, B., McCoy, R., Schuchardt, K., Stephan, E., Windus, T., Amin, K., Bittner, S., Lansing, C., Minkoff, M., Nijsure, S., von Laszewski, G., Pinzon, R., Ruscic, B., Wagner, A., Wang, B., Pitz, W., Ho, Y.L., Montoya, D., Xu, L., Allison, T.C., Green Jr., W.H., Frenklach, M.: Metadata in the collaboratory for multi-scale chemical science. In: Proceedings of the 2003 International Conference on Dublin Core and Metadata Applications: Supporting Communities of Discourse and Practice—Metadata Research & Applications, pp. 13:1–13:9. Dublin Core Metadata Initiative (2003)
47. Park, J., Nguyen, D., Sandhu, R.: A provenance-based access control model. In: Proceedings of the 10th Annual International Conference on Privacy, Security and Trust (PST), pp. 137–144 (2012). doi:10.1109/PST.2012.6297930
48. Pohly, D.J., McLaughlin, S., McDaniel, P., Butler, K.: Hi-Fi: collecting high-fidelity whole-system provenance. In: Proceedings of the 2012 Annual Computer Security Applications Conference, ACSAC '12. Orlando, FL, USA (2012)
49. Postel, J.: RFC 791: Internet Protocol (1981)
50. Revkin, A.C.: Hacked E-mail is new fodder for climate dispute. New York Times **20** (2009)
51. Sailer, R., Zhang, X., Jaeger, T., van Doorn, L.: Design and implementation of a TCG-based integrity measurement architecture. In: Proceedings of the 13th USENIX Security Symposium. San Diego, CA, USA (2004)
52. Sar, C., Cao, P.: Lineage file system. http://crypto.stanford.edu/cao/lineage.html (2005)
53. Shamir, A., Tauman, Y.: Improved online/offline signature schemes. In: Advances in Cryptology—CRYPTO 2001 (2001)
54. Silva, C.T., Anderson, E.W., Santos, E., Freire, J.: Using vistrails and provenance for teaching scientific visualization. Comput. Graph. Forum **30**(1), 75–84 (2011)
55. Sion, R.: Strong WORM. In: Proceedings of the 2008 The 28th International Conference on Distributed Computing Systems (2008)
56. Spillane, R.P., Sears, R., Yalamanchili, C., Gaikwad, S., Chinni, M., Zadok, E.: Story book: an efficient extensible provenance framework. In: First Workshop on the Theory and Practice of Provenance. USENIX (2009)
57. Sundararaman, S., Sivathanu, G., Zadok, E.: Selective versioning in a secure disk system. In: Proceedings of the 17th USENIX Security Symposium (2008)
58. Symantec: Symantec security response. http://www.symantec.com/security_response (2015)
59. The Netfilter Core Team: The netfilter project: packet mangling for linux 2.4. http://www.netfilter.org/, http://crypto.stanford.edu/~cao/lineage.html (1999)
60. U.S. Code: 22 U.S. Code §2778—control of arms exports and imports. https://www.law.cornell.edu/uscode/text/22/2778 (1976)
61. Xie, Y., Muniswamy-Reddy, K.K., Long, D.D.E., Amer, A., Feng, D., Tan, Z.: Compressing provenance graphs. In: Proceedings of the 3rd USENIX Workshop on the Theory and Practice of Provenance (2011)

62. Xie, Y., Feng, D., Tan, Z., Chen, L., Muniswamy-Reddy, K.K., Li, Y., Long, D.D.: A hybrid approach for efficient provenance storage. In: Proceedings of the 21st ACM International Conference on Information and Knowledge Management, CIKM '12 (2012)
63. Zanussi, T., Yaghmour, K., Wisniewski, R., Moore, R., Dagenais, M.: Relayfs: an efficient unified approach for transmitting data from kernel to user space. In: Proceedings of the 2003 Linux Symposium, pp. 494–506. Ottawa, ON, Canada (2003)
64. Zhang, X., Edwards, A., Jaeger, T.: Using CQUAL for static analysis of authorization hook placement. In: Proceedings of the 11th USENIX Security Symposium (2002)
65. Zhou, W., Sherr, M., Tao, T., Li, X., Loo, B.T., Mao, Y.: Efficient querying and maintenance of network provenance at internet-scale. In: Proceedings of the 2010 ACM SIGMOD International Conference on Measurement of Data (2010)
66. Zhou, W., Fei, Q., Narayan, A., Haeberlen, A., Loo, B.T., Sherr, M.: Secure network provenance. In: ACM Symposium on Operating Systems Principles (SOSP) (2011)
67. Zhou, W., Mapara, S., Ren, Y., Haeberlen, A., Ives, Z., Loo, B.T., Sherr, M.: Distributed time-aware provenance. In: Proceedings of VLDB (2013)

Conclusion

Yong Guan, Sneha Kumar Kasera, Cliff Wang and Ryan M. Gerdes

Abstract We identify a series of research questions for further work in the broad area of fingerprinting.

1 Overview

Device fingerprinting shows considerable promise, as demonstrated in the laboratory, for use in authentication, forensics, intrusion detection, and possibly assurance monitoring. However, to establish practical and secure deployment of this technology will require a concerted, multi-year effort to answer several questions, including

1. What are the origins of fingerprints, e.g., what circuit and device components are the main sources of that fingerprint in the case of RF fingerprinting?
2. Which approach is better for finding the origins of fingerprints and understanding the ground truth? Black box testing, enumeration or white box reverse engineering to explore the origin? Use of intrusive, semi-intrusive or non-intrusive strategies for reverse engineering and exploring the origins?
3. How to formulate the problem of forensic fingerprinting for a particular context; e.g., how can we be sure the evidence is enough in court?
4. How to evaluate and quantify the forensic capability of a vector of features for forensic fingerprinting?

Y. Guan (✉)
Iowa State University, Ames, IA 50011, USA
e-mail: guan@iastate.edu

S.K. Kasera
University of Utah, Salt Lake City, UT 84112, USA
e-mail: kasera@cs.utah.edu

C. Wang
Army Research Office, Research Triangle Park, NC 27709, USA
e-mail: cliff.x.wang.civ@mail.mil

R.M. Gerdes
Utah State University, Logan, UT 84341, USA
e-mail: ryan.gerdes@usu.edu

© Springer Science+Business Media New York 2016
C. Wang et al. (eds.), *Digital Fingerprinting*,
DOI 10.1007/978-1-4939-6601-1_9

177

5. What if anti-forensic techniques are involved in forensic fingerprinting? What are the threat model and capabilities of the adversary?
6. Hypothesis testing is hard in forensic fingerprinting given the versatile capability of the suspect. How to prove something is impossible, given the vast space of possibilities?

Answering the above will require a sustained effort and innovations in the areas of fingerprint measurement, integration of cryptographic methods, the science of fingerprints, and the security of fingerprinting.

2 Measurements of Fingerprints

The effort expended in collecting data about various communications and sensor devices would not only allow researchers the opportunity to further validate existing fingerprinting techniques but the resulting data would inform and motivate efforts in understanding the science, origin, and resiliency of fingerprints. We should thus view measurement as a not only being necessary to establish the scientific validity of fingerprinting but also as a critical component of a self-sustaining feedback loop in fingerprinting research: data gathered on new and exiting technologies, under differing deployment scenarios, would need to be examined using existing fingerprinting theories and frameworks, and if our ability to fingerprint the data should be negatively affected new methods could be proposed and tested.

Currently, fingerprinting researchers are working in isolation with small, disparate datasets, collected using different experimental methodologies, under different environmental conditions, and scenarios that may not reflect real-world use. This makes it difficult to compare the relative merits of each approach and judge their ability to scale (i.e. the ability to identify many devices). What is needed is a statistically valid sample of a device population for a given technology, acquired at different times and from differing deployments, and available to all interested researchers. Such a dataset would allow us to investigate (1) channel effects due to device mobility, (2) device aging, (3) experiment with methods for tracking devices after they have been absent from, and then returned to, the network, (4) and fingerprint drift.

Researchers should also propose new deployment scenarios that require measurement, e.g. if devices are mobile is the Doppler effect significant? It is also probable that environmental factors that impact our ability to fingerprint devices will not become apparent until researchers have analyzed large amounts of data. Uncovering such impacts would then suggest new scenarios for measurement.

Gathering such data will most likely require assistance from manufacturers, as we would be interested in, for instance, dates of manufacture, information on device architecture, and insight into the manufacturing process. This information would be useful for creating device models that could then be used to inform us about which aspects of device behavior should be fingerprinted and how. However, we have identified several reasons why manufacturers may be unwilling to lend their assistance: (1) privacy (users of a device could be identified); (2) liability (a user could be tracked and then harmed in some way using fingerprinting); (3) trade secrets (inner-working of devices revealed); and (4) cost (to not only provide data but changes to the manufacturing process if extrinsic fingerprints are used). A possible way to interest manufacturers in fingerprinting work would be to focus research efforts on reducing costs associated with acquiring and processing fingerprints to accelerate deployment of fingerprinting technology in the enterprise. This would open another revenue for sales, as manufacturers would be able to expand the sale of fingerprinting beyond the military and government (where the hitherto high costs associated with fingerprinting can be justified).

3 Fingerprints and Crypto-Based Methods

Integration of fingerprints into security protocols and applications needs further investigation. One may be able to modulate and amplify the physical properties to get an improved fingerprint. However, integrating the physical constraints such as spatial or temporal properties could be a great enabler for actual protocol implementation. The hardware/software co-design has been identified, by many including those in industry, as a promising approach because hardware is perceived to be less vulnerable. However, there is a fundamental problem of extracting and digitally integrating the hardware fingerprints into the software. The low power, potential unclonability, and the inherent resiliency to attacks are the key advantages of hardware-based fingerprinting and solutions. A fundamental problem is how you manage so many potential fingerprints. The cost maybe an issue, if there is a need for precision measurement devices, how much we get stronger by applying the fingerprint? How much do we gain in security by integrating the fingerprints? How can we quantify the confidence in the PUF-based embedded systems? Reliability, security, resilience, and robustness aspects have trade-offs. They need to be thoroughly investigated, quantified, and addressed.

4 Science of Fingerprints

Development of generalized information models and identification of important performance metrics is key to building the science of fingerprints. Among the important components in relation to science of fingerprints are the generalized information models for extrinsic and intrinsic fingerprints. These models include the parameters and their variations that identify the different sources, the measurements of these parameters through sensors, models of channel variations, and feature extraction from measurement samples. Other related issues include classification bounds, multi-mode sensors, and timing (e.g., real-time, asynchrony). These models must be integrated with some logic, and statistical and domain reasoning. The generalized information models can be applied to specific application scenarios to create application specific models (e.g., one for "forensicability"). Fingerprint models can also be used to determine the space of the source fingerprints. The performance metrics of fingerprinting systems can be characterized in the three dimensions: robustness, stealth, and security. The tradeoffs along these three dimensions and their limits are fundamental to the design, evaluation, and applicability of fingerprinting systems.

5 Security of Fingerprints

Device fingerprinting, as a technique for intrusion detection, authentication, or forensics, depends upon variability in device behaviour, classifier sensitivity, and the inability of an attacker to adequately emulate device behaviour (for assurance monitoring only the first two are of consequence). Before the security of a particular approach can be evaluated, it is necessary to determine whether devices vary significantly and consistently enough across a given population for a particular identification methodology to reliably differentiate them. Having established this, we must then consider whether device behaviour can be readily emulated. It must be emphasised that the self-evident claim that no two devices can be made to produce exactly the same networking signals is not in itself enough to prove the validity of fingerprinting—signal variation is itself defined with respect to the discriminatory methodology used in identifying devices, while its relevance is determined by the ability or inability of an attacker to produce high fidelity forgeries.

There are three aspects of device variability that need to be considered in relation to fingerprinting schemes, namely its extent, consistency, and origin. Whether or not we are able to profile and track a device depends upon the device exhibiting its unique behaviour in a consistent manner. To account for the observable amount of change a device undergoes during the course of operation, we must capture the velocity and degree of change during steady state operation and after the device has lost and re-established connectivity. While understanding the origin of such variations may be of use in modelling device behaviour, and hence aid in the construction of device profiles and tracking regimes, it also bears directly upon the security of fingerprinting. Consider that if an attacker understands the degree to which individual components contribute to differences in device behaviour, they could attempt to engineer devices that conform to known devices by targeting just those components most responsible for expressing identifiable characteristics. Of course, the job of imitating a particular device is considerably easier if the extent of observed variation of a population of devices is not appreciable enough to be discerned by the identification methodology. Determining whether a given methodology is even practicable requires that we test it via application to a statistically significant sample of devices and calculate the theoretical number of devices it is capable of distinguishing between. Such a theoretical analysis is dependent upon the sensitivity of the underlying classification technique(s). The term sensitivity is meant in this context to denote *population* sensitivity, or the number of devices that can be distinguished using a particular methodology.

While establishing that a fingerprinting methodology is capable of distinguishing between and tracking a population of devices is necessary to prove the security of a particular approach, it is not sufficient. To achieve sufficiency it must be determined, according to some measure, how different two signals need be before they can be identified as such. Again, this calculation is dependent upon the sensitivity of the classifier, though in this case sensitivity refers to how close two signals must be in order to produce identical results (we will use the term *difference* sensitivity to avoid ambiguity with population sensitivity). Once this is decided, we must resolve whether an attacker, using current technology, is able produce an acceptable forgery using either a signal generator or by modifying an existing device.

Index

Note: Page numbers followed by f and t indicate figures and tables respectively

A

ABCD parameters, 33, 37
Access points (APs), 23
    wireless, 132
Access Vector Cache (AVC), 165
ACP scan, 120
Acquisition setup, 13, 15, 16
Active fingerprinting, 119–122
Active identification, 13
Advanced Persistent Threat (APT)
    detection, 148
Analog VHF transmitters, 8
AND gate transitions, 42–43
Asymmetric key cryptography, 40
Authentication, 1–2, 39–40
Authentication schemes, conventional, 72
Authentication system, 57–58
    receiver, 74–76
    transmitter, 73–74
Automatic provenance-aware systems, 144
    in applications, 145–147
    in middleware, 145
    in operating systems, 144

B

Background on fingerprinting, 93–94
Beacon-enabled IEEE 802.15.4 network,
    56f
BEEP systems, 146, 148
Bluetooth transceivers, 8, 20

Boolean satisfiability (SAT) problem, 96,
    97f
Bring Your Own Device (BYOD) policies,
    117

C

Certificate of authenticity, 62f
Certified code execution, 52
Challenge-response models, 39
Challenge-response pairs, obtaining, 51–52,
    51f
Channel state information (CSI), 74, 78
    precoding and power-allocation with
        CSI, 85–86
Characteristic frequency components, 126,
    129
Circuit model, 31
Classification error rate, 15, 24
Clock skew, 23, 52
    definition, 52–53
    estimation, 53–54
    exploiting, 55–57
    network authentication, 55
    pitfalls, 57–58
Collusion attack, 109, 113
Communications channels, 71
Compact discs (CDs), 61
Component behaviour, 31
Component significance, determining, 36
    constructing model input, 36
    evaluating model output, 37–38

© Springer Science+Business Media New York 2016
C. Wang et al. (eds.), *Digital Fingerprinting*,
DOI 10.1007/978-1-4939-6601-1

identity, 38
    significance, 37–38
  producing model output, 36–37
Conceptual fingerprint, 91f
Constraint-addition, fingerprinting with,
    98–100
Constraint-based watermarking technique,
    90, 94
Controlled physical unclonable functions,
    49
  certified code execution, 52
  challenge-response pairs, obtaining,
    51–52
  initialization, 50
  primitives, 49
  secret key establishment, 50
Core Provenance Library (CPL), 145, 146
Core root of trust for measurement (CRTM),
    164
Core under test (CUT), 110
CPU heat pattern, 3
Crypto-based methods and fingerprints, 39,
    179
  authentication, 39–40
  key generation, 40
    asymmetric keys, 40
    symmetric keys, 40
  techniques, 41
    clock skew, 52–58
    controlled physical unclonable
    functions, 49–52
    physical unclonable functions
    (PUFs), 41–49
      software control, 63–64
      Trojan detection, 63
      wireless devices, 58–63
  tradeoffs, 64
    benefits, 64
    drawbacks, 65

D
Data collection, 178
  setup, 132f
Data-dependency, 13
Data provenance, 142, 143, 144, 147, 148
DBNotes, 145
Delay-based implementation, 42–44
Denial, of fingerprint, 112
Device fingerprints, 2, 3, 12–13, 41, 177,
    180
Device measurement and origin of variation,
    31–38

ABCD parameters, 33
component significance, determining,
    36
  constructing model input, 36
  evaluating model output, 37–38
  producing model output, 36–37
measuring parameters, 34–35
proposed model, 33–34
Device under identification, 7, 8–9, 25
D-flip flop, 41–42, 110
Digital Signature Algorithm (DSA)
    signatures, 163
Digital versatile discs (DVDs), 61
Disclosed Provenance API (DPAPI), 145,
    146
Disclosed provenance-aware systems, 143
Discrete Fourier Transform (DFT), 130
Discrete model, 31
Discrete Wavelet Transform (DWT), 11
Don't Fragment (DF) bit, 118
Doppler effect, 179

E
Earth Science System Workbench, 143, 145
Embedded authentication, 72
  framework for, 72
    authentication performance, 77
    receiver, 74–76
    transmitter, 73–74
    system diagram, 73f
Embedded fingerprint authentication,
    metrics for, 77
  authentication performance, 78
  impact on data BER, 77–78
  security analysis, 79
    complexity, 81–82
    impersonation and substitution
    attacks, 81
    key equivocation, 79–81
Encrypted traffic, analysis of, 124
End of Option List (EOL), 118
Equal Error Rate (EER), 15
Equivocation, 79, 82–84
  multiple observations, 80–81
  noiseless observations, 79–80
  noisy observations, 80
Error correcting syndrome values, 45–46
Error correction, 46
Error-tolerance assumption, 93, 94
Execution partitioning (EP) step, 146

F

Fast Fourier Transform (FFT), 11, 25
Feature selection, 16
Fingerprint detection, 108
Fingerprint location, 104, 105
    defined, 101
Fingerprinting by design, 69
    embedded authentication, 72
        framework for, 72–77
    experimental results, 82
        authentication performance, 82
        impact on data BER, 84
        key equivocation, 82–84
    fingerprint embedding, 70–71
    fingerprinting and communications, 71
    intrinsic fingerprints, 69–70
    metrics for, 77
        authentication performance, 78
        impact on data BER, 77–78
        security analysis, 79–82
Fingerprinting protocol, 95
Fingerprints
    applications and requirements of, 2
    and crypto-based methods, 179
    measurements of, 178–179
    science of, 179–180
    security of, 180–181
Fingerprints, types and origins of, 2–3, 5
    attacking physical-layer device
        identification, 23–24
    device fingerprints, 12–13
    features, 9–11
    future research directions, 25–26
    identification signals, 9
    physical-layer device identification, 6,
        13–14, 22–23
        device under identification, 8–9
        general view, 6–8
        improving, 15–17
    state of the art, 17
        modulation-based approaches, 21
        transient-based approaches, 17–21
    system performance and design issues,
        14–15
Flooding Time Synchronization Protocol,
    55
Fourier transformation, 11
Frequency error, 58, 59f

H

HF RFID, 8, 22–23
Hidden services, 123

Hi-Fi, completeness analysis of, 165
    exfiltration, 168
    persistence and stealth, 166–167
    recording malicious behavior, 165–166
    remote control, 167–168
    spread, 168–169
High-fidelity whole systems provenance,
    150, 160
    design of Hi-Fi, 150–151
    implementation of Hi-Fi, 154
        bootstrapping filesystem provenance,
            155–156
        earlyboot provenance, 154–155
        opaque provenance, 156
        OS integration, 155
        provenance logging, 154
        socket provenance, 156–158
    limitations of Hi-Fi, 158
    system-level objects, handling of,
        151–154
Host discovery, 120

I

ICBM Echo request, 120
ICBM messages, 119
ICMP timestamps, 33
Ideal fingerprint, 91
Identification signals, 7, 9
IEEE 802.11a device identification, 22
IEEE 802.11 transceivers, 8, 8f, 20
IEEE 802.11 transient signals, 20
IEEE 802.15.4 transceivers, 8
IEEE 802.15.4 wireless sensor node
    network, 55
Inferred features, 9, 11, 12f, 24
Inferring users' online activities through
    traffic analysis, 123
In-specification characteristics, 9
Integrated circuits (ICs), 89
Integrity Measurement Architecture (IMA),
    163
Intrinsic fingerprints, 69–70
IP intruder, 90
IP protection, digital fingerprinting for, 93
    background on fingerprinting, 93–94
    constraint-addition, fingerprinting with,
        98–100
    iterative fingerprinting techniques,
        95–98
    need and challenge of digital
        fingerprinting IPs, 94
    requirements of digital fingerprinting,
        94–95

ISO 14443 RFID transponders, 21
Iterative fingerprinting techniques, 95–98

K
K-bit fingerprints, 106
Key extraction, 60f, 61
Key generation, 40
    asymmetric keys, 40
    symmetric keys, 40

L
LineageFS, 160
Linear programming method, 53–54
Linksys CompactWireless USB adapter
    (WUSB54GC), 132
Linux Integrity Measurement Architecture
    (IMA), 163
Linux kernel's boot-time initialization
    process, 154
Linux provenance modules (LPM), 159
    augmenting whole-system provenance,
        159–160
    deploying, 164–165
    design of, 161, 161f
        netfilter hooks, 162–163
        provenance hooks, 162
        workflow provenance, 163–164
    security analysis of, 169
        authenticated channel, 170
        authenticated disclosures, 170–171
        complete, 169–170
        tamperproof, 170
        verifiable, 170
    threat model, 160–161
Linux Security Module (LSM), 150
LogGC system, 146, 148

M
Mandatory Access Control (MAC), 148,
    158, 165
Marking assumption, 93
Maximum Segment Size (MSS), 118
Measurements of fingerprints, 178–179
Memory-backed "pseudo-filesystems", 154
Message authentication code (MAC), 51–52
Messages, authenticating, 71
MIMO systems, 16, 26
MIMO transmission, 72
Modification, fingerprint, 112
Modulation-based identification techniques,
    21

Multiplexer-based arbiter implementation,
    41–42

N
Network analysers, 35
Network authentication, 55
Network traffic fingerprinting, 3
NI-USRP software-defined radios, 82
nmap program, 120
Noise, 45–48
Noise frequency components, 126, 129
No-Operation (NOP), 118

O
Observability Don't Care (ODC)
        fingerprinting, 100
    conditions, 101
    determining potential fingerprinting
        modifications, 102–103
    finding locations for circuit modification
        based on, 101–102
    illustrative example, 100
    ODC trigger signal, 102
    overhead constraints, maintaining, 103
    security analysis, 103–104
Operating System (OS) fingerprinting, 115
    active fingerprinting, 119–122
    detection, 120
    encrypted traffic, analysis of, 124
    future directions, 135
    packet-content agnostic traffic analysis,
        122
        hidden services, 123
        inferring users' online activities
            through traffic analysis, 123
        website fingerprinting, 122–123
    passive fingerprinting, 117–119
    smartphone OS reconnaissance, 124
        empirical evaluation, 132–135
        identifying, 128–132
        system model, 127
        threat model, 127
    smartphone traffic, analysis of, 123–124
Optical disc fingerprints, 62f
Optical media, 61–63
Oscillator implementation, 44–45
Out-specification characteristics, 9
Oven controlled crystal oscillators
    (OCXOs), 57

P

Packet-content agnostic traffic analysis, reconnaissance through, 122, *see also* Reconnaissancehidden services, 123
  inferring users' online activities through traffic analysis, 123
  website fingerprinting, 122–123
Passive fingerprinting, 117–119
Passive identification, 13
PERM (Provenance Extension of the Relational Model), 145
Physical-layer device identification, 5–6, 13–14, 18t–19t, 22–23
  attacking, 23–24
  device under identification, 8–9
  entities involved in, 7f
  general view, 6–8
  improving, 15–17
  system performance and design issues, 14–15
  uses of, 6
Physical realizations, 45
Physical unclonable functions (PUFs), 41, 63, 91
  controlled PUFs, 49
    certified code execution, 52
    challenge-response pairs, obtaining, 51–52
    initialization, 50
    primitives, 49
    secret key establishment, 50
  delay-based implementation, 42–44
  improvements, 49
  multiplexer-based arbiter implementation, 41–42
  noise, 45–48
  oscillator implementation, 44–45
  privacy, 48
Platform Configuration Registers (PCRs), 148
Platform Control Register (PCR), 163
Population sensitivity, 180–181
Port scanning, 120
POSIX shared memory, 153
Post-silicon design phase, 92, 100
Potential fingerprinting modifications, determining, 102–103
Predefined features, 9, 11, 12f, 24
Pre-silicon design phase, 92
Primitives, cryptographic, 49
Privacy, 26, 48
Probabilistic neural network (PNN), 14, 20

Propagating lineage information as datasets, 145
Provenance-aware application (PAA), 146, 148, 163
Provenance-Aware Storage System (PASS) instruments, 144, 160
Provenance-aware systems, 142
  automatic provenance-aware systems, 144
    in applications, 145–147
    in middleware, 145
    in operating systems, 144
  disclosed provenance-aware systems, 143
Provenance-based access control schemes (PBAC), 147
Provenance collection, security challenges to, 147–149
Provenance monitor concept, 149–150, 158
Provenance monitors, analyzing security of, 165
  Hi-Fi, completeness analysis of, 165, *see also* High-fidelity whole systems provenanceexfiltration, 168
    persistence and stealth, 166–167
    recording malicious behavior, 165–166
    remote control, 167–168
    spread, 168–169
  Linux provenance modules (LPM), security analysis of, 169, *see also* Linux provenance modules (LPM)authenticated channel, 170
    authenticated disclosures, 170–171
    complete, 169–170
    tamperproof, 170
    verifiable, 170
Pseudo-filesystems, 154

R

Radio frequency, 58–59
Rayleigh fading, 78
Received signal strength indicator (RSSI), 60
Receiver Operating Characteristic (ROC), 15
Reconnaissance, 117, 127, *see also* Smartphone OS reconnaissance, case studythrough packet-content agnostic traffic analysis, 122
  hidden services, 123
  inferring users' online activities through traffic analysis, 123

website fingerprinting, 122–123
Regular files, 152
Relay, defined, 154
Removal, fingerprint, 112
Request for Comments (RFC), 120
Requirements of digital fingerprinting,
        94–95
Reuse-based IP business models, 90
RFID device, 8
RFID transponder, 8f, 14
Ring oscillators, 44f, 47
Robust fingerprints, 26
Robustness, 13, 25

S
Satisfiability Don't Care (SDC) fingerprint-
        ing, 104
    assumptions for, 105–106
    fingerprint embedding scheme, 107–108
    and illustrative example, 104–105
    security analysis, 108–109
    technique, 106–107
Scalar network analysers, 35
Scan chain fingerprinting, 109, 111
    basics on scan chain design, 110–111
    illustrative example, 109–110
    security analysis, 111–113
Science of fingerprints, 179–180
SCTP scan, 120, 157
Secret key establishment, 50
Secure and trustworthy provenance
        collection for digital forensics, 141
    analyzing security of provenance
        monitors, 165
        completeness analysis of Hi-Fi,
        165–169
        security analysis of LPM, 169–171
    ensuring trustworthiness of provenance,
        147
        provenance monitor concept,
        149–150
        security challenges to provenance
        collection, 147–149
    future challenges, 171–172
    high-fidelity whole systems provenance,
        150
        design of Hi-Fi, 150–151
        handling of system-level objects,
        151–154
        Hi-Fi implementation, 154–158
        limitations of Hi-Fi, 158
    Linux provenance modules, 159 see
        also Linux provenance modules

(LPM)augmenting whole-system
        provenance, 159–160
        deploying LPM, 164–165
        design of LPM, 161–164
        threat model, 160–161
    provenance-aware systems, 142
        automatic provenance-aware
        systems, 144–147
        disclosed provenance-aware
        systems, 143
Security and privacy of device identification,
        26
Security of fingerprints, 180–181
Selective Acknowledgement (SackOk), 118
Self-timed delay, 43f
SELinux Access Vector Cache (AVC) Log,
        170
Shared secret keys, 49, 51, 71
Simple modification attack, 109
Simple removal attack, 108
Smartphone OS reconnaissance, case study,
        124
    empirical evaluation, 132
        experiment setup, 132
        identification of minor versions of
        smartphone OSes, 134
        length of traffic traces, 133–134
        performance metrics, 133
        running time, 135
    identifying, 128
        identification algorithm, 129–132
        rationale, 128–129
    system model, 127
    threat model, 127
Smartphone traffic, analysis of, 123–124
Socket identifiers, 154
Socket provenance, 151, 156–158
    TCP sockets, 157
    UDP sockets, 157–158
Software control, 63–64
SPADE, 144, 148, 159, 171
S-parameters, 34, 35
Specifications, 9
Statistical feature extraction, 16–17
Steganography, 71
Support Vector Machines (SVM), 14
    SVM classifier, 21
Symmetric keys, 40
SYN-ACP packet, 118
SYN packet, 117, 118
System on a chip (SoC) paradigm, 89

T
TCP NULL, FIN, and Xmas scan, 120
TCP scan, 120
TCP signatures, 117
TCP SYN scan, 120
TCP timestamps, 55, 56
TCP Window scan, 120
Time domain methods, 59
Time synchronization, 57f
Time Synchronization Function, 55
Time-to-Live (TTL), 117
Timestamps, 55, 55f
Tmote Sky sensor devices, 21
Tor network, 56, 123
TPM Platform Control Register (PCR), 163
Tradeoffs, 64
    benefits, 64
    drawbacks, 65
Transient-based device identification, 17,
    20–21
Trojans, 93
    detection, 63
Trusted Platform Module (TPM)
    attestations, 148, 164
Two-port model, 32
Type of Service (ToS) flags, 118

U
UDP scan, 120
UHF RFID tags, 22
UHF RFID transponders, 8
UHF sensor nodes, 8

Unique identification, causes of, 25–26
USRP1 devices, 82
UUIDs, 151, 153, 154

V
Vector network analysers, 35
Version detection, 120
VHF FM transmitters, 17, 20
VLSI design cycle, 92, 92f

W
Watermarking, 3, 90
Wavelet analysis, 17
Wavelet transformations, 11
Website fingerprinting, 122–123
WiFi communication, 127
Window Scale value, 118
Wireless devices, 58
    classes of, 8f
    optical media, 61–63
    physical-layer identification of, 7f
    radio frequency, 58–59
    wireless link key extraction, 59–61
Wireless link key extraction, 59–61
Write once read-many (WORM) storage
    system, 151

Z
Zab trojan, 167